75803

D0949006

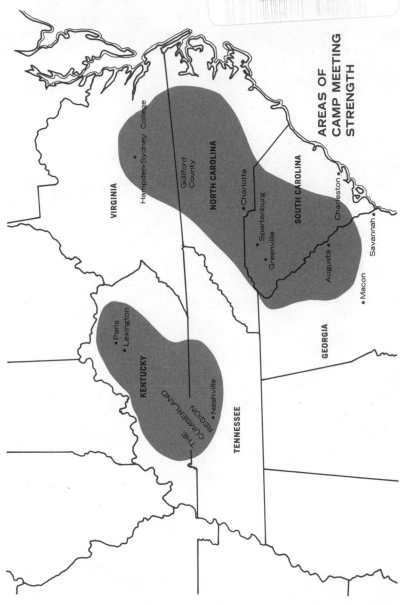

AREAS OF
CAMP MEETING
STRENGTH

The Great Revival

1787-1805

*The Origins of the Southern
Evangelical Mind*

John B. Boles

The Great Revival
1787-1805

The University Press of Kentucky

ISBN: 0-8131-1260-5

Library of Congress Catalog Card Number: 77-183349

A statewide cooperative scholarly publishing agency
serving Berea College, Centre College of Kentucky,
Eastern Kentucky University, Kentucky State College,
Morehead State University, Murray State University,
University of Kentucky, University of Louisville,
and Western Kentucky University.

Editorial and Sales Offices: Lexington, Kentucky 40506

for Nancy

Contents

Preface

*Even the skeptical historian
develops a humble respect
for religion, since he
sees it functioning, and
seemingly indispensable, in
every land and age.*

Will and Ariel Durant

The genesis of the great revival of religion which swept across the South in the opening years of the nineteenth century has been explained primarily in terms of geography and emotion. Too often students have focused only on the immediate beginnings of the revival in the Cumberland region of Kentucky. The frontier aspect of this interpretation includes the declining threat of Indian attacks, the relative scarcity of churches, the loneliness of thinly settled pioneer families, the materialism and acquisitiveness of those persons clearing wilderness farmlands, and the ever-present physical violence that seemed part and parcel of western life. The second part of this current interpretation emphasizes the emotional response to the hard, bitter, monotonous life on the western frontier. The camp meeting revival which erupted is portrayed as a welcome catharsis for socially and emotionally starved pioneers. The constant nearness of death, the absence of law and order, the lack of educational opportunities, all contributed to a people who wanted and needed a religion that appealed to the heart, not the head.

By combining this emotionally charged populace with a frightening theology emphasizing damnation and hellfire, the popular interpretation is complete. Abstract thought is conspicuously missing from the causative ingredients. Yet this narrow frontier thesis fails to explain how the revival actually began, or why it began when it did. Neither does this analysis account for the rapid spread of the revival throughout the entire South, the older parts of which possessed few frontier characteristics. Many of the leading promoters of the revival were too new to the frontier to have been strongly molded by it. And it is difficult to understand how the influence on people of something as vague and geographically imprecise as the frontier could have produced such a dynamic religious movement.

The origin of the Great Revival is complex, involving the total world view of the participants. It includes their concept of the sovereignty of God and their overall cosmology. I was totally unaware of these complications when I began this work, for I simply intended to do a monographic, institutional study of the beginning and development of the revival. But when I realized that the old explanations were insufficient, I started to read more avidly the general religious literature of the southern evangelicals. Slowly an entire new intellectual world that I had never imagined—the religious sphere of the southern mind—came into focus. I came to see nuances and implications that seemed in large part to explain the origins of the revival. Yet this became clear only after I had in a sense reentered the evangelicals' world.

In the view of the evangelicals, God controlled minutely the ordering of all earthly events, from the falling of a sparrow to a widespread decline of religion. Everything had meaning, even the devastating drought the churches were then suffering, and God ultimately turned all things to his purpose. Their belief system provided a role of service for man—repentance, obedience, consecration, prayer—and a role of deliverance for God. This expectation of God's ultimate triumph and Jesus Christ's eventual second coming was the keystone of their theological arch.

The participants' faith in prayer, their belief in biblical prophecy, and their overall will to believe were, given the contours of their comprehension, essential factors of the revival. They helped prepare the state of mind necessary for the revival's beginning and proliferation. With this understanding then, a tremendous upsurge of spirituality anywhere—but particularly on the frontier—would seem to presage the determined efforts of God to effect his purpose. Such a revival would seem the vanguard of a new dispensation, a creative display of God's wonder-working powers.

When news arrived elsewhere of what was happening in Kentucky— tales of extraordinary crowds and strange exercises, inexplicable conversions and miraculous transformations of entire communities—the hopes of the faithful seemed fulfilled. Confronted by this apparently undeniable demonstration of God's sovereignty and power, individuals felt the need of conversion as never before. Throughout the South, as the news spread, neighborhoods experienced revivals beyond anything ever remembered. The Great Revival in the South, long hoped for, long prayed for, had become a reality.

Historians, in their concern with the West, have tended to ignore the less spectacular antecedents of the movement. Instead of being unique to the western frontier, the theology and techniques of the Kentucky Revival were developed, and the personnel trained, in the East. The camp meeting itself slowly evolved from a spontaneous overnight meeting to a planned, carefully executed revival technique. The Kentucky phase was most significant as a catalyst. It released the millennial hopes of the faithful. This made the "Great Revival of the West" of vast importance. Again and again, mere knowledge of what had transpired at Cane Ridge, Kentucky, in 1801 triggered an immediate revival elsewhere.

Charles A. Johnson's excellent *Frontier Camp Meeting* (Dallas, Tex., 1955) discusses their origin, but his major emphasis is upon the sophisticated camp meetings of the 1830s and 1840s. And, in the tradition of William Warren Sweet, Walter B. Posey has traced the institutional development of religion in the Old Southwest. Nothing comprehensive, however, has been done for the South of 1800–1805.

Together with the detailed analysis of the origin and growth of the Great Revival, this study will attempt to reconstruct the multifaceted religious mind of the southern evangelicals. Aspects of the theology not necessarily related to the genesis of the revival will be discussed. Not only was there a shift toward Arminianism, but the evangelical concept of the ministry gained widespread acceptance. And it was this step toward individualistic evangelism, deemphasizing creeds and formal training, which soon produced the various frontier schisms. The specialist will note my revisionist interpretation of the significant theological wrangling that preceded both the Shaker intrusion and the separation of the Cumberland Presbyterians and the Disciples of Christ.

The evangelists were well aware of the sociological implications of their message—and the sociology of its acceptance. They recognized the restrictions and opportunities which gradations in affluence and social status placed before their particular denominations. Although the ministers never silently acquiesced in the obvious injustices of their communities, they were little concerned with ameliorating the general state of society. Contrary to what Perry Miller has suggested in *The Life of the Mind in America: From the Revolution to the Civil War* (New York, 1965), the foremost goal of southern evangelicals was converting the individual sinner.

The theology and sociology of the revival, combining a salvation achieved by personal commitment with an awareness (and often criticism) of the differences in social standing, realized almost none of their potential political results. Alan Heimert in his sometimes cryptic, sometimes illuminating *Religion and the American Mind* (Cambridge, Mass., 1966) has shown once again that religion and politics often share basic beliefs. However, the empirical evidence for his conclusions about the southern revivals is, at best, insufficient. The southern pietists were too otherworldly to be much concerned with politics. Heimert's monumental work also deals almost entirely with New England printed sources. In this study I attempt to draw out, through an analysis of the memoirs, journals, diaries, letters, sermons, and church records, the subtle relationships between the revivalistic religion that swept the South after 1800 and the surging strength of Jeffersonianism.

In the concluding chapter I try to show the impact pietistic religion has had on the subsequent history of the South. The growing religious orthodoxy contributed to the freedom-of-thought crisis that Clement Eaton has so ably discussed, and it helped shape the unchanging distinctiveness of southern history that has prompted so many investigations. Extrapolating from concepts discussed in this study, I suggest in the final chapter what amounts to another "central theme" of southern history.

The study will emphasize white Baptists, Methodists, and Presbyterians in the six states of Virginia, North Carolina, South Carolina, Georgia, Kentucky, and Tennessee. The time span, for the major portion of the work, will be from shortly before the Hampden-Sydney revival in 1787 to the ebb of the principal revival surge in 1805. One basic assumption—that the three denominations shared certain tenets of a large, overarching belief system—is valid, I think, despite their differences on church polity, open communion, and foreordination. Their theological differences were often subordinated in the midst of the revival. Again and again, sermons at a camp meeting purposely disregarded theological niceties. Orthodox Calvinism was blended with fervent Arminianism, election with near universalism, in the effort to produce conviction. Perhaps these denominational characteristics can best be pictured as epicycles rotating around a circumference containing the general belief in the role of Providence, repentance, and prayer. It is this central belief structure, around which the particular beliefs orbited, that the study will elaborate.

The friendliness, cooperativeness, and interest shown by library personnel made research a pleasure. Among those individuals who afforded me unusual kindness and assistance were Miss Helena Koiner of the Interlibrary Loan Department, Alderman Library, University of Virginia; William H. Runge, Curator of the Rare Book Room, Alderman Library, and his staff; the Reverend Robert Stuart Sanders of Lexington, Kentucky; and Professor Walter B. Posey, formerly of Agnes Scott College and Emory University.

I would like to express my deepest gratitude to two foundations for their financial support: The Thomas Jefferson Memorial Foundation and the Woodrow Wilson Foundation. Barbara Murray, Kathie Young, and especially Peg Ashe have helped with the typing. I have discussed different sections of this study with Professor Richard E. Ellis and at that time fellow graduate students William J. Gilmore, John H. Schroeder, and Myron F. Wehtje. They often forced me to consider aspects I had overlooked. I appreciate also the readings given by Professors William H. Harbaugh, Joseph H. Kett, and Mary Catherine Kahl. Professor W. W. Abbot has, as always, been a source of solid advice on the normal problems of graduate school and professional life.

Everyone who has worked with Professor Bernard Mayo understands the debt of gratitude I owe him. His enthusiasm, creativity, patience, and scholarly and stylistic perfectionism have inspired me to do my best. His generous concern both for me and this project merits an appreciation I cannot adequately express.

Professor Merrill D. Peterson likewise has given me the benefit of his acute criticism and insight. Professor Paul M. Gaston taught me much about southern history. And in a special way I am indebted to Professor Henry F. May, who volunteered to read the manuscript at an early stage and share his knowledge of religion in the early republic. My colleagues at Towson State College have provided a very congenial working atmosphere for bringing this study to completion.

These scholars have all been of inestimable aid. But the one person to whom I owe the greatest appreciation is my wife Nancy. She never grew tired of the subject or my fascination with it; she never became impatient. Without her warm cooperation I would never have been able to finish this work. I alone, of course, am responsible for any errors, oversimplifications, or exaggerations.

The Great Revival
1787-1805

Chapter One

The Setting

The two decades following the American Revolution were years of transition for the major religious denominations in the South. The Anglican Church, enervated before the Revolution largely by a debilitating blindness to popular needs, emerged from the conflict in a precarious position.[1] Long associated with dry-as-dust sermons, lackadaisical piety, and the fopperies of tidewater society, the orphaned Church of England was a victim of change. The times simply demanded what the state church was not. Dilapidated buildings and vacant pulpits, a Tory label and an aristocratic past, offered scant hope for the new era. The evangelical inroads of the Baptists, Methodists, and Presbyterians had drawn off the most zealous believers. When released from coerced support, the lower classes, the backcountry folk, and the seekers of heart-warming religion largely transferred to more relevant denominations. The well-bred and educated who, even though only nominally devout had maintained the prewar Establishment, were now just as often unconcerned or openly interested in the deistic vogue. Caught between pietism on one side and rationalism on the other, the erstwhile Church of England would inevitably face lean years.

The Episcopal Church's misery was its competitors' boon. The rector of stuffy stereotype was no match for the ebullient evangelist. The Episcopal Church too often smacked of England and the colonial dependency. Even had the church escaped the ravages of war unscathed, it would have been hard-pressed to meet the challenge of a backcountry filling rapidly with war veterans and opportunists. Distrusted, depressed, and perhaps a little disdainful, the once ascendant church saw its position drop precipitously. Its fate mirrored the growing domination of the popularly supported churches: Baptist, Methodist, and Presbyterian.

A century before the Revolution the vanguard of the Presbyterian Church entered the Chesapeake society of Virginia and the low country of Carolina.[2] These small settlements, having come directly from Scotland, Ireland, or the Continent, planted the seed of their church in fertile southern soil, but sustained growth was not soon forthcoming. A half century later, Scotch-Irish Presbyterians began migrating southward from Pennsylvania down the broad Valley of Virginia, and within twenty years they had fanned out over the piedmont and near backcountry of Virginia, both Carolinas, and Georgia. Everywhere they went these hard-working, strong-willed people built Presbyterian churches along with their cabins. Their reaction to the Great Awakening was neither uniform nor substantial, simply because they were too widely dispersed. But the energizing currents of evangelism radiated from north-central Virginia, where an indigenous revival, beginning in the mid-1740s, had been stoked first by a Presbyterian missionary, William Robinson, and then by the enormously gifted Samuel Davies. From the experience and inspiration of this Hanover County revival came many of the evangelical New Side Presbyterian ministers who preserved their denomination in the South despite discrimination, the deprivations of war, and widespread indifference to religion.

The structure and characteristics of Presbyterianism which, by traditional standards, seemed to promise great success, proved in the new national experience to be a liability. By temperament and precedent dedicated to an educated clergy, their admirable ideal produced numerous schools, academies, and learned clergymen, but made inevitable a crippling shortage of ministers in the backcountry and on the frontier. This was true despite the number of ministers graduated from Hampden-Sydney and Liberty Hall (later Washington and Lee College). Their rigid, circumspect creed was both a stabilizing force for immigrants and satisfied settlers and a

[1] For the faltering progress of the Anglican (reorganized as Episcopal after the Revolution) Church see Raymond W. Albright, *A History of the Protestant Episcopal Church* (New York, 1964); James Thayer Addison, *The Episcopal Church in the United States, 1789–1931* (New York, 1951); William Wilson Manross, *A History of the American Episcopal Church*, 3d ed. (New York, 1959); H. J. Eckenrode, *The Separation of Church and State in Virginia* (Richmond, Va., 1909); G. MacLaren Brydon, *Virginia's Mother Church*, 2 vols. (Richmond, Va., 1947); William Warren Sweet, *Religion in the Development of American Culture, 1765–1840* (New York, 1952); and Francis L. Hawks, *Contributions to the Ecclesiastical History of the United States of America*, 2 vols. (New York, 1836), 1. Basic background information on all the major denominations can be found in such general texts as Sweet, *The Story of Religion in America* (New York, 1950), and Winthrop S. Hudson, *Religion in America* (New York, 1965).

[2] Among the works detailing the history of the Presbyterian Church, I have found the following most helpful: Ernest Trice Thompson, *Presbyterians in the South, 1607–1861* (Richmond, Va., 1963); William Henry Foote, *Sketches of North Carolina, Historical and Biographical* (New York, 1846), and *Sketches of Virginia, Historical and Biographical*, 2 vols. (Philadelphia, 1850–1855); Robert Ellis Thompson, *A History of the Presbyterian Churches in the United States*, vol. 6, *American Church History Series*, 2d ed. (New York, 1902); and Wesley M. Gewehr, *The Great Awakening in Virginia, 1740–1790* (Durham, N. C., 1930).

stumbling block for egalitarian seekers and upcountry plainfolk. The tightly knit federal system of local presbytery, regional synod, and national General Assembly (established in 1787) could provide intelligent and united direction, but it could also be dictatorial and detrimental to healthy congregational autonomy. In a South overwhelmingly rural, simple in taste, and habituated to little government supervision of any kind, the immense Presbyterian influence was to be dependent upon a relatively small group of unusually able men. The Presbyterian did not become the archetype of the southern church.

Three distinct strains of Baptist heritage are represented in the South.[3] Between 1682 and 1696 a small group of Particular (or Calvinist) Baptists from Maine arrived in the Charleston, South Carolina, region. They struggled with slight success and were kept alive only by the transitory preaching of George Whitefield's itinerant evangelism until Oliver Hart's invigorating leadership began about 1750. His able ministry produced the Charleston Association of Baptist Churches, whose constituents thrived into the nineteenth century.

It was about 1700 that the Arminian (free will) General Baptists immigrated to eastern Virginia from England. In 1720 economic hardships and in the early 1740s an epidemic forced most of these General Baptists to move into north-central and eastern North Carolina, where for a time they enjoyed modest success. In 1750 Robert Williams, who had spent five years among the Calvinistic (Particular) Baptists in South Carolina, returned to his native North Carolina and began converting his Baptist friends to the Calvinist doctrines. He, along with Oliver Hart of Charleston, appealed to the strong Particular organization in Philadelphia for aid in proselytizing. The Philadelphia Association sent John Gano, and later two other missionaries, who successfully converted most of the former General Baptist ministers and church leaders to the strict Calvinism of the Particular

[3] The intricate story of the Baptists in the South is best told by William L. Lumpkin, *Baptist Foundations in the South: Tracing through the Separates the Influence of the Great Awakening, 1754–1787* (Nashville, Tenn., 1961); Noel Ray Lykins, "North Carolina Separate Baptists: A Study in Frontier Expansion in the Eighteenth Century" (Th.M. thesis, Southeastern Baptist Theological Seminary, 1961); Robert G. Torbet, *A History of the Baptists* (Philadelphia, 1950); David Benedict, *A General History of the Baptist Denomination in America*, 2 vols. (Boston, 1813), 2; Robert Baylor Semple, *A History of the Rise and Progress of the Baptists in Virginia* (Richmond, Va., 1810). C. C. Goen, *Revivalism and Separatism in New England, 1740–1800* (New Haven, Conn., 1962), and William G. McLoughlin, *Isaac Backus and the American Pietistic Tradition* (Boston, 1967), are best for the northern origins of the Separate Baptists.

Baptists. But relatively few of the actual members joined the reconstituted churches. The majority of the General Baptists were left without a viable church organization.

At the same time in Connecticut, two Congregational brothers-in-law, Shubal Stearns and Daniel Marshall, had reexamined their beliefs in the midst of the Great Awakening and, along with many others, had shifted from Congregationalism to Separatism to the Baptist faith. These Separate Baptists held to a Calvinism liberally tinctured with fervent evangelism. Both Stearns and Marshall felt a call to the frontier. Consequently the ministers, with a handful of followers, left Connecticut in 1754. After a brief stay in Virginia, the group settled at Sandy Creek, in north-central North Carolina. Here, under the remarkably charismatic leadership of Stearns (and to a lesser extent Marshall), the Separate Baptists enjoyed great success. They quickly converted a cadre of enthusiastic evangelists and proceeded to bring several thousand under their banner in southern Virginia and North Carolina.

Governor William Tryon of North Carolina blamed the Separates for the insurgent Regulator movement, and fear of persecution drove huge numbers of them from North Carolina in 1771 and 1772. The exiles settled in South Carolina, Georgia, Tennessee, and Kentucky, further spreading their beliefs. This surging Separate Baptist movement absorbed most of those General Baptists who had not been converted to the rigorous Calvinism of the Particulars. The less evangelistic Particular Baptists, now also threatened with assimilation, first began calling themselves Regular Baptists in an attempt to defend their position. When the Revolution intervened, the Regulars were already pushing for a merger with the Separates—a move completed soon after the close of the war everywhere but in Kentucky, where it was not effected until 1801.

The Baptist faith that emerged was an effective blend: active evangelism, voluntary associations for unity of effort, democratic control, a popular base of support. The liberal stand taken, particularly by the Virginia Baptists, on the Revolution and disestablishment, gained fame for their denomination and the warm support of the common people who had bristled under the restrictions and failures of the Anglican Church. The Baptists, with their unpretentious farmer-ministers drawn from among the congregation, were destined to share southern leadership with the Methodists.

Although organized Methodism first appeared in America in 1766 under the ministry of Philip Embury in New York, it did not reach the South until 1773.[4] In that year Robert Williams arrived in the southeastern

---

[4] For the spectacular growth of the Methodist Church, see James Monroe Buck-

Virginia parish of Devereux Jarratt, an evangelistic Anglican. Jarratt, a Methodist in everything but name, had been preaching emotional, hard-hitting sermons to his flock, and their response was encouraging. He willingly gave Williams his support and permitted the new Methodist congregations to use his barn as a meetinghouse. Since the Methodist itinerants at this time remained nominal members of the Church of England, and were not ordained, they did not administer the sacraments. They depended on the local Anglican ministers to perform this function—a duty the zealous Jarratt was only too happy to fulfill.

With Jarratt's aid, the Methodist Church grew more rapidly in Virginia than anywhere else. Thomas Rankin was sent into the district and with Jarratt itinerated throughout the region, even spreading their message to North Carolina. A powerful revival developed under their tutelage, an awakening that lasted several years into the American Revolution. But the Revolution so disrupted the Anglican Church and its ministers that the Methodists soon found it almost impossible to have the sacraments administered. By 1779 Methodists in both Delaware and Virginia were considering an organization independent of the Church of England, one authorized to perform all ministerial functions.

Immediately after the conclusion of the Revolution John Wesley drew up plans for the establishment of a truly autonomous and indigenous church in America. He proposed an abbreviated liturgy, a de-Calvinized theology, and an evangelistic hymnody. He sent his revisions to America by Thomas Coke, whom he had chosen along with Francis Asbury to be superintendents of the newly independent church. Meeting in Baltimore at the famous "Christmas Conference" of December 1784, a convention of Methodist ministers accepted the proposals, established the Methodist Episcopal Church, and persuaded Coke and a reluctant Asbury to accept the superintendency. Asbury's able, long, and energetic leadership insured the success of Meth-

---

ley, *A History of Methodists in the United States,* vol. 5, *American Church History Series,* 2d ed. (New York, 1907); Jesse Lee, *A Short History of the Methodists in the United States of America, Beginning in 1766, and Continued till 1809* (Baltimore, Md., 1810); Emory Stevens Bucke, ed., *The History of American Methodism,* 3 vols. (New York, 1964); William Warren Sweet, *Men of Zeal: The Romance of American Methodist Beginnings* (New York, 1935), and *Virginia Methodism: A History* (Richmond, Va., 1955); Wesley M. Gewehr, "Some Factors in the Expansion of Frontier Methodism," *Journal of Religion* 8(January 1928):98–120; Francis Asbury, *The Journal and Letters of Francis Asbury,* ed. Elmer T. Clark et al., 3 vols. (London, 1958); and for Jarratt, see Nancy Gaebler, "Devereux Jarratt: Anglican Evangelist of the Virginia Great Awakening" (M.A. thesis, University of Virginia, 1967).

odism, a movement destined to dominate American Protestantism in the nineteenth century.[5]

A prodigious organization remarkably attuned to the American environment was responsible for Methodism's meteoric growth. Asbury took Wesley's scheme of rotating ministers and elaborated it to include regular circuits. Each Methodist minister was assigned a route, along which he would preach at stated intervals. This made possible an enormously expanded audience for Methodist preaching. Circuit riders could be found in the most forlorn backcountry settlements. Inclement weather, poverty, and distance were ignored. Although the method of assigning circuits and regulating ministers was decidedly autocratic, the individual ministers were men of the people: homely, often unlettered, pious, and given to unbending labor for minuscule pay. Asbury tempered his autocracy by itinerating thousands of miles yearly himself, thereby experiencing the hardships and sufferings common to his brothers of lesser fame and responsibility. He represented the devotion to cause which helped the Methodists, along with the Baptists, conquer the South.

Despite the presence of the three denominations in the region, their existence did not mean that the South was religious. Revival fervor was a comparatively recent development, and much of it was confined to portions of North Carolina and especially Virginia. The backcountry Anglican itinerant Charles Woodmason exaggerated little when he wrote of the Carolinas in the mid-1760s: "How many thousands . . . never saw, much less read, or ever heard a Chapter of the Bible! How many Ten thousands who never were baptized or heard a Sermon! And thrice Ten thousand, who never heard of the Name of Christ, save in Curses and Execrations! Lamentable! Lamentable is the situation of these people."[6] The colonial South never had regionwide revivals; its Great Awakening was not to come until after 1800. The local seasons of religious prosperity only helped prepare the leadership and background of vague beliefs which eventually made

[5] The following works discuss the "Methodist Age": Thompson, *A History of the Presbyterian Churches*, p. 34; Winthrop S. Hudson, *American Protestantism* (Chicago, 1961), pp. 33, 96–97, 128; and C. C. Goen, "The 'Methodist Age' in American Church History," *Religion in Life* 44 (Autumn 1965): 562–72. For an extensive account of the "Christmas Conference," see N. C. Hughes, Jr., "The Methodist Christmas Conference: Baltimore—December 24, 1784–January 2, 1785," *Maryland Historical Magazine* 54 (September 1959): 272–92.

[6] *The Carolina Backcountry on the Eve of the Revolution: The Journal and Other Writings of Charles Woodmason, Anglican Itinerant*, ed. Richard J. Hooker (Chapel Hill, N. C., 1953), p. 77. Cf. Carl Bridenbaugh, *Myths & Realities: Societies of the Colonial South* (New York, 1963), pp. 30–31, 75, 97, 180–83.

possible the great revival floods. These local revivals merit attention more for what they promised than for what they achieved.

By the end of the Revolution, each of the three popular denominations in Virginia had enjoyed separate periods of revival and rapid growth. Wesley M. Gewehr has traced the development of what he calls the three phases of the Great Awakening in Virginia: the Presbyterian, from the middle of the 1740s until almost 1760; the Baptist, which began in the middle 1760s and did not fade until the early 1770s; the Methodist, gaining strength in the early 1770s and climaxing in 1776. Although by almost any standard, religion was still very weak in Virginia at the opening of the Revolution, it lost during the ensuing decade much of whatever influence and support it had gained. But in 1785 there were indications of a resurgence, which peaked in 1787 and 1788. Unlike the earlier revivals, this quickening was experienced by all three major groups concurrently. And all cooperated to an unprecedented degree in their efforts to produce the best results.[7]

The Baptist and Methodist participants in the 1787 awakening exhibited the same highly emotional, bizarre manifestations of conversion usually associated with the camp meetings of the later Great Revival. Jesse Lee, the first historian of Methodism, tells of a congregation so exercised that it was genuinely oblivious to everything but religion:

> The poor awakened sinners were wrestling with the Lord for mercy in every direction, some on their knees, others lying in the arms of their friends, and others stretched on the floor, not able to stand, and some were convulsed, with every limb as stiff as a stick. In the midst of this work several sleepers of the house broke down at once, which made a very loud noise; and the floor sunk down considerably; but the people paid but little or no attention to it, and many of them knew nothing of it, for no one was hurt.[8]

John Leland, the famous Baptist leader of Virginia and later Massachusetts, reported that it was "nothing strange, to see a great part of the congregation fall prostrate upon the floor or ground; many of whom, entirely lose the use of their limbs for a season."[9] From these emotional meetings several thousand converts were added to the church rolls.

The revival ferment induced by the Methodists and Baptists contributed to a rising interest in spiritual matters among three students at

[7] Gewehr, *The Great Awakening in Virginia*, gives a very complete account of all these revivals. See also Gaebler, "Devereux Jarratt."

[8] Lee, *A Short History of the Methodists*, pp. 130–31.

[9] John Leland, *The Virginia Chronicle* (1790), in Leland, *The Life and Writings of Elder John Leland*, ed. L. F. Greene (New York, 1845), p. 114.

Hampden-Sydney, a Presbyterian college. These youths, William Hill, Cary Allen, and James Blythe, were discovered praying in their room, and from the publicity that followed there developed a collegewide revival. Under the direction of the Reverend John Blair Smith, energetic president of the school, the currents of revivalism swelled far beyond the campus. The nearby counties were soon all engaged in a renewal of religious vigor; shortly Liberty Hall was involved. The zeal of the Presbyterians exceeded anything they had known for four decades, but the resolute Smith kept the enthusiasm under control. Never in this revival did it erupt among the Presbyterians as it had with the Methodists and Baptists.[10]

As a result of this interdenominational revival, the forces of religion were greatly strengthened for a time. A large enough body of believers was created to enable the denominations to survive the drought ahead—the decline would not completely extinguish the fires of religious enthusiasm. A large number of Methodist and Presbyterian ministers emerged, providing the personnel to spread the rudiments of Christian belief across the South.[11] And perhaps most important for the future, the success at Hampden-Sydney irrevocably impressed the efficacy of revivalism upon the mind of visiting James McGready, a young Presbyterian minister on his way to North Carolina from Pennsylvania.[12] He would eventually carry the evangelical message to Kentucky.

By 1787 the three denominations which would shape the future of southern religion had formed their personalities and organizational structures. Yet, except for the short-lived revival in Virginia at the beginning of the period, and much smaller revivals in North Carolina and Kentucky, the next decade offered little evidence to the contemporary observer that genuine, sustained piety would ever thrive in the southern climate. It simply required several years of unrewarding preaching, weary missionary

[10] Foote, *Sketches of Virginia*, 1: 412–30, covers the Presbyterian revival, reprinting most of the relevant source materials. See also William Hill, *Autobiographical Sketches and Other Papers of William Hill of Winchester* (Richmond, Va., 1968), pp. 7–15 and 107–16. Hill of course was a participant in the revival.

[11] See Gewehr, *The Great Awakening in Virginia*, pp. 172–73, for the Methodist increase; and Robert Stuart, "Reminiscences, Respecting the Establishment and Progress of the Presbyterian Church in Kentucky," in Robert Stuart Sanders, *The Reverend Robert Stuart, D.D. 1772–1856; A Pioneer in Kentucky Presbyterianism and His Descendants* (Louisville, Ky., 1962), p. 69, who counted forty Presbyterian ministers resulting from the revival. For some reason, however, relatively few Baptist ministers emerged, though church membership grew. See Leland, *Virginia Chronicle*, in *Life and Writings*, p. 116.

[12] Foote, *Sketches of North Carolina*, p. 370.

tours, and the mechanics of church formation to build the organizational and theological groundwork necessary for a lasting revival.[13] These years of pioneering effort, during which rather vaguely defined religious ideas were planted in the minds of most southerners, offered little comfort to the clergy. These were years of boiling political activity, frenetic land grabbing, and frontier Indian skirmishes. The entire era was one of intensive constitutional theorizing. The period began with ratification debates and ended with manifestoes of state nullification. Whiskey rebels and British impressment, the French Revolution and Hamiltonian economics, Genet's perambulations and Yazoo land frauds kept public opinion agitated. These issues alone would have distracted minds from religion, but even more powerful was the lure of greener pastures.

Thousands of acres of uncleared virgin land beckoned the dissatisfied and footloose. Even the seaboard states had wide expanses of rich, easily owned soil, but their bounteous offerings were nothing compared to the prodigality of Kentucky and Tennessee.[14] Multitudes of people—growing families, Revolutionary War veterans rewarded with western land, younger sons without an inheritance, adventurers—swarmed westward, crowding such gateways as Pittsburgh and the Cumberland Gap. One already in Tennessee noted: "To a person who observes the migration to this country, it appears as if North and South Carolina, and Georgia, were emptying themselves into it."[15]

This migration left older churches in the seaboard South bereft of many active members.[16] Pioneers on the western fringe often realized they had moved beyond the reach of their familiar church, and the sparsity of their settlements made local church organization difficult. Although by

---

[13] One of the few scholars to point out this necessary background for a revival is Donald G. Mathews, who in his article "The Second Great Awakening as an Organizing Process, 1780–1830: An Hypothesis," *American Quarterly* 21 (Spring 1969) : 23–43, wrote "it is simply impossible to have a revival unless there is some institutional and ideational framework that has provided a meaningful context for the revival in the first place. That is, one cannot have a revival without churches," p. 25.

[14] David Barrow, "Diary," July 30, 1795; typescript copy in the collection of the Filson Club, Louisville, Ky.

[15] [Daniel Smith], *A Short Description of the State of Tennessee* (Philadelphia, 1796; Boston reprint, 1938), p. 33.

[16] Hence a South Carolinian explained why religion was very dull in 1798: "Congregations are not very stable in this country at this time. [A] spirit of emigration prevails." Robert Wilson to Rev. Samuel Wilson, Abbeville County, S. C., March 27, 1798; in the L. C. Glenn Collection, Southern Historical Collection, University of North Carolina, Chapel Hill, N. C.

1799 the three major denominations had managed to reach nominally almost the entire western population, many families still had no opportunity to attend religious services. Two Brethren missionaries in Tennessee found a strong desire for preaching of any kind. Immediately after one of their services near Nashville in 1799, two parents "begged that in course of the week a service might be conducted in their home, so that the many children in their neighborhood might, for once, have the opportunity to hear something of the Saviour." [17]

Nowhere was the post-revolutionary South a Puritan "city on a hill." When travelers tired of describing the uncouthness, inquisitiveness, and barbarity of Southerners, they usually berated the irreligiosity of the region. The French nobleman Duc De La Rochefoucault typically observed that "religion is one of the objects which occupies the least of the attention of the American people," and particularly, "few nations are less addicted to religious practices than the Virginians." [18] David Barrow, a Baptist, thus summarized the result of his tour of Kentucky in 1795: "Of all the denominations I can remember to have seen in that country, the Deists, Nothingarians and anythingnarians are the most numerous." [19] Nineteen-year-old William Ellery Channing, Harvard-educated tutor in Richmond, Virginia, complained, "Christianity is here breathing its last. I cannot find a friend with whom I can even converse on religious subjects." [20]

Yet beneath the placid surface of this apparently profane society forces were at work which promised to evoke a spiritual quickening. Each of the three major denominations had developed an institutional framework that allowed them to prepare for and promote a revival. The intense but local interdenominational revival of 1787–1789 in Virginia produced many evangelical ministers and proved the efficacy of revivalistic preaching. The burgeoning Methodist and Separate Baptist movements were gradually infusing new vigor and expectations in the southern religious leaders. The perseverance of a few fervent ministers maintained the body of theological beliefs shared, albeit passively, by most people of even the slightest religious background. The existence of widely scattered churches, such as the one

---

[17] [Abraham Steiner and Frederick C. De Schweinitz], "Report of the Journey of the Brethren Steiner and Schweinitz . . . 1799," in *Early Travels in the Tennessee Country, 1540–1800*, ed. Samuel Cole Williams (Johnson City, Tenn., 1928), p. 510; see also pp. 455, 511–12.

[18] Duc De La Rochefoucault, *Travels Through the United States of North America . . . In the Years 1795, 1796, and 1797*, 2 vols. (London, 1799), 2: 50, 669.

[19] Barrow, "Diary," July 30, 1795.

[20] *Memoir of William Ellery Channing, With Extracts from His Correspondence and Manuscripts*, 2 vols. (Boston, 1848), 1: 126.

near Winchester, Virginia, visited by Ferdinand Marie Bayard in 1791 kept alive a loosely defined belief system out of which a revivalistic frame of mind could develop:

> The preacher [was] a Presbyterian minister . . . his sermon turned entirely upon the principles of the evangelical doctrines: he recommended the practice of those abstruse virtues, of general usefullness, and which society disposes with less than those which make extraordinary men. He spoke with impressive simplicity; his voice became soft and sweet when he described the love of the Creator for man, and his unceasing solicitude for his daily needs: he was listened to by a congregation absorbed in deep mediation [*sic*] . . . . As I came back from the church I noticed that the doors of the houses were closed: they remained closed throughout the day. Everyone seemed lost in meditation.[21]

The self-examination and rigorous moral policing which the Methodists experienced weekly in their class meetings, the Baptists monthly at their business meetings, and the Presbyterians quarterly at their synods maintained a pure remnant.[22] In periods of materialism and general irreligion, church minute books contain little else than the record of those excluded from fellowship. Alcoholism, profanity, mistreatment of slaves, and sexual immorality were common malfeasances. Some churches, in their rigid observance, almost decimated their own membership. Thus was produced a large body of churchless people who desired reconciliation and renewal of religious fellowship. Backsliders purged from membership were ready for a religious revival. But the prerequisite condition for an impending revival was a clerical preoccupation with the apparent decline in religion. Their deep concern led them to seek the causes of the decline, and therein they discovered a theological basis for hope.

[21] Ferdinand Marie Bayard, *Travels of a Frenchman in Maryland and Virginia . . . in 1791*, trans. and ed. Ben C. McCary (Ann Arbor, Mich., 1950), p. 87. See also Nathl. Harris to Stith Mead, May 3, 1793, Stith Mead Letterbook, p. 80, Virginia Historical Society, Richmond. The various letters to and from Mead richly document the existence of local awakenings in individual churches and at the same time portray the general deadness in religion.

[22] This examination of members is exhibited in any church or associational minutes chosen during the period under discussion. For an analysis of the social control practiced by the evangelical churches in a slightly later period, see W. W. Sweet, "The Churches as Moral Courts of the Frontier," *Church History* 2 (March 1933): 3–21; and Cortland Victor Smith, "Church Organization as an Agency of Social Control: Church Discipline in North Carolina, 1800–1861" (Ph.D. diss., University of North Carolina, 1967).

Chapter Two

The Feeling of Crisis

For most American clergymen, the final years of the eighteenth century were freighted with despair. These were the suspicious times when orthodox New Englanders saw a Tom Paine deist behind every door and a French infidel lurking in the shadows. Lyman Beecher found the Yale of 1793 "in a most ungodly state" and forever wondered how he had escaped the "intemperance, profanity, gambling, and licentiousness" that were so rampant.[1] Crotchety, outspoken Jedidiah Morse preached a Fast Day sermon in Massachusetts warning of a secret conspiracy of the "Bavarian Illuminati" which threatened to topple the Republic.[2] The deistic publications and activities of Paine, Elihu Palmer, and Ethan Allen gave some credence to clerical fears. The intemperate charges of the so-called infidels were matched in intensity only by the counterattacks of the orthodox. For example, the distinguished Presbyterian Ashbel Green generously characterized Paine's *Age of Reason* as "a book in which the most contemptible ignorance, the grossest falsehood, the most vulgar buffoonery, the most unblushing impudence, and the most daring profaneness are united [to] make up its contents."[3]

In the South the gravest danger perceived to Christianity was a rather prosaic irreligiosity. One September day in 1793, after a parched summer, Drury Lacy, a teacher-minister at Hampden-Sydney College in Prince Edward County, Virginia, described local conditions to a former student:

> The dry fields & languishing Vines, exhibit a too striking picture of the present State of the Church. Refreshing Showers and fruitful Seasons have been restrained, both in the Fields & in the Assemblies. We but seldom have the pleasure to see persons deeply affected, and tears streaming from their Eyes. The Harvest seems to be past. God has called his Labourers out of this part of his Vineyard, and I am left here like an Old Servant upon a desolate Farm. I go around once in a while to keep up the Fences; and in good Weather I try to thresh a little. But I have so many complaints, & lazy to boot, that very little is done.[4]

Lacy's concern was repeated throughout the South. Though here and there rather muted notice of deism was made, the preeminent emphasis was on the distressing coldness of religious interest. The fact that Lacy, an evangelistic Presbyterian at a denominational college with a revivalistic heritage, found the outlook bleak shows how dramatically the decline made itself felt. Yet Lacy was not alone in his views. He represented the overwhelming consensus of southern evangelicals—Baptist, Methodist, and Presbyterian—in every southern state. The same clergymen who were unknowingly on the verge of unprecedented success saw only desolation.

The Reverend Devereux Jarratt, an early promoter of Methodism who had remained in the Episcopal Church primarily because he loved its stately ritual, found the entire religious situation of Virginia in 1796 sadly bleak. "The prospect," he wrote, "is gloomy and truly suspicious and discouraging." The churches of his own denomination were little attended; its ministers were not, "in reality, gospel ministers." [5] Nor did this fiery-tongued Episcopal rector "find the aspect of religious affairs much more encouraging in other societies, or denominations. There is an awful falling off on every hand. . . . By a letter from a pious Presbyterian minister, I learn that religion is at a low ebb among them. The baptists, I suppose, are equally declining . . . the Methodists are splitting and falling to pieces." [6]

Only the year before, the Circular Letter of the Goshen Baptist Association of Virginia had warned that this was "a dark time with the church, and many false teachers are gone out into the world." [7] A devout Georgia Presbyterian minister confessed in 1794 that he was "greatly distressed in mind, from a view of the present apparent languishing state of religion in this country. Coldness and formality prevails." [8] In 1801, just before the

[1] Quoted in G. Adolf Koch, *Republican Religion: The American Revolution and the Cult of Reason* (New York, [1933]), p. 242. Koch and Herbert M. Morais, *Deism in Nineteenth Century America* (New York, 1934), give detailed coverage of the northern fear of infidelity and deism.

[2] Conrad Wright, *The Beginnings of Unitarianism in America* (Boston, 1966), pp. 244–55. This fear of an international revolutionary organization was no less real for being groundless.

[3] *A Sermon Delivered . . . in the City of Philadelphia on the 19th of February 1795* (Philadelphia, 1795), p. 19n.

[4] Lacy to William Williamson, September 18, 1793, Williamson Papers, Shane Collection, Presbyterian Historical Society, Philadelphia.

[5] Jarratt to John Coleman, January 28, 1796, in Jarratt, *The Life of the Reverend Devereux Jarratt* (Baltimore, Md., 1806), p. 128.

[6] Ibid., p. 180.

[7] Goshen Baptist Association Minutes, 1795, "Circular Letter," p. 7, microfilm, Historical Commission, Southern Baptist Convention, Nashville, Tenn.

[8] [Rev.] John Newton to Rev. Samuel Wilson, July 14, 1794, L. C. Glenn Collection.

revival erupted in Georgia, the state Baptist association attacked the current worldliness, dissipation, materialism, and total absence of Christian piety.[9] Baptist minister Edmund Botsford of South Carolina grew so desperate in the spring of 1796 that he seriously considered leaving his congregation. Lack of interest, bad crops, and floods left his people with no way and no inclination to pay him. Few came to hear his sermons, "infidelity" seemed on the increase; he had even lost his respect for the congregation. Coldness and darkness reigned: "I was in hopes some time ago it was midnight with us, but I now begin to fear I was mistaken ... in cold winter nights, it often seems a long time from midnight to morning." [10] His metaphor, however, strongly implied a dawn.

In every southern state, representatives of each denomination voiced similar concern. Methodist itinerant Jeremiah Norman recorded in his diary again and again the evidence of a religious slump in North Carolina.[11] Lemuel Burkitt, a Baptist minister and historian from North Carolina, could find no indication of a resurgence of piety: "It appears generally cold amongst Professors, and but few Additions to the Churches." [12] Five years later, after the revival had begun, Burkitt and his co-author retrospectively surveyed "the long and tedious night of spiritual darkness and coldness in religion" when "the churches appeared to be on a general decline." [13]

As Isaac Weld, a British traveler, made his way across Virginia in the spring of 1796, he noted the natives' open hospitality, their contentment, and their indolence, dissipation, and widespread addiction to liquor. But more than personal ruin he remembered the decayed and empty churches: "Indeed, throughout the lower parts of Virginia, that is, between the mountains and the sea, the people have scarcely any sense of religion, and in the country parts the churches are all falling into decay. As I rode along, I scarcely observed one that was not in ruinous condition, with the windows broken, and doors dropping off the hinges, and lying open to the pigs and cattle wandering about the woods." [14] Rochefoucault had summarized the surface situa-

[9] Georgia Baptist Association Circular Letter, 1801, in C. D. Mallary, *Memoirs of Elder Jesse Mercer* ([n.p.], 1844), p. 141.

[10] Botsford to Richard Furman, April 10, 1796, and May 3, 1796, in the Edmund Botsford Letters, South Carolina Baptist Historical Collection, Furman University, Greenville, S. C.

[11] "Diary," pp. 935, 938, 943, 963, in the Stephen B. Weeks Collection of the Southern Historical Collection, University of North Carolina, Chapel Hill, N. C.

[12] Burkitt to Richard Furman, January 11, 1798, Richard Furman Papers, South Carolina Baptist Historical Collection, Furman University, Greenville, S. C.

[13] Lemuel Burkitt and Jesse Read, *A Concise History of the Kehukee Baptist Association* (Halifax, [N. C.], 1803), p. 138.

[14] *Travels Through the States of North America, and the Provinces of Upper*

tion three years earlier: "few nations are less addicted to religious practices than the Virginians." [15] Even a decade before Weld's observations, the prominent Baptist leader of Massachusetts, Isaac Backus, commented upon the great extent to which "irreligion hath prevailed" in Virginia. And Robert Baylor Semple, the contemporary historian of Virginia Baptists, dwelt at length on the waning interest of the faithful during the general decline. "Some of the watchmen fell, others stumbled, and many slumbered at their post. Iniquity greatly abounded. Associations were but thinly attended, and the business badly conducted." [16] William Hill, a Presbyterian missionary, actually gave up on portions of Virginia:

> We reached Col. Burgess Balls at Chatham immediately opposite Fredericksburg, where we received gentiel treatment, but no room for religion, no, not even prayers in the family. I should have been glad to have preached in Fredericksburg but from the unsuccessful attempts I had made in Richmond, Williamsburg, Norfolk & Petersburg—knowing that there was not a presbyterian in the place—having no acquaintance, nor letter of introduction—hearing that they had refused to let Mr. Whitfield preach, & that he had shaken off the dust of his feet against them & hearing from all quarters their character for drinking, gaming, & horse racing, I concluded there was no work for me to do there, & so passed by on the other side.[17]

At the official meetings of the Presbyterian Church in the South careful attention was given to the state of religion. The factual evidence for this church's concern is more widely available than the other denominations, simply because the regularly scheduled presbytery and synod meetings provided a convenient platform for the statement and preservation of views. For example, the Synod of the Carolinas heard and recorded the results of the Reverend Robert Wilson's 1794 missionary tour to portions of South Carolina. "It is truly lamentable," he reported, "to see and hear of the great profanation of the Sabbath that is every where practised even among those who make a profession of the Christian religion. Hunting shooting & all kinds of amusements is engaged in, on the Sabbath day." [18] That same year

---

and Lower Canada, during the Years 1795, 1796, and 1797, 1 vol. ed. (London, 1799), pp. 101 and 118. Probably most of the churches in actual ruins were those of the collapsing Episcopal Church.

[15] Rochefoucault, *Travels Through the United States,* 2:50.

[16] Semple, *History of the Baptists in Virginia,* pp. 35–36; Backus is quoted in McLoughlin, *Isaac Backus,* p. 205.

[17] William Hill, *Journal,* January 10, 1792, in Hill, *Autobiographical Sketches and Other Papers,* p. 91.

[18] Synod of the Carolinas, "Minutes," 1:187, Ms in Union Theological Seminary in Virginia, Richmond.

to the north, the Pastoral Letter of the Virginia Synod spoke of the "deep affliction" the church was suffering, and sorrowfully noted that "Vice & wickedness in some of their most insulting & infamous forms abound in our Country." Yet the situation deteriorated even further during the next three years. The decline and obvious lack of interest in religion had proceeded to such a point that barely a quorum attended the 1797 synod meeting in Winchester, Virginia. The alarmed (and rather piqued) moderator of the synod wrote a pastoral letter to each presbytery, urging that they pressure their members to be more diligent in attendance. After all, the disturbed author wrote: "We cannot suppose they have concluded to let the authority of Jesus Christ as King in his Church fall to the ground. Yet if the members of each Presbytery should become a little more careless, we will cease to have Synodical meetings.—Already the reduced state of our body occasioned by the delinquincy of its members, sinks our dignity; weakens our influence, & greatly discourages the hearts of such as attend." [19] Perhaps the Charleston Baptist Association fairly summarized the conditions indicated by the official church records and the written testimony of numerous clergymen up and down the seaboard South: "That religion is in a low and languishing state throughout the continent, admitting a few exceptions, and that it is greatly so with us, is evident," concluded their Circular Letter of 1793, "from the best testimony and our own observation." [20]

As gray and wintry as the religious season appeared to the representatives of the major denominations in the older states of the South, the western states of Kentucky and Tennessee exhibited even less religious vitality. Here too, despite occasional murmuring against deism and infidelity, the primary complaint was of simple apathy to religion. Francis Asbury, molder of American Methodism, confessed to himself while in Tennessee that "Good religion and such good land are not so easily matched together." [21] Peter Cartwright recorded in a famous passage from his classic *Autobiography* that Logan County, Kentucky, in 1793 was infamous as a "rogues' harbor"; law was unheard of, thieves and ruffians predominated. Sunday was spent at everything except worship, and in such an environment, Cartwright piously recalled that he was quite "naturally a wild, wicked boy." A 1794 letter from Kentucky to John Rippon's international yearbook of Baptist activ-

[19] Synod of Virginia, "Minutes," 1:137, 184–85, photocopies in Union Theological Seminary in Virginia, Richmond; originals at Historical Foundation of the Reformed and Presbyterian Churches, Montreat, N. C.

[20] Charleston Baptist Association, "Minutes, 1790–1804," p. 6, microfilm, Historical Commission of the Southern Baptist Convention, Nashville, Tenn.

[21] Asbury, *Journal and Letters*, April 25, 1796, 2:83.

ities informed the editor "with concern . . . that religion appears to be at a very low ebb with every denomination in this state."[22]

On a later trip to Tennessee, Asbury tried to understand why it was so difficult for religion to flourish among the people of the West: "When I consider where they came from, where they are, and how they are, and how they are called to go farther, their being unsettled, with so many objects to take their attention, with the health and good air they enjoy; and when I reflect that not one in a hundred came here to get religion, but rather to get plenty of good land, I think it will be well if some or many do not eventually lose their souls." He had to confess three years afterwards, on the very eve of the revival, that it was "plain there are not many mighty among the Methodists in Kentucky."[23] Andrew Fulton, a missionary of the Seceder Presbyterian Church of Scotland, discovered that in Nashville, "and indeed almost all the newly formed towns in this western colony, there are few religious people."[24] The minutes of the Transylvania Presbytery reveal that they were anxious about the "prevalence of vice & infidelity, the great apparent declension of true vital religion in too many places."[25]

The decline of religion made southern ministers of every denomination uneasy. Many feared that religion, which had only comparatively recently showed the first signs of potential vigor in the South, was collapsing amid the birth pangs of a new nation. Avaricious land-grabbing and a propensity to alcoholism were often cited as contributing factors to the religious illness. And a small but significant number of solicitous clergymen perceived the emergence of deism and an undefined infidelity as the insidious disease sapping the strength of religion. This interpretation of the religious crisis, though not at all dominant in the South, created a disproportionate degree of apprehension. Rather typically, the Methodist itinerant James Smith, traveling near Lexington, Kentucky, in the autumn of 1795, feared that "the Universalists, joining with the Deists, had given Christianity a deadly

[22] Anonymous letter, to Rippon, September 15, 1794, in John Rippon, *The Baptist Annual Register*, vol. 2, *For 1794, 1795, 1796–1797* ([London], n. d.), p. 201; and Peter Cartwright, *Autobiography of Peter Cartwright, the Backwoods Preacher*, ed. William P. Strickland (Cincinnati, Ohio, 1856), pp. 24–27.

[23] Asbury, *Journal and Letters*, March 26, 1797, 2:125; October 13, 1800, 2:254.

[24] "Extract of a Letter from Fulton to Rev. Mr. Alexander Pringle, Perth. Canerun, Ky. January 9, 1799," in *New York Missionary Magazine* 1 (1800):122.

[25] Transylvania Presbytery, "Minutes," October 8, 1800, reprinted in William Warren Sweet, *Religion on the American Frontier*, vol. 2, *The Presbyterians, 1783–1840* (New York, 1936), pp. 185–86; see also p. 144. The original minutes are in the Louisville Presbyterian Seminary Library, Louisville, Ky.

stab hereabouts." [26] The preceding summer David Barrow, who said deists, nothingarians, and anythingnarians were predominant in Kentucky, reported that the western deists had recently been much strengthened by the "late publication of Thomas Paine." [27]

Although today the brief outburst of deism and anticlericalism never appears to have threatened seriously the citadels of religion, at the time the danger seemed real and menacing. The gales of European liberalism and revolt ruffled orthodoxy in the United States. The outpouring of books and pamphlets from Paine, Palmer, and Allen that scared New Englanders also quickened southern pulses. Forty years later the Reverend Robert Stuart of Kentucky still remembered the deistic persuasion that gripped him and his ministerial brethren with fear: "The writings of Infidels, and particularly *Tom Paine's Age of Reason* [sic], was extensively circulated, and his principles imbibed by the youth particularly, with avidity; so that Infidelity, with all its concomitant evils, like a mighty tide, was desolating the land, with respect to religion and morals. Youth became scoffers at religion and blasphemers against God. Such a thing as a young man of talents turning his attention to the ministry was so rare, that it would have excited astonishment." [28]

Steiner and Schweinitz, the two Brethren missionaries to Tennessee, were told by a respected citizen of Nashville that in that region, "especially among the upper classes, deism and irreligion ruled beyond all bounds." [29] From Richmond, William Ellery Channing wrote, "Infidelity is very general among the higher classes; and they who do not reject Christianity can hardly be said to believe, as they never examine the foundations on which it rests. In fine, religion is in a deplorable state." [30] The depressing secularism of society led Presbyterian minister David Rice to complain: "By adopting and acting upon the principles & maxims of this world Christians & ministers contribute more to the spread of infidelity & impiety than all the infidel writers of Europe and America. O for purity of heart and life." [31]

[26] "Tours into Kentucky and the Northwest Territory: Three Journals by the Rev. James Smith of Powhatan County, Virginia, 1783–1795–1799," *Ohio Archaeological and Historical Publications* 16 (1907): 374.

[27] Barrow, "Diary," July 30, 1795.

[28] Stuart, "Reminiscences of the Presbyterian Church in Kentucky," p. 68. Deism does appear to have presented more of a threat in Kentucky and Tennessee than elsewhere in the South.

[29] [Steiner and Schweinitz], "Report of the Journey of the Brethren," p. 513.

[30] Channing, *Memoir*, 1 : 126. See also Frederic Beasley to Charles Pettigrew, February 6, 1797, Pettigrew Papers, North Carolina State Archives, Raleigh, N. C.

[31] Rice to Ashbel Green, March 4, 1796, Gratz Collection, Historical Society of Pennsylvania, Philadelphia.

Devereux Jarratt, the evangelical Episcopalian, argued very similarly about the Virginia situation in 1794: "The general neglect of the public worship of God, at this day, is truly lamentable, and is really distressing to every pious and considerate man; because this neglect too plainly shows men to be utterly destitute of all true religion, and is the plentiful source of that *infidelity*, which is now growing and spreading through the *State*. When men neglect frequenting the house of the Lord, . . . it is no wonder that all sense of religion should die away, and the traces thereof be erased." [32] And in Midway, Georgia, Cyrus Gildersleeve delivered a New Year's Day sermon in which he warned each friend of the Christian cause, in the evil days upon them, to use "extraordinary vigilance in guarding his own mind, and especially those of our youth, from the contagious influence of vice, and in counteracting the malignant poison of infidelity." [33]

This awareness of religious decline, this fear that Christianity was losing out to indifference and infidelity, this sense of near-desperation, was in many ways an accurate characterization of the religious condition. The clerical preoccupation with the coldness of vital piety was far from a mere figment of ministerial imaginations. The colonial South had by no means been renowned for its devout stature, but the brief outbreak of religious fervor in Virginia before the Revolution and the scattered revivals after 1787 left an exaggerated memory which made the 1790s seem bleak in comparison. Moreover, the dynamic new organizational strength of the popular churches helped them to realize just how irreligious most of the South was.

Some of the religious malaise can be explained by the secularizing influence of the Revolution. [34] After the war soldiers returned to neglected farms and crops, depleted savings, rotting fences, and fields turned to weed. Perhaps there was an unwillingness on the part of numerous war veterans

[32] Jarratt, *Sermons on Various and Important Subjects in Practical Divinity, Adapted to the Plainest Capacities, and Suited to the Family and Closet*, 3 vols. (Philadelphia, 1793–1794), 3: 223–24.

[33] Gildersleeve, *A New-Year Sermon, Delivered at Midway, January 1st, 1798* (Savannah, Ga., [1798]), p. 16. Although later, as Martin E. Marty has suggested in *The Infidel: Freethought and American Religion* (Cleveland, Ohio, 1961), ministers probably used the threat of infidelity and deism to frighten people into church, at the period under consideration the clergy appear to have been honestly alarmed. Nevertheless, indifference was still more of a problem than infidelity. For a similar analysis, see Richard Hofstadter, *Anti-Intellectualism in American Life* (New York, 1966), p. 120.

[34] Robert Baird, *Religion in America* (New York, 1844), p. 102. We recognize today that since the South had not possessed a strong religious tradition before the Revolution, the Revolution could not have been the major cause of the apathy observed in the 1790s.

to face the morally serious decisions and demands necessary for religious vitality. According to historian William Henry Foote, "Many considered freedom from moral obligation as part of civil liberty." [35] And too, the making of peace opened millions of acres of virgin soil to would-be takers. In the westward onrush religion was liable to be placed along with education and culture as a future commitment. Virginia Baptist historian Robert B. Semple discussed another postwar development which often proved detrimental to religion: "The opening of a free trade by peace, served as a powerful bait, to entrap professors who were in any great degree, inclined to the pursuit of wealth. Nothing is more common, than for the increase of riches, to produce a decrease of piety. Speculators seldom make warm Christians." [36] Emigration from the seaboard states often weakened eastern churches, and for many years the churches collectively were unable to provide adequate religious coverage for the frontier settlements. This extraordinary mobility was cited by the 1799 Circular Letter of the Charleston Baptist Association as one of the contributing factors to the decline of religion: "that prevailing spirit of moving from place to place, just as fancy, whim, or supposed interest may dictate, without a due regard to the call of providence, or the interests of religion; by which churches are often greatly weakened, or, as it were, wantonly, and sacrilegiously, broken up." [37] This profound social disruption—the result of war, population growth, migration, and the vagaries of time and circumstance—intensified the deep longing for a strong, settled, secure religious life.

The religious fervor in the Virginia churches during the 1787–1789 revival soon wore off in the tumultous era of the 1790s. The concerned evangelicals never accepted the lowered intensity of piety as natural, as indeed it was for the South. Instead they mythologized their region's religious past. If according to their mental picture of a previous era of piety the present seemed less than devout, then there must be some cause for the "declension." One today might well question whether there was in fact a decline or a return to normality. A cynical observer might also question the honesty of the ministerial concern and their implied references to an earlier South of peace and piety. Yet such a creation and use of myth would not be alien either to the South or to ministers. The region, as George B. Tindall has pointed out in another context, is peculiarly "susceptible to mythol-

---

[35] Foote, *Sketches of North Carolina*, p. 371.

[36] Semple, *History of Baptists in Virginia*, pp. 35–36.

[37] Wood Furman, comp., *A History of the Charleston Association of Baptist Churches in the State of South-Carolina; with an Appendix Containing the Principal Circular Letters to the Churches* (Charleston, S. C., 1811), p. 145.

ogy." [38] It has often been a characteristic of Protestant clergy to assume or believe that all their people had originally (or at some period not far removed) been pious and were currently backsliders. Certainly this mental image of a decline had a functional truth which the historian must accept, for much of the immediately subsequent religious history of the South revolves around the sincerely believed concept of "declension."

Whatever the long-range empirical validity of the clerical fears, in reality church membership *was* slumping. For example, during the six years preceding 1800, the Methodist Church—most popular among the expanding middle and lower classes—declined in national membership from 67,643 to 61,351. In booming frontier Kentucky the population almost tripled in the 1790s, but the woefully small Methodist membership decreased. [39] With the other denominations doing no better, overall church attendance reflected the apparent fate of religion.

As for the authenticity of the deistic threat, Elihu Palmer, Ethan Allen, and others were publishing, speaking, and gaining adherents. The deistic enterprise was extensive: clubs were formed and newspapers were published. [40] Their activities were almost entirely confined to New England and the Middle Atlantic states, but their reputations penetrated to every corner of the young nation. The speculation that regional leaders (some of national import like Thomas Jefferson) trafficked with deistic ideas fueled southern fears.

The French Revolution played a small role in this emerging southern awareness of deism and infidelity. Perry Miller, in his discussion of the prelude to the revivals which opened the nineteenth century, wrote that he believed it "unrealistic to represent the majority of Christian Americans . . . as primarily worried in the 1790's about a threat from European infidelity." He did not deny that Protestants, especially in New England, were worried about French affairs. But, he stated, "the central fact is that the disturbing

---

[38] George B. Tindall, "Mythology: A New Frontier in Southern History," in *The Idea of the South*, ed. Frank E. Vandiver (Chicago, 1964), pp. 1–15; see also Paul M. Gaston, *The New South Creed: A Study in Southern Mythmaking* (New York, 1970), pp. 4–12.

[39] Lee, *A Short History of the Methodists*, pp. 363–64; and A. M. Redford, *The History of Methodism in Kentucky*, 4 vols. (Nashville, Tenn., 1866), 1:249.

[40] Koch, *Republican Religion*, and Morais, *Deism in Nineteenth Century America*, passim. Many clergymen and laymen were to some extent worried about the several "Jacobin" societies organized in Kentucky. For example, see the letter to James Madison describing the "Democratical Society of Kentucky," John Lee to Col. James Madison, February 3, 1794, in the Shane Collection, Presbyterian Historical Society, Philadelphia.

bulletins from Europe fed an appetite for self-examination and self-recrimination which had been born in America long before the fall of the Bastille."[41] The French Revolution must have seemed remote to most Southerners.

Political strife, Indian terrorism on the trans-Appalachian frontier, the threat of war first with England and then with France, land scandals and some evangelical opposition to slavery, all combined to distract folk from single-minded devotion to religion. Yet just as important for the declining interest in the "true faith" was the intradenominational feuding which marred the reputation of organized religion in the South. In Kentucky, the Regular and Separate Baptists disagreed over the acceptance of the Philadelphia Confession of Faith (which was rigidly Calvinistic), the laying on of hands after baptism, the washing of feet, and the morality of slavery.[42] In the seaboard South, one can also detect the existence of a subtle rivalry between the older, more establishment Regular Baptists in the vicinity of Charleston and Savannah, and the upcountry Separate Baptists with their unlettered evangelism.[43]

One Kentucky Presbyterian, Adam Rankin, brought disruption over the issue of singing. Rankin was such a straight-laced Bible literalist that he would have congregations sing only the Psalms, the Songs of David. He fought his case all the way to the General Assembly in Philadelphia to have repealed the ruling allowing the use of Watts's hymns. His opposition to songs referring to the Christ he professed to preach knew no bounds. After he had alienated many of his congregation, Transylvania Presbytery was forced to depose him of his ministerial office. But Rankin persisted in his crusade, gathered a small group of supporters, temporarily affiliated himself with a fledgling Seceder Presbyterian movement, and managed to make

[41] Perry Miller, *The Life of the Mind in America, from the Revolution to the Civil War* (New York, 1965), pp. 4–5. The easily documented absence in the South of widespread clerical attacks on the French Revolution is in contrast to the New England situation. For one thing, there was no established clergy in the South who could interpret French events as a threat to their official position. And, as Genêt's travel route and Jefferson's near anglophobia indicate, France was held in higher regard in the South. For comparison with New England, see Gary B. Nash, "The American Clergy and the French Revolution," *William and Mary Quarterly*, 3d series, 22 (July 1965): 395–412, which, despite its title, ignores the South.

[42] For an extended discussion of these disputes, see J. H. Spencer, *A History of the Kentucky Baptists from 1769 to 1885*, 2 vols. (Cincinnati, Ohio, 1886), 1:175–84.

[43] See Edmund Botsford to [Rev. William Rogers?], November 1, 1809, and Botsford to Richard Furman, February 28, 1803, in the Edmund Botsford Letters.

religion look ridiculous to impartial observers.[44] (Later Rankin was to be a bitter opponent of the revival because, among other reasons, revival hymns were sung enthusiastically.)

The Methodist Church was momentarily staggered by a schism which erupted over Asbury's authority. The rapid growth of the Methodist movement had complicated their annual governmental meetings. Since the number of ministers involved made a completely democratic general conference unwieldy, Asbury proposed a substitute: a council composed of the bishops and elders, most of whom, incidentally, had been chosen by Asbury. This extreme centralization proved so unpopular that the council met only twice, in 1789 and 1790. It was also the beginning of James O'Kelly's opposition to Asbury.

O'Kelly, a determined Virginia Methodist, fought with the council and later the reconstituted General Conference to permit an aggrieved minister to seek repeal of the appointment handed him by his local bishop. The Asbury-dominated General Conference overwhelmingly turned down O'Kelly's petition. Thereupon O'Kelly in 1792 withdrew and formed a "Republican Methodist" group, soon to number several thousand throughout the South. For several years following the split, feelings were harsh between the two groups of Methodists.[45] Such feuding and internal opposition hindered the expansion of the Methodist Church.[46]

Intradenominational bickering and deistic propaganda, postwar materialism, and westward migration lent credence to the worst fears of the ministers. Nothing they could see promised immediate improvement. In the face of solid facts, optimism was guarded. There was an overwhelming, devastating, oppressive sense of the current failure of Christianity to prosper. The more they became aware of the problem, the more severe it

[44] Robert Davidson, *History of the Presbyterian Church in the State of Kentucky* (New York, 1847), pp. 88–98.

[45] For a brief history of the O'Kelly schism, see Lee, *A Short History of the Methodists*, pp. 149–59, 176–93, 202–6; William Warren Sweet, *Religion on the American Frontier*, vol. 4, *The Methodists* (Chicago, 1946), pp. 39–40; and Charles F. Kilgore, *The James O'Kelly Schism in the Methodist Episcopal Church* (Mexico City, 1963), passim. See also Asbury to [Thomas Morrell], November [15], 1792, in Asbury, *Journal and Letters*, 3: 113.

[46] Stith Mead wrote fellow Methodist Hope Hull a long letter criticizing the "very harmful" effects of the "Republican" (or, as he sometimes called it, the "OKellean") schism: "But Alas! By reason of Divisive spirit, and aspiring notions, their [*sic*] appears to be almost a universal stab to Religion; the Cause of God is betrayed into the hands of sinful men, Dear Zion Groans." Mead to Hull, July 7, 1794, Mead Letterbook, p. 97.

suddenly became. Out of this domineering preoccupation with a mission seemingly gone awry emerged an intense introspection. Anthropologists have shown that quite often when a society's traditions, ideals, or hopes seem threatened, the severe anxiety results in a susceptibility to what Anthony F. C. Wallace has termed a revitalization movement. These are attempts to "create a more satisfying culture" by purposely reviving real or idealized conditions of the past, especially those traditional customs that appear near extinction.[47] The southern conditions at the end of the eighteenth century and the stance of the concerned clerics make it possible to see what followed as a powerful revitalization movement. It was this very despair, extruded through their belief system, that ultimately produced the intellectual conclusions conducive to a regional revival of startling intensity.

[47] See Wallace, "Revitalization Movements," *American Anthropologist* 58 (1956): 264–81; Wallace, "Handsome Lake and the Great Revival in the West," *American Quarterly* 4 (Summer 1952): 149–65; and Edward Norbeck, *Religion in Primitive Society* (New York, 1961), pp. 229–32.

Chapter Three

The Theory of Providential Deliverance

For the southern clergymen apprehensive about the future of Christianity, their fears had a significance much larger than mere personal worry. This perception was integrated into their overall belief system. Their understanding of how God worked in this world and how man erred in life ultimately produced very similar conclusions among ministers of each denomination. Repeatedly these conclusions led to a generalized remedy for the situation. That fears felt by each denomination could produce such a remarkably uniform theory of action is evidence of how similar their central beliefs were. The apprehensions about religion constituted a problem to be solved. For some Christians their beliefs were so well developed that the articulation of the problem almost automatically resulted in a solution. That is, given their way of looking at God working in history, any event or situation necessarily and irrevocably was destined to bear the imprint of Providence. Sometimes such a person would state the entire proposition in a sentence or two—God would simply be victorious.

Among other individuals the perceived problem would set into motion all their accepted ideas about God, man, and history. From this process of thought would come an interpretation of the situation based on belief in divine omnipotence. With this understanding there followed a hypothesis for rectifying the spiritual dilemma. Very often the philosophical problem posed by an undeniable decline of religion allowed by a loving God was discussed in detail—partly a way the clergy had of convincing themselves that what they believed was reasonable, and partly a method of convincing others that their interpretation of events was demonstrable. As the ministers became aware of the decline of religion, the problem was analyzed on the basis—sometimes unconsciously—of their preconditioned beliefs, attitudes, and ideas. From this process emerged an axiomatically valid answer to the problem of coldness in religion.

The heart of the widely accepted belief system was the assurance common among orthodox Christians everywhere that a benevolent God controlled all events in this universe. In an age when most men could resort to no scientific explanation for widespread illness, unexpected death, crop failures, and natural disasters, it was easy for them to accept an omnipresent God. Everything took place under God's minute supervision. He controlled the falling of a sparrow, numbered the hairs on their heads, and regulated the fortunes of organized religion. Obviously this was a view of God far removed from the Newtonian model which was gaining acceptance among many well-educated deists as well as others in the upper South and farther northward. This rival system wherein God had removed himself from active interference in a clockwork universe was alien to the southern pietistic mind.

Given the existence of such a providential theory about God's role in the life of man, it was but a short step to full confidence that God could and would, in his own good time, deliver man from whatever afflictions he suffered. For many, the uniting of God's providence and God's deliverance was seemingly unconditional. Even if there were a decline of religion, God nevertheless in some manner still controlled the trials of man and would, at the proper time, provide a means of revitalizing religion. This statement of a providential solution posed no conditions to be met by man—this is not to say none was recognized. They were considered part of the process by which God would effect the revival of vital piety. In a letter to Methodist minister Archibald Robert of Prince Edward County, Virginia, Devereux Jarratt expressed this dual belief—concern about the present, yet faith that God would be victorious: "My mind is not a little affected with ye [the] prospect of religion & morals at this day; and I cannot avoid gloomy & distressing apprehensions respecting consequences.—However, I know ye foundation of God standeth sure,—that his counsel shall stand, & he will fulfill all his pleasure."[1]

Such faith in the face of apparent ruin was common among the evangelicals. In 1795 the Reverend James Smith, a Methodist passing through Kentucky, noted that the infidels in the region had "given Christianity a deadly stab." "But, 'the Lord hath his way in the wilderness and all things obey his might.' I trust he will yet bring good out of this evil, and that the glory of scriptural religion, [though] obscure for the present, will shine forth hereafter with redoubled luster."[2]

Richard Furman, a Baptist leader in South Carolina, admitted in 1792 that the state of religion was "truly melancholy," but despite this he felt well assured that there were some remaining who feared God, "and as the Lord is

[1] Jarratt to Robert, January 11, 1800, Gratz Collection.
[2] Smith, "Tours into Kentucky and the Northwest Territory," p. 374.

great in his Mercies, we are thereby encouraged to hope, that he will once more return and look with Mercy on his languishing and almost expiring Church." And no matter how bleak the future seemed for religion, Furman remembered that "God has promised Strength equal to the Day of Trial," and in proportion to the troubles, "so will the Glory and Joy of Victory be to the faithful soul."[3] Jeremiah Norman, a Methodist circuit rider in North Carolina, often noted the extent to which fervent religion was dead, yet he also wrote confidently that "if the Lord will lay to his helping hand the work will soon be wrought."[4]

From the testimony of numerous private letters and diaries, it is evident that many pietistic evangelicals felt that God would provide relief. Man's role was minimized in their expression of confidence in the future. This was so because they were not communicating with the public, and hence were not urging a course of action. Among themselves and intimates, ministers sometimes simply stated their belief in God's benevolence without going into detail about the conditions to be met. As the ministers' public words show, man's role and duty were silently recognized although not always explicitly stated. The important thing is that they never, even privately, gave up hope.

When speaking to laymen, ministers carefully explicated their reasons for believing God would change man's infidelity into faith. They attempted to demonstrate how eminently reasonable it was to trust God to deliver them from the present declension, once the root causes of the decline were recognized and faced by Christians. The occasional absence in private writing of any emphasis on the role of man in the deliverance process in no way decreases the importance, indeed the necessity, of the human response. This was seen by the clergy as the way in which God would create the conditions worthy of an outpouring of his forgiveness and spiritual blessings.

By theorizing from the general belief in a God both omnipotent and omniscient, the ministers discovered a vital role for Christians which at the same time made allowance for the preeminent role of God. God's control over all matters concerning man was still the deciding element. No one could know when or where he would begin to work. But now Christians could reasonably expect a certain, if unappointed, result if they responded in the right way to the felt needs of the hour. This was not a confidence conveniently worked out to improve morale in a period of stress; the theology

---

[3] Furman to Sarah Furman Haynsworth, August 23, 1792, and Furman to his brother, January 19, 1789, Furman Family Papers, South Carolina Baptist Historical Collection, Furman University, Greenville, S. C.

[4] Norman, "Diary," August 13, 1800, Mss in Stephen B. Weeks Collection. Cf. John Kobler to Stith Mead, January 15, 1795, Mead Letterbook, pp. 142–43.

of hope was inherent in their most central beliefs.[5] The decline merely called forth what was subconsciously there. The presentation of this under-standing of events was the primary concern of countless sermons, circular letters, committee reports, and private correspondence in the decade before the revival.

In seeking to comprehend and explain the low state of vital piety, most ministers seem to have decided that an erring mankind was involved. The Synod of Virginia probed this problem in a pastoral letter of September 1794. First the vices, the irreligion, and the disruptions of the period were cataloged, then an explanation based on God's omnipotence was formulated: "Surely we ought to inquire why it is, that the sword of the Lord is un-sheathed, & suspended over our own happy country. We ought by no means to confine our views to the immediate causes of our distress. They are the Sword, the hand is thine! Yes we with our Fathers have sinned. In how many instances is the standard of revolt lifted up against the Throne of God himself?"[6]

Inherent in this search for causation was the belief that man had done something wrong, since a benevolent, reasonable God would not have al-lowed such a deplorable decline to occur unless he had some justification. In this sense, the causation was sought primarily in the ways that men had failed God. As the Reverend Sanders Walker argued before the Georgia Baptist Association in 1800, "An earnest solicitude to know the causes of this declension, should exercise every Christian heart. Perhaps among many, that of the *neglect* of family worship and *secret* prayer may not be the least."[7] Robert B. Semple described how the Roanoke Baptist Association

---

[5] Perry Miller has described and analyzed the much earlier Puritan "Jeremiad" literature—structurally similar to the southern evangelical sermons berating the "declension" and calling for repentance—and found that it served a very different purpose. He believed these sermons to be a complex sort of psychological purgative making possible the transition from Puritan to Yankee. See his essays "Errand into the Wilderness," in his *Errand into the Wilderness* (New York, 1964), pp. 1–15; and "Declension in a Bible Commonwealth," *Proceedings of the American Anti-quarian Society* 51 (1941): 37–94; and his *The New England Mind: From Colony to Province* (Cambridge, Mass., 1953). Of course the Puritan community had far more precise notions of group mission than the southern evangelicals, and com-mercial development was effecting more disruptive change from the old Puritan cultural patterns.

[6] Synod of Virginia, "Minutes," Vol. 1, September 26, 1794, Mss photocopies at Union Theological Seminary in Virginia; originals at Historical Foundation of the Reformed and Presbyterian Churches, Montreat, N. C.

[7] In Jesse Mercer, *A History of the Georgia Baptist Association* (Washington, Ga., 1838), p. 151.

attempted to come to grips with the dilemma: "Every circular letter contained some exhortation to the churches to search for the cause, to endeavour to rouse up, from their lethargy."[8] That is, the immediate reason for the apparent near collapse of religion should be sought in the hearts of Christians.

Pushing their analysis still farther, the clergy tried to explain why God would permit, or cause, such a falling off on the part of those who professed religion. If God had withdrawn his mercies from Christians temporarily because they had grown lax and accustomed to the ways of the world, why in the first place did an all-powerful God allow such a falling away? Francis Asbury hypothesized that God was simply teaching men not to glorify human abilities: "Mr. Wesley, in his Journal, seems to think that the cause of the hindrance of the work of God is wholly and entirely in man. But may we not ask, with reverence, hath not God sometimes, for his own purposes, withheld his power, that no flesh might glory in his sight, but feel that he is all in all?"[9] According to this view, God was looking after man's interest by encouraging him to place his total reliance in the hands of Providence.

The circular letter written by Silas Mercer in 1795 for the Georgia Baptist Association contains one of the most complete attempts to unravel just what God was doing. Mercer portrayed the distressing state of religion, the indifference, the coldness of the times which made Christians apprehensive.

> But why are these things so? To which we answer. The great Governor of the Universe does not always work by miracles, neither offers violence to the human will. It cannot be thought, but that he could have made his people perfect in soul, body and spirit, at the same time when he converted their souls. But it appears to us, that Jehovah, in his wise providence, saw proper to continue them in connection with an old corrupt nature, in order to properly discipline them, that by the various combats between flesh and spirit, they may be weaned from sensual delight, and learn to trust their all in him. But again: in a lively time of religion, hypocrites and formalists are apt to creep into the Church, therefore, a time of trial is necessary to purge these, as dross from the pure gold or real Christians. And further: the Lord intends, it may be, by this way to prove that salvation is by grace alone; for in a time of declension no man or set of men, no, not all the people in the world, can make a stir of religion. So this proves that religion is of the Lord.[10]

[8] Semple, *History of the Baptists in Virginia*, p. 238.
[9] Asbury, *Journal and Letters*, February 22, 1795, 2:43.
[10] Mercer, *History of the Georgia Baptist Association*, pp. 145–46.

As David Barrow wrote to his fellow minister Richard Furman, God was showing how mistaken man was to trust human power, and thus rob God of his "divine Prerogative." [11]

In his great love for man, God had let his creatures sink into dissipation and irreligion so that they would experience the futility, the absence of fellowship, that always accompanied separation from God. Frustration, mental depression, contention would be the immediate result of this alienation, but out of this experience men would achieve a renewed awareness of the importance of God and of godliness in their lives. Drury Lacy, a Presbyterian minister of Virginia, explained to a former student how God used hardship to produce better Christians: "You know the Love a Parent has for a child. Now if the child be sick & requires Physic, the parent will force it down however disagreeable it may be to Taste. God loves his children with a Love infinitely more tender than any Parent does his child, and he will take care of the Health of the Soul, whatever sufferings it may cost the Body. O that we might be converted & become as little children to take what is given without resistance." [12] Out of disappointment and pain came patience and strength—lessons long taught by Christianity.

This assurance was the basis for the clergymen's expectations that religion would be revived. The falling away which God had permitted for larger purposes presented a tangible human failing against which the clergy could remonstrate. Since God determined the background and future of the decline, men's deliverance would be assured if they would only recognize their mistakes, repent of their sins, then turn to and call upon God. The duty of the clergy now was to exhort men to repent and reform; God, if entreated by sincere prayer, would remove the coldness of heart and effect a resurgence of vital piety. The path to revivalism was clear. An omnipotent Creator manipulating the entire mechanics of the decline would surely—if only certain conditions were met—effect an overwhelming revival.

When the immediate human causes of the decline (man's displeasing of God) were ended, then the antecedent cause (God's use of means to point up man's dependence and impotence) would be satisfied. The avoidance of "sin" would effect this reconciliation. All man had to do was recognize the ways he sinned, sincerely repent of his error, supplicate God by prayer, and then conform by grace to the ways of God. God would give man the power to live the kind of life he should. "Brethren, what can we expect," reproved the Bethel Baptist Association immediately before the revival in South Carolina,

[11] Barrow to Furman, July 25, 1793, Richard Furman Papers.
[12] Lacy to William Williamson, June 6, 1796, Shane Collection.

if we live in disobedience, if we backslide in heart and depart from God? will he not chastise us with the rod of blindness and barrenness? can we expect any thing but a declension? Is it not owing to such conduct that our congregations from year to year complain of coldness and deadness. . . . The truth is, we do not cry to him with sufficient fervency and zeal: we do not plead the promises with sufficient faith: we are too much at our ease: we see cause for lamentation, but we do not lament: It will not be better with us until we alter our conduct and reform our lives.[13]

This point that present sinning had to be stopped in order that God might bless was emphasized again and again. Awareness of the hurtful effects of living estranged from their Creator was the lesson intended by the religious depression. The recognition that sin was the root of their troubles would mean that God's lesson was learned. Once the "covetousness, worldlymindness, slothfulness, omission of duty, indifferency about gospel ordinances" were removed, and glory was given to the Heavenly Father, then see " 'saith the Lord of Hosts, if I will not open you the windows of Heaven, and pour you out a blessing, that there shall not be room to receive it.' "[14] Very often Christians were called upon to be humiliated at the ways in which they failed to live a gospel life.[15] This feeling of humiliation, a recognition of the extent to which man had let himself be separated from God, was part of the repentance-reform process whereby reconciliation with God was achieved.

As a symbolic representation of the giving up of worldliness, the religious fast played a significant part in repentance. The fast was the ritual wherein repentant sinners demonstrated to God that they were willing to forsake their old form of life and accept the sacrifices and moral discipline of Christianity. Admission of wrongdoing was the heart of repentance, and the fast was a public confession. Prayer then was needed for calling upon God for forgiveness and for spiritual aid. Fasting meant that one desired to change his way of life and was willing to serve God, not the world. The act of praying signified that one accepted the necessity of dependence upon God. Thus would men fulfill the conditions intended by the Creator when he decided to allow a great falling away.

The practice of fasting and prayer traced back to Old Testament days. Belief in its efficacy can be followed throughout the entire formative period

[13] Bethel [S. C.] Baptist Association, *Circular Letter, 1802* ([n.p., n.d.]), p. 6, in South Carolina Baptist Historical Collection, Furman University.

[14] Bethel [S. C.] Baptist Association, *Circular Letter, 1794* ([n.p., n.d.]), pp. 7–8.

[15] For example, see the "Circular Letter for 1799" of the Georgia Baptist Association, in Mercer, *History of the Georgia Baptist Association*, p. 141.

of southern religion. Before the Revolution the first Baptist church in Albe-marle County, Virginia, felt the need of divine aid: "And proposals [were] made for a Fast. . . . Thinking it a duty that the Lord required of us And that it was anciently Practiced by the Sants [*sic*] of old and by Common People in Distress (And we read of none but had their request answered)."[16] A decade after the Great Revival, when James McGready, one of the preeminent leaders of that revival, was faced with another dark period in the progress of the church, he preached once more a fast day sermon: "If we will glance over the history of the Church in all ages of the world, we will discover that fasting and prayer have been the means to which the people of God have resorted, that they might cast themselves upon his protection, and obtain from his Omnipotent Arm deliverance in times of public judgements, and of great national calamity."[17] A forgiving, loving God would certainly accept man's apologetic fasting, and God could be expected to hear and act upon heartfelt prayers for such spiritual requests as forgiveness and guidance. A Methodist sermon by George A. Reed delivered several times in the 1790s argued that God always answered reasonable prayer: "For those blessings GOD has promised absolutely to give, such as pardon, grace, & eternal life, we cannot be too earnest, or explicit in our prayer."[18] Asbury posed for himself a rhetorical question, "Does God always hear prayer, and answer it? If it is in the Spirit's groaning, and in purity of intention, and in faith, doubtless he does."[19]

The next logical step for the revival-hungry ministers was to urge widespread fasting as a symbol of public repentance and general prayer as supplication for God's forgiveness and blessings. None could know when God would begin the reformation: one could only be patient, continue days of petitioning, and look forward to the time when the Spirit would work anew. The manner in which the clergy persevered in their exhortations of prayer and fasting was a measure of their confidence both in God's benevolence and their understanding of his ways. Here they found the strength to maintain their expectation that when Christians had fulfilled these preparations, God would reply in kind. For in a very real sense, they had constructed a covenant relationship with respect to the idea of revivalism. Once

[16] Chestnut Grove Baptist Church, "Minute Book, 1773–1811," May 1773, Virginia Baptist Historical Society, University of Richmond.

[17] McGready, *The Posthumous Works of the Reverend and Pious James M'Gready, Late Minister of the Gospel, in Henderson, Kentucky*, ed. James Smith, 2 vols. (Louisville, Ky., 1831–1833), 2: 313.

[18] From an untitled sermon preached four times in 1793, and once in 1796, by Reed, in his "Papers," Duke University Library, Durham, N. C.

[19] Asbury, *Journal and Letters*, March 5, 1806, 2: 497.

men had done their duty toward God, he could certainly be trusted to restore the season of religious plenty. The ministerial purpose now was to lead individuals to fulfill the conditions for God's mercy.

The multitude of pastoral and circular letters, sermons, and calls to repentance that resulted never expressed more than a small portion of the theory behind expected providential deliverance. But what they said illustrates the belief that out of the decline would come a religious resurgence. As early in the period as 1793, the Synod of Virginia appointed a day to be set aside for "fasting & prayer to supplicate the influence of the holy Spirit to be poured out upon our Churches & to awaken & convert Sinners, & to quicken the children of God in their respective duties."[20] In that same year Richard Furman of Charleston described a "general Fast" that the South Carolina Baptist Association had sponsored: "May God of his Great Mercy hear the Prayers of his People, and not only avert national Calamities, but revive a Work of Grace in his Churches, and all our Souls."[21]

In one church organization after another—the Synod of the Carolinas in 1795; Hanover Presbytery in 1800; Kentucky's Transylvania Presbytery in 1800; Bear Creek, North Carolina, Baptist Church in 1801— members were called upon to plead with God for divine aid. Rarely, however, did the request for congregational cooperation express the entire theological interpretation as completely as did that of the Hanover Presbytery in 1799 after several of its leading ministers had died. Its pastoral letter read in part: "The Synod being deeply affected with the great loss which the Church has sustained, . . . at a time when their labors seemed more needful than ever; and conceiving that such Dispensations of Providence call for Humiliation before God, accompanied with earnest prayer that he would rise up others to supply their place; and having appointed . . . a day of Fasting & prayer for the above purpose, the Presbytery resolved to comply with the said appointment."[22]

Quite obviously then, ministers and congregations across the South were seeking reconciliation with God and anticipating his forgiveness and blessings. The religious had convinced themselves that the existence of an observable decline in religious interest somehow foreshadowed a resurgence, for "All the dispensations of Providence refer to, tend to promote, and shall finally terminate in, the advancement of the best interests of his

[20] Synod of Virginia, "Minutes," Vol. 1, September 23, 1793.

[21] Furman to Rachel Furman [his mother], December 10, 1793, Furman Family Papers.

[22] Hanover Presbytery, "Minutes," Vol. 4, October 25, 1799. Photocopy in Union Theological Seminary in Virginia, original at Historical Foundation of the Reformed and Presbyterian Churches, Montreat, N. C.

church and people."[23] The absence of religious vitality awakened Christians to their mistakes and frailties.

This, it was thought, was what God had intended; and since God answered prayer, deliverance would certainly follow. "Render to Jehovah his unquestionable and too long detained due," urged the Charleston Baptist Association, "and prove him herewith, if he will not, in such a case, according to his word, open the windows of heaven and pour you out a blessing, that there even shall not be room sufficient to hold it."[24] In one church after another, prayer societies were organized in an effort to accelerate the beginning of God's deliverance.[25] Their faith in God's benevolence provided hope; their understanding of the conditions to be met gave perseverance. Before a revival could occur, the true believers had to generate a certain attitude among the nominal Christians. Despite the present calamitous condition of religion, God could be expected someday to begin working anew. The beliefs and efforts of the North Carolina Kehukee Baptist Association portray this evangelical consensus and illustrate the mental attitude so conducive to revivalism that had developed.

> As early as the year 1778, a revival was greatly desired, and a fast was proclaimed, to humble ourselves before the Lord, and to solicit the throne of grace for a revival. In 1785 ... another fast was proclaimed. . . . [I]n 1794, the Association agreed to appoint the Saturday before the fourth Sunday in every month, a day for *prayer-meetings* throughout the Churches . . . to make earnest prayer and supplication to Almighty God for a revival of religion. Thus the means were used, and the request was so laudable, that there was no doubt but the Lord would grant the *desires* of the righteous . . . . For the Lord has promised, *ask and ye shall receive.*[26]

In addition to all the foregoing, there also existed a quiet undercurrent of speculation about the millennium to come. Virtually none of this chiliastic thought was expressed before the revival began. Then the momentous-

---

[23] Presbyterian Church, *Minutes of the General Assembly, A.D. 1789 to A.D. 1820 Inclusive*, "Pastoral Letter, May 22, 1799" (Philadelphia, 1847), p. 178.

[24] Charleston Baptist Association, *Minutes*, "Circular Letter, November, 1795" ([n.p., n.d.]), pp. 6–7, South Carolina Baptist Historical Collection, Furman University, Greenville, S. C.

[25] See, for example, Rev. Archibald Alexander [president of Hampden-Sydney College] to Rev. Nathan Strong, January 25, 1802, in the *Connecticut Evangelical Magazine* 2 (March 1802): 354; Eli Caruthers, "Richard Hugg King and His Times. Reminiscences of Rev. Eli Caruthers of Orange Presbytery, N. C., 1862," pp. 23–24, typescript, North Carolina State Archives, Raleigh, N. C.; and Foote, *Sketches of North Carolina*, p. 343.

[26] Burkitt and Read, *History of the Kehukee Baptist Association*, pp. 139–40.

ness of the revival itself seemed to release the more extravagant hopes that Jesus Christ was preparing to return. That this idea could appear simultaneously throughout the South indicates that the germinal beliefs were already present. Derived from an interpretation of the Scriptures, this belief held that there would be a falling away, accompanied by the unspiritual reign of an antichrist. Yet eventually, by this interpretation, Richard McNemar wrote, "there would be glorious times upon earth, and Christ would appear again, and set up his kingdom, and gather the nations into it." Near the end of the disastrous decade of the 1790s, according to McNemar—perhaps the preeminent contemporary exponent of millennialism—many began to wonder when the antichrist regime would fall, to be succeeded by Jesus Christ's return and the establishment of his true kingdom. "And many," he wrote, "began to apprehend that this period was not far off; and concluded it was time to leave off their vain disputes, and unite in prayer, for Christ to come and pour out his spirit, gather his people into one, make an end of sin, and fill the earth with his glory."[27] This probably rare thought only added another element of that hope which confidently expected imminent fulfillment.

Like a room filled with oil-soaked cloths, the South was primed to blaze with the fires of religious zeal. Once an outbreak occurred of sufficient intensity and size to attract more than local attention, the revival spark would sweep across the South. The extravagant camp meeting revivals in Kentucky were perfectly suited to perform that function. With them the Great Revival, long sought after, long prayed for, was to begin.

[27] M'Nemar, *The Kentucky Revival* (New York, 1846), pp. 11–12. The work was first published in Cincinnati in 1807.

Chapter Four

Portents of Revival

The climate of ideas, beliefs, and hopes out of which the Great Revival in the South developed is more important than the location or circumstances of its actual beginning. Yet from a small start in Logan County, Kentucky, the revival gained momentum and symbolic meaning until it was powerful enough to sweep across the South. It was only through an unusual combination of personality, theology, time, society, and coincidence that a remarkable outbreak of religious emotion erupted in Logan County. The leading personality in this particular beginning was James McGready.[1] More than any other single individual, McGready, a Presbyterian, transferred the evangelistic New Side doctrines of the Great Awakening to frontier Kentucky. In his career both technique and theology were ideally united for revivalism. His success at igniting a congregation to high intensity proved to be the catalyst that triggered a southern epidemic of religious enthusiasm. His ministerial accomplishments illustrate how one man, propitiously placed, could initiate a broad social movement.

James McGready was probably born of Scotch-Irish parents in western Pennsylvania about 1760. In 1778 his family migrated to Guilford County, North Carolina, and settled near the congregation of David Caldwell, a respected Presbyterian of evangelical persuasion.[2] James McGready, Sr., was probably a farmer; at any rate we do know that his large family was poor, and the youthful James had to work long, tiring hours in the fields with his brothers. Reputedly he was quiet, thoughtful, desirous of an education, and extremely punctual in the performance of his religious duties. He seemed to be destined for the ministry, for, in the inimitable way of devout denominational biography, it is said of him that "he never omitted private prayer from the time he was seven years old, and having been preserved from outbreaking sins, from profane swearing, from intoxication, and sabbath breaking, and other excesses, he had begun to think that he was sanctified from his birth."[3]

Although it is difficult to imagine such a saintly youth, his religious bent vividly impressed a visiting uncle. The relative persuaded McGready's parents to let young James accompany him back to Pennsylvania to receive theological training. The first year there, probably 1784, McGready boarded with and helped operate the farm of John McMillan, the first Presbyterian minister to have a regular congregation west of the Alleghenies. McGready undoubtedly received private tutoring in the home of McMillan, a graduate of the College of New Jersey (Princeton). In the fall of 1785 Joseph Smith, another Presbyterian minister—and also product of the College of New Jersey—opened an academy nearby to prepare young men for the ministry. McGready immediately enrolled, but shortly afterwards, when McMillan also opened a "log college," he transferred there.[4] This literary and theological academy was subsequently famous for the large number of Presbyterian ministers it provided for the rapidly developing West. McMillan taught by means of written lectures arranged in the form of questions and answers. The students took notes and were expected to memorize and recite the lectures. This system, though undoubtedly dull and dogmatic, has been characterized as "concise, condensed, *multum in Parvo*, lucid, and forceful."[5] It was here that McGready learned to present his thoughts in clear, logical, ordered form.

Though McGready had long considered himself sanctified, it was around this time (1786) that he—or so the story goes—heard several friends discussing his religious condition. Upon overhearing their conversation, he realized that he had never experienced a vivid new birth. John McMillan was among the New Side Presbyterians who believed that religion was more a matter of the heart than the head. Consequently he emphasized the necessity of a vigorous conversion experience. McGready, now doubting his own position, earnestly sought a spiritual rebirth. According to the Reverend James Smith, "in the year A. D. 1786, on a Sabbath morning, at a

[1] James Smith, *History of the Christian Church* (Nashville, Tenn., 1835), p. 562.

[2] Foote, *Sketches of North Carolina*, pp. 368–70; William B. Sprague, *Annals of the American Pulpit*, 7 vols. (New York, 1859), 3:278; Smith, *History of the Christian Church*, p. 561; S. M. Rankin, *History of the Buffalo Presbyterian Church and Her People* (Greensboro, N. C., 1934), p. 48. David Caldwell was a graduate of Pequea Academy, a revival-oriented log college in southeastern Pennsylvania. John McMillan, who would be McGready's spiritual mentor, was also a Pequea alumnus. See Dwight Raymond Guthrie, *John McMillan: The Apostle of Presbyterianism in the West, 1752–1833* (Pittsburgh, Pa., 1952), p. 12.

[3] Foote, *Sketches of North Carolina*, p. 368.

[4] Ibid.; Joseph Smith, *Old Redstone; or, Historical Sketches of Western Presbyterianism* (Philadelphia, 1854), pp. 361–62; Sprague, *Annals of the American Pulpit*, 3:278; Sweet, *The Presbyterians*, p. 26.

[5] Quoted by Sweet, *The Presbyterians*, pp. 77–78; see also Guthrie, *John McMillan*, pp. 85–88.

Sacramental meeting, near the Monogahala [*sic*], he was savingly converted to God." [6] This riverside sacramental occasion could very well have been a revival meeting, for the Presbyterian strongholds of western Pennsylvania were then undergoing a prolonged period of religious vitality. Many came from considerable distances to hear the sermons of evangelists such as McMillan. These revival meetings sometimes lasted all night, and "Frequently the exercised could not suppress their feelings of joy or distress, but gave them vent in groans and cries." [7]

Thus in the mid-1780s, McGready was learning the technique, perhaps unconsciously, of practical revivalism. Soon thereafter he completed his formal education and was licensed to preach by the Presbytery of Redstone (in Pennsylvania) on August 13, 1788. [8] That fall the new minister departed for his parents' home in North Carolina. On his way he traveled through the region of Virginia then experiencing an interdenominational revival. McGready stayed for some time at Hampden-Sydney College, where the Presbyterian phase of this Virginia movement had begun. The unusually effective preaching of John Blair Smith, combined with his admirable prevention of emotional excesses, fired McGready to emulation. For him, the efficacy of pungent revivalistic preaching was proved. [9]

Guilford County, North Carolina, was in sad religious condition when McGready arrived. Partly as a result of the disruptive powers of war, congregations were scattered, irreligion was widespread, and materialism seemed rampant. Backcountry mores had little to recommend them to ministers, especially the boisterous custom of guzzling whiskey at funerals. McGready gained local repute when, upon being asked to deliver thanks over the refreshments at a wake, he obstinately and scathingly refused. His caustic rebuff created a sensation, but once the furor had subsided, and with the county's attention now focused upon him, his preaching was remarkably effective. In his own congregations of Haw River and Stoney Creek, he was particularly successful. He pointed out the formalism, hypocrisy, and

[6] Smith, *History of the Christian Church*, p. 562; slightly different accounts are in Robert V. Foster, "A Sketch of the History of the Cumberland Presbyterian Church," in *American Church History*, 13 vols. (New York, 1904), 11:261; and Herschel S. Porter, "History of the Cumberland Presbyterian Church," in *An Original History of All the Religious Denominations in the United States*, ed. I. Daniel Rupp (Harrisburg, Pa., 1849), p. 500n. For McMillan's views on conversion, see Guthrie, *John McMillan*, p. 66.

[7] William Speer, *The Great Revival of 1800* (Philadelphia, 1872), pp. 19–20, quoting the *Western Missionary Magazine*, 1803.

[8] Sprague, *Annals of the American Pulpit*, 3:278.

[9] Ibid.; and Foote, *Sketches of North Carolina*, p. 370.

sin of the people and preached the overriding necessity of a new birth. He made his congregations feel, as he himself had earlier felt, that they were unfit to be acknowledged church members. "An unworthy communicant in such circumstances as yours," he would grimly exhort, "is more offensive to Almighty God than a loathsome carcass crawling with vermin set before a dainty prince." [10] He was adamant in his insistence upon the importance of knowing the exact time and place that the saving experience had occurred.

About the year 1790 McGready married and with his bride made his home midway between his two congregations. Like most Presbyterian ministers, he soon opened a school in his home. Frequently he preached in the Buffalo and Alamance churches of David Caldwell—McGready was soon a great favorite of the students at Caldwell's "Guilford Academy." [11] One can easily understand why the young and impressionable students were so affected by McGready. A very plain dresser, he was a large, rather portly man, six feet tall, with prominent features. His grave appearance and piercing eyes chained one's attention; his voice seemed unearthly, coarse, and tremulous. Thunderous tones and jerky gesticulations increased his hypnotic ability to sway an audience. The preacher usually began very calmly, but as he progressed he increased in tempo, volume, and enthusiasm—his conclusions never failed to be fervent and fiery. Especially did he excel in public prayer; congregations were often brought to tears by his long, original, and poignant "wrestlings with God." [12] Barton W. Stone, later one of the outstanding revivalists in Kentucky, remembered first hearing McGready preach at Caldwell's academy: "Such earnestness, such zeal, such powerful persuasion, enforced by the joys of heaven and miseries of hell, I had never witnessed before. My mind was chained by him, and followed him closely in his rounds of heaven, earth, and hell with feeling indescribable. His concluding remarks were addressed to the sinner to flee the wrath

[10] Foote, *Sketches of North Carolina*, p. 372; E. W. Caruthers, *A Sketch of the Life and Character of the Rev. David Caldwell, D.D.* (Greensboro, N. C., 1842), p. 252; Smith, *History of the Christian Church*, p. 562; Guion Griffis Johnson, "Revival Movements in Ante-Bellum North Carolina," *North Carolina Historical Review* 10(January 1933): 27–28.

[11] Foote, *Sketches of North Carolina*, p. 373.

[12] Ibid., p. 372; Barton W. Stone, *A Short History of the Life of Barton W. Stone*, in James R. Rogers, *The Cane Ridge Meeting-House* (Cincinnati, Ohio, 1910), pp. 119–21, hereafter listed as Stone, *Autobiography*; Davidson, *History of the Presbyterian Church in Kentucky*, p. 132; F. R. Cossitt, *The Life and Times of Rev. Finis Ewing* (Louisville, Ky., 1853), p. 45; Richard Beard, *Brief Biographical Sketches of Some of the Early Ministers of the Cumberland Presbyterian Church* (Nashville, Tenn., 1867), pp. 16–17.

to come without delay. Never before had I comparatively felt the force of truth. Such was my excitement that, had I been standing, I should have probably sunk to the floor under the impression."[13]

McGready was more interested in the salvation of his listeners than in constructing a formal creed—he was first and foremost a revivalist—but his carefully prepared sermons do reflect the theological subtleties of evangelical Calvinism.[14] His most effective homiletic technique was the intensification of his listeners' fears of damnation. The glowing beauty and tranquillity of heaven were starkly contrasted with the miseries of hell. Such eternal topics, expounded with his oratorical skills, totally engrossed each member of the congregation. From the testimony of the Reverend William Barnet, "Father McGready would so describe Heaven, that you would almost see its glories, and long to be there, and he would so array hell and its horrors before the wicked, that they would tremble and quake, imagining a lake of fire and brimstone yawning to overwhelm them, and the wrath of God thrusting them down the horrible abyss."[15]

How could one escape this burning damnation? On this issue, McGready was quick and to the point—man must experience new birth. This regeneration, which imprints the image of God upon one's soul, is of utmost importance, for, "In that awful day, when the universe, assembled, must appear before the quick and dead, the question brethren, will not be, were you a Presbyterian—a Seceder—a Covenanter—a Baptist—or a Methodist; but, did you experience a new birth? Did you accept of Christ and his salvation as set forth in the Gospel?"[16] Those dead to sin receive this new spiritual life only—in an ultimate sense—through the power and will of God, but men have a necessary subsidiary role in the sanctification process. This human role is to repent of past and present sin and consequently recognize that God must have man's complete obedience and subservience. Yet God, in his merciful providence, generated within the sinner the feelings of contrition which lead to human repentance.[17]

It is in this manner that a religious decline eventually effects among individual Christians a greater dependence upon God. But this providentially evoked sense of guilt requires an act of personal volition.

[13] Stone, *Autobiography*, p. 121.

[14] McGready, *Posthumous Works*, 1:318. For another analysis, see John Opie, Jr., "James McGready: Theologian of Frontier Revivalism," *Church History* 34 (December 1965): 445–56.

[15] Cossitt, *The Life of Finis Ewing*, p. 43.

[16] McGready, *Posthumous Works*, 2:71.

[17] Ibid., 1:92.

You must attend to the business of your salvation. . . .

You must forsake your vain companions, vain conversation, and every known sin; you must diligently attend to the performance of every known duty. . . . Thus you must pray in your family and in secret; you must reflect on your dreadful condition. . . .

Lie at the feet of Jesus, and like an humble penitent, plead his gracious free offers of mercy to the chief of sinners; plead the infinite, all-sufficiency of that atoning blood which has washed away the sins of millions.[18]

"It is the will of God that the sinner should try to forsake his sins, and as a guilty, condemned criminal, fall at the footstool of sovereign mercy, crying for pardon." Thus humbly supplicated, God made possible the saving faith.[19] This faith, to which the sinner is led by the Holy Spirit, is the condition for salvation. Man's belief in Jesus Christ's redemptive death on the cross justifies man in the eyes of God. Thus by simple faith are men saved.[20]

The orthodox Presbyterian interpretation of election had little meaning for McGready. Although he occasionally used the term, and never denied it as a principle, for him it meant little more than that God, from the beginning, had known those who would eventually achieve justification. There was no sense of this being a small group, limited in number. Nor was there a feeling on his part that individual salvation was really a matter of inevitability. Rather, McGready believed that gospel ministers had an essential role to perform in leading their listeners to an earnest consideration of their spiritual condition.

[The minister] must use every possible means to alarm and awaken Christless sinners from their security, and bring them to a sense of their danger and guilt. He must use every argument to convince them of the horrors of an unconverted state; he must tell them the worst of their case —roar the thunders of Sinai in their ears, and flash the lightenings of Jehovah's vengeance in their faces. . . . Let them hear or not, though the world scorn and revile us, call us low preachers and madmen, Methodists —do this we must, or we will be the worst murderers; the blood of sinners will be required at our hands—their damnation will lie at our door.[21]

Motivated by such a concept of his ministerial duty, fired with zeal, eloquent and extremely energetic, McGready soon produced a vigorous renewal of interest in religion. Beginning about the year 1791, the McGready-led revival spread across north-central North Carolina, generating repentant fervor throughout the congregations of Hawfields, Cross Roads, Alamance, Buffalo, Stoney Creek, Bethlehem, Haw River, Eno,

[18] Ibid., 1:119–20.   [19] Ibid., 1:73; 1:126.   [20] Ibid., 1:286.
[21] Ibid., 1:316–17.

and those in Granville, and on the Hico and Dan rivers.[22] Like the Virginia revival of 1787–1789, this North Carolina awakening (remembered by David Caldwell as "McGrady's revival") did not achieve the fame, fervency, or widespread results of those to come after 1800. It did, however, enable the churches to gain enough strength to survive the emigration and lean years of the decade to follow. Of greater significance for the future, the charismatic McGready induced many able young men to enter the ministry. "There never was a time," wrote the Reverend Robert Wilson in 1793, "in which so many young men were turning to the ministry. . . . makes me think one of two things will inevitably follow—either they will be dispised & loaded with reproaches from every quarter or they will be instruments in the hand of God in producing a glorious revival."[23] Five of these young licentiates who shared the evangelistic zeal and theology of their mentor subsequently migrated to Kentucky, there to play an indispensable role in the development of the Great Revival: William McGee, Barton W. Stone, William Hodge, Samuel McAdow, and John Rankin.[24]

In the process of promoting this local revival, McGready vigorously attacked the materialism and immorality of the piedmont society. He was especially careful to assail the irreligion and hypocrisy of the better classes. Soon afterward opposition erupted, for his blistering attacks on the sins of the wealthy greatly offended several families of influence at his Stoney Creek congregation. Their counterattack was climaxed by upsetting the pews, burning the altar, and, in a final effort to drive him away, they sent him a letter written in blood, threatening death if he did not leave. The next Sunday he replied to his detractors with a sermon based on Jesus' famous lament: "O Jerusalem, Jerusalem, thou that killest the prophets and stonest them which are sent unto thee, how often would I have gathered thy children together even as a hen gathereth her chickens under her wings, and ye would not. Behold, your house is left unto you desolate."[25]

Whether McGready was intimidated or not, he quickly requested an

---

[22] Jethro Rumple, *The History of Presbyterianism in North Carolina* [Reprinted from the *North Carolina Presbyterian*, 1878–1887] (Richmond, Va., 1966), p. 64.

[23] Wilson to Reverend Samuel Wilson, Crowders Creek, N. C., September 30, 1793, L. C. Glenn Collection.

[24] Foote, *Sketches of North Carolina*, p. 376; and Caruthers, "Richard Hugg King," p. 40.

[25] Smith, *History of the Christian Church*, pp. 563–64; Foote, *Sketches of North Carolina*, p. 375. Perhaps most of the opposition arose from those of anti-revivalist, Old Side persuasion, for this had been the viewpoint of the region before Caldwell. See Rankin, *History of Buffalo Church*, pp. 19, 151–52.

intermediate presbytery to release him from his position as soon as he received a call from former members of his congregation who had moved to Kentucky. Although the special presbytery disapproved of his "hasty preparations for a removal," they permitted his retreat. McGready, with well-chosen discretion and speed, promptly removed himself from immediate danger and, in August 1796, prudently departed for Kentucky. On the way he preached several months in Knoxville, Tennessee, but soon thereafter reached his destination, Logan County—in the heart of the untamed Cumberland country.[26]

Religion was obviously languishing in the Kentucky of late 1796. The consensus of travelers, ministers, and common citizens was that irreligion and heathenism were in close competition. Kentucky was experiencing a staggering growth of population—from 73,677 in 1790 to 220,955 in 1800. This onrush of settlers had simply outgrown the ability of the churches to keep up. The first ministers had come to Kentucky immediately after the Revolution, and during the 1780s both the Baptists and Presbyterians had established a foothold. Methodist circuit riders had soon added these western districts to their itinerary, but the efforts of all three denominations had not kept pace with the booming development of the state.[27] The internecine feuding over hymns, footwashing, and centralized authority further minimized the effectiveness of the meager religious institutions.

Most of the Presbyterian ministers who preceded McGready to Kentucky seem to have had rather mediocre ability. Even Robert Davidson, a staunch defender of orthodoxy and critic of the revival, admitted that these early clergymen were "past their prime" and "accustomed to a certain fixed routine."[28] Over the past decade they had managed to establish a loose network of churches and three presbyteries across the breadth of Kentucky, but the times now called for energetic preaching. This the older clergy, most of whom were from Virginia and Pennsylvania, seemed unable or unwilling to do. Their formal, uninspiring sermons contributed to

[26] Foster, "A Sketch of the Cumberland Presbyterian Church," p. 261; Orange Presbytery, "Minutes," September 27, 1796, pp. 7–8, Ms in the Historical Foundation of the Reformed and Presbyterian Churches, Montreat, N. C.

[27] The following illustrate the foundations of the denominations in Kentucky: John M. Peck, "Baptists of the Mississippi Valley," *Christian Review* 17 (October 1852): 482–514; Spencer, *A History of Kentucky Baptists*, vol. 1; Davidson, *History of the Presbyterian Church in Kentucky*; Robert H. Bishop, *An Outline of the History of the Church in the State of Kentucky* (Lexington, Ky., 1824); Redford, *History of Methodism in Kentucky*, vol. 1.

[28] Davidson, *History of the Presbyterian Church in Kentucky*, p. 103.

the loss of interest in religion. Perhaps some depended too heavily on God's role, to the detriment of human efforts. Or just as likely, the long period of decline, combined with needless intradenominational feuding in the face of a materialistic society deficient in religion, had drained away their zeal. The few sacramental occasions that the Presbyterian Church recognized were seldom observed. The Lord's Supper was the preeminent sacrament among each of the evangelical denominations—so preeminent that it had become synonymous with the term "sacramental meeting." In this secular Kentucky environment, communion was rarely taken, the ceremony itself had become tedious and stylized, and most significantly, it had gradually become an institution with little appeal to young people.

Very probably as the lean years lingered, the more rigid Presbyterian ministers sought to preserve what seemed to be left of professing Christians by tightening the admission requirements for the sacraments. One of the unfortunate results of such a policy was the limiting of participants according to age. The Reverend Thomas Cleland remembered that as a youth in Kentucky, he rarely saw people of his age welcome at the communion exercise. The "action sermons" preparing the congregation for the ritual seemed to debar almost everyone, but they so severely decreased adolescent involvement that Cleland "had long since come to the conclusion that *young people* had nothing to do with the sacrament, that it was intended for old people only." [29] The historian Robert Davidson was even more explicit: "The approach of young persons to the communion was a rarity never expected. It was the general impression that none but elderly persons, who from their years had acquired steady habits and were out of the way of temptation, should partake of the ordinance. As a natural consequence the young felt at ease, and gave themselves no concern about religion; and the Church, gaining no accessions, was in a fair way of becoming extinct through natural decrease." [30] Quite understandably, such a church would not seem relevant to the young people of Kentucky.

As a result, even in those sections where there was an organized Presbyterian Church, many youths were excluded. In many other regions, parents in all denominations decried the absence of any sort of religious training for their children, as well as for themselves. Hence in a literal sense, this brash new society coming of age in Kentucky included a large, youthful segment that was virtually unchurched. In a rural environment, this underage group represented a very substantial portion of the total population. As early as

---

[29] Edward P. Humphrey and Thomas A. Cleland, *Memoirs of the Rev. Thomas Cleland: Compiled from his Private Papers* (Cincinnati, Ohio, 1859), p. 37.

[30] Davidson, *History of the Presbyterian Church in Kentucky*, p. 104.

1790, the percentage of the white population under sixteen was higher in Kentucky than in any other state except Tennessee, which was even less developed. (While the national figure was 49 percent, 54.5 percent of Kentucky's white population was under sixteen, and 55 percent of Tennessee's.) By 1800 this youthful percentage in Kentucky had increased to 55.2 percent.[31] Such figures are not unusual for rural areas where every child was another farmhand, but they graphically illustrate why the absence of a vigorous religious establishment was resulting in a continually increasing body of potential converts. Further, the great bulk of Kentucky families were small farmers who owned no slaves.[32] It was for just such people, with little education, wealth, or pretensions, that evangelical religion was most attractive.[33]

Turnerian interpretations notwithstanding, the inhabitants of Kentucky had neither a unique inclination to emotionalism nor a quenchless thirst for hard liquor. "One half of the white people, at least," in the words of the early Kentucky historian, Humphrey Marshall, "and probably, three-fourths of the slaves, were from Virginia."[34] Indeed, wrote Davidson, Kentucky was "but the Old Dominion expanded. They cherished the feelings and the name of Virginians."[35] The majority of those who had not come from Virginia were once natives of the Carolinas. The trek across the mountains, while difficult, could hardly have served, in Oscar Handlin's words, as a "brutal filter" to produce a people of strikingly different characteristics in the trans-Appalachian region. Many of the preachers were Virginians as well.

[31] [U.S. Census for 1800], *Return of the Whole Number of Persons Within the Several Districts of the United States* (Washington, D. C., 1800), p. 2P; and *A Century of Population Growth, From the First Census to the Twelfth, 1790–1900* (Washington, D. C., 1909), pp. 200 and passim.

[32] Ibid. Computations derived from census figures. The southern states in 1790 averaged 53 slaves for every 100 white persons. Kentucky at this time had only 20 slaves per 100 whites (and Tennessee had 11). In 1800 the proportion of slaves to the total population of Kentucky was 18.3 percent, but in the region around Logan County, the percentage was only 11.1 percent. Thus this section, in particular, was a region of "plain folk."

[33] Although discussing another region in a later era, Whitney R. Cross has shown that there exists a direct relationship between rurality and a susceptibility to religious enthusiasm. A commercial, more cosmopolitan environment, on the other hand, retards such enthusiasm. *The Burned-Over District: The Social and Intellectual History of Enthusiastic Religion in Western New York, 1800–1850* (Ithaca, N. Y., 1950), esp. chapt. 4.

[34] Humphrey Marshall, *The History of Kentucky*, 2 vols. in 1 (Frankfort, Ky., 1824), 1:441–42. This passage is not in the original, 1812 edition.

[35] Davidson, *History of the Presbyterian Church in Kentucky*, p. 56.

Most of the early Presbyterian ministers had been trained in the Old Dominion. So many Baptist leaders had come from there that Robert Semple called Kentucky "the cemetery of Virginia Baptist preachers." [36] Besides the growing ranks of Methodist circuit riders who were active in the West, a large number of former Virginia-based itinerants had settled in Kentucky. [37] The background of most of the people in Kentucky, then, was very similar to those throughout the seaboard South.

Furthermore, many members in Kentucky had been purged from the church rolls in the time of apathy. These people had a vague relationship with religion. As in other states, clergy and conscientious Christian laymen were concerned about the declining state of religion. Church organizations such as the Transylvania Presbytery called for days of public fasting and prayer, as well as personal repentance and reformation. [38] Social conditions and religious climate both called for a revival of religion.

Kentucky had not experienced an awakening since the closing years of the 1780s, when the Methodists and Baptists enjoyed a brief period of growth. [39] But if Kentucky, along with the rest of the South, seemed ripe for a revival in the years after 1795, certain factors made the area south of the Kentucky River and just north of the Tennessee border—the Cumberland region—particularly primed for an explosion of religious fervor. The overwhelming majority of Baptist ministers in the state were of revivalistic Separate Baptist heritage. Most had migrated west after the union of Baptists in Virginia and had therefore adopted the more conciliatory term Regular Baptists. The only Baptist association in the South that still retained the name of the zealous Separate Baptists was the South Kentucky Association, [40] centered in the section containing Logan County. This area of Kentucky was not dominated by towns, where law suits, politics, and merchandizing might monopolize one's attention.

Yet of even greater immediate importance was the skilled phalanx of

---

[36] Semple, *History of the Baptists in Virginia*, p. 354.

[37] W. E. Arnold, *History of Methodism in Kentucky*, 2 vols. (Louisville, Ky., 1935–1936), 1: 174–75.

[38] Transylvania Presbytery, "Minutes," April 25, 1794, and October 8, 1800, reprinted in Sweet, *The Presbyterians*, pp. 144, 185–86.

[39] James Haw to Francis Asbury, 1789, in *Arminian Magazine* 2 (April 1790): 202–4; William Hickman, "A Short Account of My Life and Travels" (1828), p. 15, typescript at Southern Baptist Theological Seminary, Louisville, Ky.; and Spencer, *History of Kentucky Baptists*, 1: 174.

[40] Ibid., pp. 107, 211, 480–81; Peck, "Baptists of the Mississippi Valley," p. 485. In 1800 the Separates represented about one-fifth of the churches and members in Kentucky.

revivalistic Presbyterians who entered Kentucky from North Carolina after 1796. These six men of zeal, including McGready, more than doubled the proportion (from one-seventh to one-third) of evangelical Presbyterian ministers in the state.[41] Five of these six located in the Cumberland region, where the Separate Baptists and the Methodist circuit riders were already established. And James McGready, their leader in Kentucky, had been instrumental in turning these Presbyterian evangelists to the ministry. Each member of this group—William McGee, William Hodge, John Rankin, Barton W. Stone, and Samuel McAdow—was trained in the theology and techniques perfected by McGready. Each emphasized the importance of being able to date the conversion experience. Each participated in the camp meeting revivals which later swept across the state.

Hence through a unique chemistry of situation, demography, ministerial training, and popular desire, the Cumberland region of Kentucky after the mid-1790s was a fertile seedbed of revivalism. In the late autumn of 1796, James McGready arrived there. In January 1797 he took charge of three small congregations—Red River, Muddy River, and Gasper River, all in Logan County. The prevailing "universal deadness and stupidity" continued until that May, when as a result of his persuasive sermons the first "outpouring of [God's] Spirit" occurred.[42] At this time McGready was emphasizing the tripartite theology of repentance, faith, and regeneration. During the spring and summer the people were moved—eight or nine claiming conversion—but by winter the old deadness returned, and the general falling away almost negated the previous growth.[43]

The few steadfast "praying Christians" were greatly alarmed. During the winter McGready and his sparse congregations adopted the following covenant, binding themselves to pray for an outpouring of the Holy Spirit:

> We feel encouraged to unite our supplications to a prayer hearing God, for the outpouring of his spirit, that his people may be quickened and

[41] Based on a study of the various biographical sketches contained throughout Davidson, *History of the Presbyterian Church in Kentucky.*

[42] James McGready, "A Short Narrative of the Revival of Religion in Logan County, in the State of Kentucky, and the Adjacent Settlements in the State of Tennessee, from May 1797, until September 1800," in the *New York Missionary Magazine* 4 (1803) : 74.

[43] Ibid.; McGready, "Narrative of the Commencement and Progress of the Revival of 1800. . . . In a Letter to a Friend. . . . Dated Logan County, Kentucky, October 23, 1801," in McGready, *Posthumous Works,* 1 : ix; also "Extract of a Letter from the Rev. James M. Gready, a Presbyterian Minister, in Logan County, Kentucky, to the Rev. Dr. Coke," in the *Methodist Magazine* [London] 26 (1803) : 181–84.

comforted, and that our children, and sinners generally, may be converted. Therefore, we bind ourselves to observe the third Saturday of each month, for one year, as a day of fasting and prayer, for the conversion of sinners in Logan county, and throughout the world. We also engage to spend one half hour every Saturday evening, beginning at the setting of the sun, and one half hour every Sabbath morning, at the rising of the sun, in pleading with God to revive his words.[44]

Thus covenanted the few sincere believers persevered throughout the cold winter, but little happened that could be ascribed to the mercies of God until the fourth Sunday of July 1798.

At a sacramental meeting of the Gasper River congregation, many felt themselves gloriously awakened, and McGready wrote that the "Lord poured out his spirit in a very remarkable manner." This heartening upsurge of spirituality spread; on the first Sunday of September the people of the Muddy River congregation were similarly moved. Soon this awakening spread among the Red River congregation, and throughout the entire region the inhabitants to an unusual degree turned their thoughts to religion.[45] The faithful confidently expected that God would begin his work among them, and as McGready's energetic efforts gradually increased their fervor, it became easier to believe that God was actually beginning his unchallengeable work of deliverance. The existence of revival sentiment at one congregation seemed to validate their religious expectations. With such substantive "proof," others were more than willing to put their reliance in their God's hands.

"But alas! danger was near—the Devil," interpreted the obviously partial McGready, "had his plan deeply laid." An opposing Presbyterian minister, James Balch, arrived and immediately ridiculed the entire work of the revival with its bare emotionalism—involving the struggling churches in dispute and confusion. The disrupting influences sown by the Old Side (antirevivalistic) Balch lasted for almost a year; in the meantime McGready's three congregations lay in a "dismal state of deadness and darkness."[46]

Yet never did McGready or the faithful remnant give up hope that God would send a restoring revival. Fasting, prayer, preaching continued, and on the last Sunday of July 1799, at a communion meeting at the Red River church, members again seriously responded to their minister's exhor-

[44] Covenant quoted by Smith, *History of the Christian Church*, pp. 565–66; see also McGready, "A Short Narrative of the Revival," pp. 74–75.

[45] Ibid.; and McGready, "Narrative of the Commencement . . . of the Revival," p. x.

[46] Ibid., pp. x–xi; and McGready, "A Short Narrative of the Revival," p. 151.

tations. Monday evening most of the congregation lingered around the door after the service, as if unwilling to leave without having their hopes fulfilled. After a brief consultation, McGready and the assisting ministers agreed to call the people back into the church, and then the preachers delivered long, passionate prayers and admonitions. Under these intense urgings, many members of the congregation felt themselves enlivened in spirit, comforted, and convicted. Their zeal increased their striving for repentance and God's forgiveness and mercy. "About this time," recorded McGready, "a remarkable spirit of prayer and supplication was given to Christians, and a sensible, heart-felt burden of the dreadful state of sinners out of Christ: so that it might be said with propriety, that Zion travailed in birth to bring forth her spiritual children." [47]

A month later, under the ministrations of McGready and one of his North Carolina converts, the Reverend John Rankin, such a revival developed at a Gasper River sacramental service that many were quite overcome with emotion and fell to the floor, so deeply were they struck with "heart-piercing conviction." [48] The uninhibited physical responses to penetrating preaching and beliefs that were soon to characterize the Kentucky phase of the Great Revival here made their first appearance. The revival now gained momentum. Enough conspicuous conversions and unusual physical phenomena had occurred to arrest attention. Unawakened neighbors were now encountering recently converted friends, and this lay cross-fertilization spread the zeal for revival far and near. Rapidly the upswing in religious feeling swept to the neighboring congregations. During the communion exercises at McGready's new church at Clay-lick, the revival again was experienced.

At each successive appearance, the awakening seemed to grow in power. The Muddy River church was the scene in late September 1799 of "the greatest, the most solemn and powerful time of any that had been before." [49] Rankin wrote in his autobiography that on this occasion he warned the hesitant with a pertinent text: "Behold ye dispisers and wonder. . . , for I work a work in your days, a work which you shall in no wise believe, though a man declare it unto you." [50] The growing numbers of converts needed

[47] Ibid., p. 152; and McGready, "Narrative of the Commencement . . . of the Revival," p. xi.

[48] Ibid., pp. xi–xii; McGready, "A Short Narrative of the Revival," pp. 152–53; and John Rankin, "Autobiographical Sketch, Written in 1845," in J. P. McLean, "The Kentucky Revival and Its Influence on the Miami Valley," *Ohio Archaeological and Historical Publications* 12 (April 1903) : 279.

[49] McGready, "A Short Narrative of the Revival," p. 153.

[50] Rankin, "Autobiographical Sketch," p. 279.

little such prodding to believe that God had begun his all-powerful work. Before winter restrained the large crowds, there was one last revival meeting in nearby Tennessee. Here McGready was joined by Rankin and by another of his North Carolina converts, the Reverend William McGee, an unusually fervent Presbyterian. During the ensuing winter nothing extraordinary occurred, but very few of those recently converted seemed to relapse into complacency. This was the proverbial calm before the storm, for the coming summer (1800) was to bring the most amazing displays of revivalistic zeal yet. As McGready said in his narrative,

> All the blessed displays of Almighty power and grace, all the sweet gales of the divine Spirit, and soul-reviving showers of the blessings of Heaven which we enjoyed before, and which we considered wonderful beyond conception; were but like a few scattering drops before a mighty rain, when compared with the overflowing floods of salvation, which the eternal, gracious Jehovah has poured out like a mighty river, upon this our guilty, unworthy country. The Lord has indeed shewed himself a prayer-hearing God: he has given his people a praying spirit and a lively faith, and then he has answered their prayers far beyond their highest expectations.[51]

The Great Revival of the South had found its beginning.

[51] McGready, "A Short Narrative of the Revival," p. 154.

Chapter Five

Kentucky Ablaze

At the close of the eighteenth century, Kentucky, with the rest of the South, had reached the point where dozens of ministers and thousands of church members were convinced that God would some day send his glorious deliverance.[1] Prayer societies, fasts, intense and urgent sermons, all were united in an effort to bring men into the necessary relationship with God. Hopeful expectation had largely subdued ministerial pessimism. Throughout the South, from the sea islands of South Carolina to the piedmont of Virginia, and even to the "Barrens" of Kentucky, the faithful remnant was waiting for God to send a revival. None could be sure where or when it would start, but all could be sure of one thing: God would do his work in strange and wonderful ways. This miraculous manifestation would be the seal, proving the authenticity of the heaven-sent revival.

During the last three years of the decade before 1800, there were small, sporadic revival outbursts scattered through the South. Yet none of these achieved the unusual fervor, duration, or fame necessary to seize the contemporary imagination. For example, the Baptists in Mason County, Kentucky, prospered in 1797 from a "manifest increase in spiritual interest." For the local churches intimately involved, these indications of renewal "afforded the eager watchmen grounds of hope." Three churches in the county baptized 277 new members,[2] but this revival was short-lived. The following year was peculiarly unpropitious for religion in the more densely inhabited regions. In the older, longer settled, and hence more populous counties of Kentucky (as with other states), political institutions were comparatively well established. Therefore a county like Mason, with the state's highest population in 1800,[3] would be particularly affected by the political agitations of a year such as 1798.

J. H. Spencer, the historian of Kentucky Baptists, sees just this as the cause for the rapid demise of the Mason County revival. During the year after its beginning, Kentuckians were distracted by politics as never before. The state was in turmoil over its proposed new constitution, which had been turned down by the state senate. Debate over the new plan of government embroiled many in the divisive issue of slavery. Furthermore, the obnoxious Alien and Sedition Acts inflamed public opinion. This political excitement drowned out the emerging religious sentiment in Mason and doubtless in other counties.[4]

In the relatively newer, more rural regions of Kentucky, where the population was sparser and political institutions were less organized, religion was better able to maintain its hold on the people. The Cumberland district was thus admirably suited for James McGready's efforts, for there was relatively little to distract men from the religious fervor and dedication he was feverishly working to promote. His increasing success in the previous three years had generated widespread excitement, and the stories of how sinners had fallen in convulsions pricked the curiosity of hundreds. The summer and autumn months of 1800 saw unparalleled crowds at the services conducted by McGready and his associates.

What were then considered the first really extraordinary manifestations of divine power occurred in the latter part of June 1800. Four or five hundred of the most devout members of the three congregations of Muddy River, Red River, and Gasper River met together at the Red River meetinghouse for a communion service.[5] For many in the group, this was the

---

[1] In most of the earlier literature, the Kentucky revival was equated with the Great Revival. The most relevant monograph, Catharine C. Cleveland's *Great Revival in the West, 1797–1805* (Chicago, 1916) suffers from her narrow focus on the frontier environment and the emphasis, so typical of her period, on the "instinctive" excitability of the Scotch-Irish who largely peopled the backcountry. Bernard A. Weisberger's *They Gathered at the River* (Boston, 1958) contains a narrative chapter on the Kentucky revival. The two best brief accounts are those of Donald G. Mathews, "The Second Great Awakening as an Organizing Process, 1780–1830: An Hypothesis," *American Quarterly* 21 (Spring 1969): 23–43; and Ralph E. Morrow, "The Great Revival, the West, and the Crisis of the Church," in *The Frontier Reexamined*, ed. John Francis McDermott (Urbana, Ill., 1967), pp. 65–78. The several well-known works of Walter B. Posey carefully describe the revival in Kentucky and Tennessee. Because I am concerned with pinpointing the men, dogmas, and events and working out their probable cause-effect relationships in the chartered dimensions of time and space, I have gone almost entirely to the primary sources for my account. Many of the facts and quotations I relate can be found in earlier works, especially Posey's. But none of these secondary sources make a sustained attempt to analyze why and how the revival developed.

[2] Spencer, *A History of Kentucky Baptists*, 1: 344–45.

[3] [U. S. Census], *Return of the Whole Number of Persons*, p. 2P.

[4] Spencer, *A History of Kentucky Baptists*, 1: 366–77.

[5] John McGee to [?], October 27, 1800, in Lorenzo Dow, ed., *Extracts from Original Letters, to the Methodist Bishops . . . Giving An Account of the Work of God, Since the Year 1800* (Liverpool, 1806), p. 10; see also John Rankin, "Autobiographical Sketch," p. 279.

third year they had been actively praying and preparing for a revival. For at least three years they had been told that faith would guarantee a strong religious resurgence and that they could expect it at any time. The three Presbyterian ministers who were energetically pressing the people toward repentance and expectation (William Hodge, John Rankin, and Mc-Gready) devoutly believed God would answer their congregational prayers. To these revival ingredients, by fortuitous circumstance, two ministerial additions injected a completely undiluted mixture of emotionalism and evangelical zeal.

These welcome newcomers were two brothers originally from North Carolina, but now stationed in Tennessee, the Presbyterian William McGee and the Methodist John McGee. Their preaching together had excited marvel in Tennessee, for their theological views had previously been thought antagonistic. John McGee wrote that brotherly love dissolved their differences in doctrine, and the Reverend James B. Finley remembered that "Nothing was discoverable in their preaching of a doctrinal character, except the doctrine of man's total depravity and ruin by sin, and his recovery therefrom by faith in Christ."[6]

In 1800 the two McGee brothers decided to make a tour through Kentucky to the Ohio Territory, and on the way they attended the large sacramental service being held by the McGready forces at Red River. They were welcomed upon their arrival, for William McGee had been a pupil and convert of McGready in North Carolina and within the past year had cooperated with him in neighboring Tennessee. William introduced his brother, and because of their kinship and McGready's friendship with William, both were invited to participate in the service.[7] The uninhibited fervor of a Methodist itinerant was thus added to the already zealous Presbyterian exhortations.

Friday, Saturday, and Sunday were marked by the congregation's close attention and reverence. But Monday, in the words of McGready, "was indeed the great day of the feast." William Hodge preached a long and powerful sermon; suddenly a woman who had long been seeking self-assurance of her salvation began shouting and singing.[8] After her inter-

---

[6] William P. Strickland, ed., *Autobiography of Rev. James B. Finley; or, Pioneer Life in the West* (Cincinnati, Ohio, 1856), p. 362. See also John M'Gee to the Rev. Thomas L. Douglas, June 23, 1820, in the *Methodist Magazine* 4 (1821): 190. In this letter, written twenty years after the event, McGee incorrectly places the year at 1799 instead of 1800.

[7] Ibid.; and Davidson, *History of the Presbyterian Church in Kentucky*, p. 263.

[8] McGready, "A Short Narrative of the Revival," p. 155.

ruption Hodge concluded his sermon, and he, McGready, and Rankin began
to leave the church. The two McGee brothers, not yet satisfied with the
results of the meeting, sat still. Most of the congregation did the same.
William McGee, the Presbyterian, was in such a state of religious excitement that he stood momentarily, then sat weeping on the floor of the
pulpit.[9] Certainly this was unusual, and the now sobbing people—fervently
seeking full security in their hopes of salvation and God's promised miracle
of deliverance from sin—immediately realized that something extraordinary
was afoot.

Recognizing the situation, Methodist John McGee rose to tell the
excited crowd that it was his turn to preach, but "there was a greater than
I preaching," he said, and then he "exhorted them to let the Lord God
Omnipotent reign in their hearts, and to submit to Him." With this sug-
gestion that God himself was at work, the people frantically, joyously, ex-
pectantly began to cry and shout.[10] By now all the preachers had returned
and stood amazed at what was happening. They were New Side, evangelistic
Presbyterians, but this was beyond their experience. Rather than try to impede the emotional outbreak, they determined after a brief conference to
stand aside and let what they felt might be God's work progress.[11]

Above the general clamor came the penetrating voice of the woman
who had first started shouting during Hodge's sermon. As John McGee,
now so enthusiastic that he seemed possessed, made his way toward her,
someone (probably his brother) cautioned him that this was a Presbyterian
meetinghouse and that the congregation would not condone such emotionalism. In his own words, John McGee said, "I turned to go back, and was
near falling; the power of God was strong upon me, I turned again, and
losing sight of the fear of man, I went through the house shouting, and
exhorting with all possible ecstasy and energy, and the floor was soon covered with the slain." [12]

McGee's unreined emotionalism, and its result, convinced those present
that this was truly a unique and marvelous occasion. Hopes and expectations
seemed to be approaching fulfillment. As John Rankin wrote, "On seeing
and feeling [John McGee's] confidence, that it was the work of God, and
a mighty effusion of his spirit, and having heard that he was acquainted with

[9] John McGee to Douglas, *Methodist Magazine* 4:190. McGready, "A Short
Narrative of the Revival," p. 150, describes the crying, but omits reference to the
McGees. Rankin, "Autobiographical Sketch," p. 280, corroborates the McGee account.
[10] John McGee to Douglas, *Methodist Magazine* 4: 190.
[11] Rankin, "Autobiographical Sketch," p. 280.
[12] John McGee to Douglas, *Methodist Magazine* 4: 190.

such scenes in another country, we acquiesced and stood in astonishment, admiring the wonderful works of God. When this alarming occurrence subsided in outward show, the united congregations returned to their respective abodes, in contemplation of what they had seen, heard, and felt on this most oppressive occasion."[13]

Evidently McGready and the other local Presbyterian ministers were convinced that the strange phenomenon they had just witnessed was a genuine work of God, for they immediately laid preparations for another sacramental service to be held at the Gasper River church the last weekend in July. One thing that seemed especially remarkable, and was constantly singled out in the reports of this and later similar occasions, was the extent of interdenominational cooperation. McGready recognized that the Red River event would give enthusiasm and hope to all neighboring congregations. He promptly set out to promote the next meeting and took great pains to circulate the news. He asked the surrounding churches, and especially their ministers, to come prepared to stay the duration of the meeting.[14] It seems, however, that little advertisement was necessary to build up an interest in the service projected for Gasper River. Rankin, an active participant, recalled that during the intervening weeks, "the news of the strange operations which had transpired at the previous meeting had run throughout the country in every direction, carrying a high degree of excitement to the minds of almost every character. The curious came to gratify their curiosity. The seriously convicted, presented themselves that they might receive some special and salutary benefit to their souls, and promote the cause of God, at home and abroad."[15]

By early Friday morning of the appointed weekend, unprecedented crowds began congregating at Gasper River. Many came from great distances, as far away as a hundred miles, expecting an extraordinary display of religious fervor.[16] This was to be the first genuine camp meeting (the term itself was not used until late 1802), although large outdoor meetings had had a long history. At this event, for the first time, members of several

[13] Rankin, "Autobiographical Sketch," p. 280. McGee, being a Methodist, was no stranger to fervent preaching and may have seen something similar to this outbreak during a brief Methodist revival in North Carolina in 1794; see Albert M. Shipp, *The History of Methodism in South Carolina* (Nashville, Tenn., 1883), p. 272.

[14] Davidson, *History of the Presbyterian Church in Kentucky*, p. 134.

[15] Rankin, "Autobiographical Sketch," pp. 280–81.

[16] Ibid., p. 281; McGready, "Narrative of the Commencement . . . of the Revival," p. xiii; McGready, "A Short Narrative of the Revival," p. 192; and McGready, "Extract of a Letter to the Rev. Dr. Coke," p. 182.

denominations came specifically prepared to encamp and sustain themselves
throughout the length of the services. These special preparations, combined
with the interdenominational nature of the affair, only served to magnify
the auspiciousness of this unprecedented occasion.

Anticipation infused the air; a willingness to believe in God's efforts
was the pervasive sentiment. Friday passed with nothing to startle the attention, and Saturday threatened to do the same. Abruptly on Saturday
night, just after the last sermon was finished, two women began talking
about how God had entered their lives. The confidence in rebirth they
exhibited instantaneously inflamed the imagination of the numerous by-
standers.[17] After years of being told by earnest ministers that God could
and would someday begin anew his work of salvation, these listeners were
totally willing to believe that this was the start of that long desired deliverance. The smallest indication that the Spirit was present proved to them
that the time had come to receive God's saving forgiveness. Having traveled
long, hard miles expecting to find a miracle, they easily, immediately, assumed success. The overheard conversation set into motion all the precon-
ceived ideas and beliefs about providential love and deliverance: "instantly
the divine flame spread through the whole multitude. Presently you might
have seen sinners lying powerless in every part of the house, praying and
crying for mercy."[18] Throughout the night ministers were kept active by
distressed and desperate penitents seeking conversion.

Sunday was most remarkable for the exercises it produced. The morning sermon evoked groans and cries from every side, but the real display
was reserved for the evening service. By then the congregation had been
there three long, tiring, exciting days. Undoubtedly the tension had slowly
increased. As the conclusion of the sacramental meeting neared, the necessity for prompt conversion seemed to heighten. At the night sermon, with
the pulpit illuminated by flaming torches, William McGee exhorted with
all his energy and persuasive oratorical powers. The text was that of a
doubting Peter sinking beneath the waves—dexterously McGee applied
this parable to the congregation's position. McGready recreated the situation:

the power of God seemed to shake the whole assembly. Towards the
close of the sermon, the cries of the distressed arose almost as loud as his
voice.—After the congregation was dismissed the solemnity increased,
till the greater part of the multitude seemed engaged in the most solemn
manner. No person seemed to wish to go home—hunger and sleep seemed

[17] McGready, "Narrative of the Commencement . . . of the Revival," p. xiii,
and "A Short Narrative of the Revival," p. 192.
[18] McGready, "Narrative of the Commencement . . . of the Revival," p. xiii.

to affect nobody—eternal things were the vast concern. Here awakening and converting work was to be found in every part of the multitude; and even some things strangely and wonderfully new to me.[19]

As at the preceding communion service in June, a disproportionate number of young people were affected. The two most extensive accounts by McGready emphasized the large role children played in the meeting[20]— this was to be a characteristic of the camp meeting revivals across the South. Quite understandably, the impressionable, easily frightened youngsters, who by virtue of their age had never experienced a period of revivalism and mass conversion, were an easy mark for the hypnotic proselytism of the camp meeting. In a rural, relatively newly settled region like the Cumberland, this ready element of the population was predominant. Youths had not felt welcome at earlier communion services, but they were eagerly accepted as revival participants. There are numerous accounts of such youngsters who, after their conversion experience and while still in a state of shock, repeated almost verbatim the frightening exhortations they had so often heard. Here, for those willing to believe, was further proof that this was the undeniable work of God.

The Gasper River sacramental revival clearly was the catalytic agent of the Great Revival. For in the succeeding months, similar camp meeting revivals erupted in congregation after congregation, even spreading into adjacent Tennessee: Muddy River, the Ridge, Mr. Craighead's church, Clay-lick, Little Muddy-Creek, Montgomery's Meeting-House, Hope-well.[21] Each seemed more dramatic than the previous; at Desha's Creek, near the end of the year, John McGee reported that "many thousands of people attended. The mighty power and mercy of God was manifested. The people fell before the word, like corn before a storm of wind, and many rose from the dust with a divine glory shining in their countenances, and gave glory to God in such strains as made the hearts of stubborn sinners to tremble; and after the first gust of praise they would break forth in vollies of exhortation."[22]

[19] McGready, "A Short Narrative of the Revival," p. 193.

[20] Ibid., pp. 193–94; and McGready, "Narrative of the Commencement . . . of the Revival," p. xiii. Cf. "Extract of a Letter from the Rev. Gideon Blackburn, dated Blount County (Tennessee), Sept. 29, 1800," in the *New York Missionary Magazine* 2 (1801): 239. John McGee pointed out that "although there were converts of different ages under this work, it was remarkable, they were generally the children of praying parents." John McGee to Douglas, *Methodist Magazine* 4:191.

[21] McGready, "Narrative of the Commencement . . . of the Revival," p. xv.

[22] John McGee to Douglas, *Methodist Magazine* 4:191.

Wherever the participants migrated, further revivals seemed to occur. No sooner had the few visiting Tennesseans returned from Gasper River than similar religious enthusiasm developed in their home churches. Even the testimony of one of the converted children produced an almost astounding upsurge in local spirituality.[23] News of the revival in Logan County seemed to evoke imitative revivals almost spontaneously. The chain reaction had begun which at its climax constituted the Great Revival in the South.

The camp meetings spread because, given the peculiar makeup of the theological belief system preached and accepted, the Gasper River exercises triggered a self-perpetuating revival. Whether the inhabitants of the western states of Kentucky and Tennessee had lived there for a decade or more, or had recently immigrated from the older southern states, they had all been subjected to the same general religious ideas, however vague, and the same absence of firm church affiliation. In Lexington, just as in Richmond, the wealthier upper-class segment was usually Episcopalian if anything, and in both cities this class ridiculed the more pietistic brands of religion. The French botanist-propagandist-traveler François André Michaux, while near Lexington, attended one camp meeting and reported that "the best informed differ from the opinion of the multitude with respect to this species of extacy." [24] These members of society, across the South, were generally immune to the appeal of the revival. But for the huge majority of people, the fantastic displays of religious affection easily seemed to fit a providential pattern.

The common people of even the vaguest religious background had long been taught that God controlled all events, including making possible their individual salvation. Many churchgoers had set aside days or certain hours for prayers, firm in their hope that God would answer them. In such manner there was built up a persuasive and widespread belief that ultimately in a strange, complacency-shattering way, divine Providence would inaugurate the miraculous work. Even those not particularly devout had some understanding of this belief. The revival began among ardent believers; their astounding fervor, the prodigious meetings with all sects, the remarkable

[23] "Extract of a Letter from the Rev. William Hodge, of Summer [sic] County, State of Tennessee, to the Rev. Francis Asbury," Methodist Magazine [London] 26 (1803): 269.

[24] Travels to the Westward of the Allegany Mountains, in the States of the Ohio, Kentucky, and Tennessee (London, 1805), p. 243. See also Robert B. McAfee, "The Life and Times of Robert B. McAfee and his Family Connections," Register of the Kentucky State Historical Society 25 (May 1927): 222.

example of families camping for days so as not to miss any of the exercises, all served to convince the doubters that here, truly, was an unprecedented phenomenon. In an age and environment that offered few alternatives, literally thousands throughout Kentucky and the South could see no explanation other than the omnipotent hand of God.

For the faithful the revival seemed an answer to prayer. Richard McNemar was an eyewitness, and he reported that the "extraordinary appearances" first began among "individuals, who had been under deep conviction of sin, and great trouble about their souls; and had fasted and prayed, and diligently searched the Scriptures; and had undergone distresses of mind inexpressively sore, until they had obtained a comfortable hope of salvation." [25] The Reverend James Welsh, writing from near Lexington, described the state of mind of the churchgoers on the eve of the revival. The members were intimately aware of the depressed position of religion.

> Under this view of things, numbers of Christians became much concerned that God would change our mournful state, and revive his cause among us.
> Many earnest prayers I believe ascended to the throne of grace, for a considerable time previous to the commencement of the work amidst many and various discouragements. [And of great importance,] It was to be observed, . . . that much greater numbers attended the ministration of the word for some time before the work began. [26]

And from a minister in northeast Kentucky whose congregation had not yet experienced a revival, there came a letter stating that notwithstanding their present lack of success, "there does of late appear to be generally more of desire, prayer for, and expectation of, a gracious visitation." [27]

It would be hard to overestimate the excitement aroused by these revivals. Repeatedly they were described as miraculous, astounding, unusual, wonderful. As a young Englishman wrote back to his relatives, "A very

[25] M'Nemar, *The Kentucky Revival*, p. 19. See also "Extract of a letter from Kentucky, dated March 30, 1801, to John Rippon," in Rippon, *The Baptist Annual Register for 1801 and 1802*, 4 vols. (London, n.d.), 4:655.

[26] "Extract from a letter of Rev. James Welsh, of Lexington, Kentucky, to one of the Editors . . . July 15, 1802," *Connecticut Evangelical Magazine* 3 (September 1802):119. See also the Reverend John Lyle's comment on those affected at the Salem Church in mid-June 1801. Lyle, "Diary, June 1801–July 1803," corrected typescript loaned by Robert Stuart Sanders, Lexington, Ky. Original in the Kentucky Historical Society, Frankfort, Ky.

[27] James Hughs to Cornelius [November 23, 1801], in the *New York Missionary Magazine* 3 (1802):128. See the same, in *Connecticut Evangelical Magazine* 2 (1802): 393, for citation of the date.

extraordinary Appearance in the moral work has taken place here."[28] Another wrote that the news of the revival filled the whole country.[29] "The excitement created by these reports," recalled James B. Finley, "was of the most intense and astonishing character."[30] A Presbyterian minister wrote to a co-worker in Philadelphia, "I never seen people so much alarmed in my life. I do think Dear Sir that God is About to work A mighty work."[31] The movement, according to Finley, "was marked by some peculiarities which had not been known to characterize any revival in former times. The nearest approximation to it . . . was the revival on the day of pentecost."[32] "The present Revival of Religion in Kentucky and Cumberland," wrote an upstate Presbyterian, "exceeds every thing of the kind I have ever heard of, in point of numbers, and differs materially as to the means whereby it has been affected."[33] The Reverend John Lyle, upon hearing by letter of the "wonderful work," concluded that "the Lord was doing terrible things in righteousness with a kind design that the nation might see and fear and flow together. That perhaps the falling down in distress &&& might answer instead of ancient miracles to arouse the attention of a sleeping world."[34] Numerous accounts indicated the consensus: "the opinion prevailed very generally that these were new revelations of the Spirit and that his religious operations were by miraculous outpouring & were known & felt in sensible feelings & strange imaginations & passions."[35]

Against the backdrop of recent deism, materialism, and widespread indifference to religion, these gigantic revival meetings with thousands in

[28] H. Anderson to Thom. Jackson, September 10, 1801, Ms in the Kentucky Historical Society, Frankfort, Ky.

[29] "Account of the Life and Writings of James Fishback, Written by Himself," p. 7, Ms in the James Fishback Collection, Bosworth Memorial Library, Lexington Theological Seminary, Lexington, Ky. Another indication that the more educated, elite, and often Episcopalian groups opposed the revival is given by their failure to discuss it in the local newspapers. "None of the News papers have even mentioned it," complained one contemporary (H. Anderson to Thom. Jackson, September 10, 1801). On the general paucity of local news coverage, see Dwight Lawrence Mikkelson, "*Kentucky Gazette*, 1787–1848: 'The Herald of a Noisy World' " (Ph.D. diss., University of Kentucky, 1963).

[30] Strickland, *Autobiography of Finley*, p. 165.

[31] Aneas McAllister to Robert Patterson, December 25, 1802, Patterson Mss, Shane Collection, Presbyterian Historical Society, Philadelphia.

[32] Strickland, *Autobiography of Finley*, p. 362.

[33] "Extract of a Letter from the Rev. Mr. John Evans Findley, of Mason-County, Kentucky," *Methodist Magazine* [London] 26(1803): 125.

[34] Lyle, "Diary," June 14, 1801.

[35] "Life and Writings of James Fishback," pp. 7–8.

attendance, multitudes falling to the ground wailing and shouting, and reports of the miraculous transformations of entire communities, seemed all the more stupendous. It appears that for a long while, revival news completely dominated the attention of the common people. The first camp meeting revivals in the Cumberland region created such an impact that even the most nominal Christians could hardly deny that God was at work. Now all those numberless congregations that had prayed for the return of God's mercy felt a new period of divine activity had begun. The entire religious community had so primed itself to expect an imminent deliverance that now the opinion was almost unanimous: the forces of God were set in motion, nothing could impede their progress. The Gasper River revivals released all these pent-up hopes.

This "proof" that a new era was beginning almost without fail elicited new evidence for the faithful.[36] To such a degree were congregations and ministers prepared for a revival outbreak that the merest mention of what had taken place in the Cumberland region served to provoke similar awakenings elsewhere. The religious fervor, perpetuating itself, quickly spread across Kentucky and neighboring Tennessee.

The Reverend Robert Stuart, describing a camp meeting, wrote that by the time the minister had closed his sermon, and some of the "exercises" were set into motion, all that was necessary for the emotional culmination was "that it should be carried on by the people."[37] The crowd enthusiastically continued the work. As a letter from Lexington in the spring of 1801 stated, "In some it appears like a fire that has been long confined—bursting all its barriers, and spreading with a rapidity that is indiscribable. . . . It may be truly said, the Lord is doing great things for us."[38] By simple communication the spark was spread.

Methodist minister William McKendree, presiding elder of the Western District, had been in the Cumberland region of Kentucky when the work began. During the winter of 1800–1801, he came to the central portion of the state to tell of the unusual meetings he had just participated in. A pseudonymous author had described the occasion:

[36] M'Nemar, *The Kentucky Revival*, p. 22; Cossitt, *Life and Times of Rev. Finis Ewing*, p. 66; and Jacob Young, *Autobiography of a Pioneer, Or the Nativity, Experience, Travels, and Ministerial Labors of . . . Young* (Cincinnati, Ohio, [1857]), p. 54.

[37] Stuart, "Reminiscences of the Presbyterian Church in Kentucky," p. 76.

[38] "Extract of a Letter from a gentleman to his friend at the city of Washington, dated Lexington, March 8, 1801," in [Anonymous], *Gospel News, or A Brief Account of the Revival of Religion in Kentucky, and Several Other Parts of the United States* (Baltimore, Md., 1801), p. 3.

He told of the happy conversion of hundreds; how the people continued in their exercises of singing, praying and preaching on the ground, surrounded by waggons and tents, for days and nights together. That many were so affected, that they fell to the ground like men slain in battle. The piercing cries of the penitents, and rapture of the healed, appeared to be brought to our view; and what was equally encouraging to the faithful, that the work instead of declining, was progressing to the interior. After this description given by him, it was unnecessary to exhort the faithful to look for the like among themselves. Their hearts had already began to beat in unison with his: whilst sinners were generally melted into tears.[39]

During the summer and fall of 1801 the revival made its appearance among the Baptists and then the Presbyterians in the Kentucky counties of Woodford, Fayette, and Jefferson. In these, as well as the other Baptist congregations throughout Kentucky, the awakening first occurred under the ministrations of former evangelistic Separate Baptist preachers,[40] most of whom were from Virginia. Although the people in these counties had heard reports of the Cumberland revival, when the phenomena broke out among them, the Presbyterians especially were still cautious. "The falling down of multitudes, and their crying out . . . was to us so new a scene, that we thought it prudent not to be over hasty in forming any opinion of it. However, a little conversation with the affected persons, induced us to believe, that in the judgement of charity, it was the work of the Lord."[41] The Baptists and Methodists, with more of an impassioned heritage, seemed less hesitant to accept wholeheartedly the genuineness of the heralded work. In early 1801, as the weather moderated, the meetings began to approach the center of the state. "Theophilus Armenius" has described their potency:

It was truly wonderful to see what an effect their approach made upon the minds of the people. Here in the wilderness were . . . thousands hungry for the bread of life! and thousands thirsting for the waters of salvation! A general move was visible in the congregations, previously to the arrival of these meetings. The devout Christians appeared to be filled with hope. Their hearts were greatly enlarged to pray for the prosperity of Zion. The formalists were troubled with very uneasy sensations: backsliders became terrified: the wicked in general were either greatly alarmed, or struck with solemn awe, whilst curiosity was general, and raised to the

[39] Theophilus Armenius, "Account of the Rise and Progress of the Work of God in the Western Country," *Methodist Magazine* 2 (1819) : 222. Redford, in *History of Methodism in Kentucky*, 1 : 358, identifies Armenius as the Reverend Thomas S. Hinde.

[40] Spencer, *History of the Kentucky Baptists*, 1 : 536–40; and "Letter from Rev. John E. Findley," *Methodist Magazine* [London] 26 (1803) : 126.

[41] Ibid.

highest degree to see into these strange things. Indeed, such was the commotion, that every circle of the community appeared to have their whole attention arrested.[42]

If the revival accounts gave energy to the laymen of the congregations, how much more did they stimulate the ministers. Although, especially in their public posture, the clergy had never given up hope, periods of clerical depression were not unusual in the decade before 1800. As a Georgia Presbyterian had confided in 1795, "I seem to labor in vain. God help me. I am dull & languid myself, & I verily believe, the people & I am mutually affected & influenced by each other in that respect."[43] Another had similarly bemoaned his own distress over the state of religion and confessed: "No doubt I contribute my part to this declension of religion as well as others."[44] As a Virginia Baptist observed, "Seldom do we see a dull preacher, and a lively church, or vice versa. Therefore, for the most part, to reform the ministry, is to revive the church."[45] Here, then, on the leadership level, is another indication of how each revival helped to spur further revivals. Exhilarated ministers preached more fervently, prayed more feelingly, worked even more tirelessly.[46] The more the revival news spread, the more universal became the awakening.

The great Cane Ridge camp meeting had its preliminary beginning when a Bourbon County Presbyterian, Barton W. Stone, first started hearing reports of religious revivals from the south. Stone, later founder of the Disciples of Christ movement, had known James McGready since hearing

[42] Armenius, "Account of the Work of God," p. 222.

[43] Moses Waddel to William Williamson, October 25, 1795, in the Williamson Papers, Shane Collection.

[44] John Newton to Revd. Samuel Wilson, July 14, 1794, in the L. C. Glenn Collection.

[45] Semple, *History of the Baptists in Virginia*, p. 239.

[46] Drury Lacy to William Williamson, July 24, 1799, Williamson Papers, Shane Collection. In another letter to Williamson, dated March 10, 1800, in the Shane Collection, Lacy very honestly discussed the ups and downs suffered by ministers: "We are poor Creatures & often attend less to the hand of providence in drawing our Conclusions, than we do to our own Feelings. When we Experience a state of considerable darkness & langor in our own Souls every thing wears a gloomy aspect. Dark prospects hang over the church. Infidelity is ready to overwhelm the Land—the Bible to be entirely rejected, and the Christian name to be forgotten. But when it pleases God to revive us a little, and we experience something of his [love?] & Faithfulness, we begin to think, he [will re]form the Earth, & the power of his word [will s]oon subdue the rebellion in humble submis[sion to] his Feet." By this time Lacy had heard of the emerging revival in the West, and this apparent religious renaissance made earlier fears seem a little overstated.

him preach at Guilford Academy in the early 1790s. Since 1798 Stone had presided over the Concord and Cane Ridge congregations in Bourbon County, in the heart of the Bluegrass. Apathy seemed to prevail there, as elsewhere through the South. Sometime during the year 1800 word reached Stone of the series of revivals being conducted with unprecedented success by McGready. Never an advocate of orthodox Calvinism with its emphasis on the elect,[47] Stone eagerly awaited an opportunity to examine the work to the south which promised to democratize salvation. In the early spring of 1801 he found his chance and traveled to Logan County. He arrived, and there, amid a forest-encircled church, the huge crowds came.

"The scene to me was new," recalled Stone in his autobiography, "and passing strange. It baffled description." Men falling deathlike, only to arise and shout hosannas; women and children exclaiming their love for Jesus Christ. After witnessing such marvels for several days, Stone wrote that his "conviction was complete that it was a good work—the work of God."[48] After the close of this camp meeting, Stone returned "with ardent spirits" to his congregations in Bourbon County, adjacent to Lexington. A huge crowd came, anxious to hear his report. Many were deeply affected by his message, and the next evening, as their minister returned, a couple rushed out of the church, embraced the startled Stone, and began praising God in loud voices. Within a few minutes, many of the congregation had fallen to the ground, pleading for mercy with the God they feared. "The effects of this meeting through the country were like fire in dry stubble driven by a strong wind."[49] After a brief revival at the Concord church, Stone made preparations for a protracted meeting to be held at Cane Ridge in early August 1801.

This Cane Ridge camp meeting, the truly Brobdingnagian meeting of the entire southern revival, immediately gained such fame and symbolic stature that it merits close description. Larger than any of the rest, nearer the center of Kentucky's population, far the best publicized, it became known all along the eastern seaboard. For countless praying congregations in the South, news of Cane Ridge was just the spark needed to ignite further revivals. This meeting was also the scene of the most bizarre of those physical manifestations of conviction which for many even today characterize the Great Revival of the South.

The plans for the meeting to be held at Cane Ridge (near Paris, Kentucky) were publicized for over a month.[50] The simple log meetinghouse

---

[47] See Chapter Two of Barton W. Stone's *Autobiography*, pp. 119–25.
[48] Ibid., p. 155.   [49] Ibid., p. 157.
[50] My discussion of Cane Ridge will be a composite of the numerous extant

was situated on the gentle slopes of a large, very gradually inclined hill. Scattered clumps of trees offered welcome protection from the hot summer sun. The crowd began gathering early on Friday, August 8, 1801. More than a year of revival rumors from the Cumberland had created an unusual interest and curiosity here in the populous central portion of the state. "The roads were literally crowded with wagons, carriages, horsemen, and footmen, moving to the solemn camp." By Saturday the throng was variously estimated between twelve and twenty-five thousand—entirely possible for this region of Kentucky.

Thousands of worshipers were scattered across the hillside. A cacophonous clamor of shouted sermons, chanted hymns, ecstatic hosannas, and mournful wailing filled the air already thick with the smell of smoke, sweat, and excitement. "The noise was like the roar of Niagara. The vast sea of human beings seemed to be agitated as if by a storm." Perched atop stumps, standing among the limbs of half-fallen trees, or astride wagons, ministers were warning of the judgment day to come with an emotional pitch proportional to the size of the assemblage. As many as eighteen Presbyterian ministers were counted, and probably more Baptist and Methodist preachers were present.

Curious listeners huddled around the ministers. In the resulting pandemonium the overwhelming majority of ministers neglected theological subtleties and tried with all their might to get these exhausted and exhil-

---

accounts. Each complements the other; putting all together fills out the story in detail. The following accounts are used: Armenius, "Account of the Work of God," pp. 272–74; Levi Purviance, *Biography of David Purviance* (Dayton, Ohio, 1848), pp. 247–50; Peter Cartwright, *Autobiography of Peter Cartwright*, ed. William P. Strickland (Cincinnati, Ohio, 1856), pp. 45–46; Redford, *History of Methodism in Kentucky*, 1:354–58; M'Nemar, *The Kentucky Revival*, pp. 26–27; John Lyle, "Diary," August 8–13, 1801; "Extract of a Letter from a gentleman to his sister in Philadelphia, dated Lexington, (Ken.) August 10, 1801," in [Anon.], *Gospel News*, pp. 4–6; the same in W. W. Woodward, *Surprising Accounts of the Revival of Religion, in the United States of America* ([Philadelphia], 1802), pp. 56–58; the following letters printed in Woodward: "Extract of a Letter from Colonel Robert Patterson, of Lexington (Ken.) to the Rev. Doctor John King, September 25, 1801," pp. 34–39; "Extract 57. of a letter from the Rev. G. Baxter . . . to the Rev. Dr. Archibald Alexander, dated January 1, 1802," pp. 105–13; letter from [the son of Rev. James Finley], September 20, 1801, pp. 225–27. Many of these letters published in Woodward, *Surprising Accounts*, were later republished in the various New England missionary magazines, such as the *New York Missionary Magazine*, the *Connecticut Evangelical Magazine*, and the *Massachusetts Missionary Magazine*. See also "Extract of a letter from Rev. John Evans Findley," *Methodist Magazine* 26 (1803): 125–27. And, of course, Stone, in his *Autobiography*, briefly discusses Cane Ridge, pp. 157–62.

arated masses to accept Jesus Christ. Almost all the revivalists at first seem to have felt that the mere existence of the current revival season proved that God's spirit was moving among the people. In fact, many ministers assumed that the miraculous size of the throngs meant that those present were earnestly aware of their failings and desired to effect reconciliation with God.

In essence, the camp meeting circumstances, in which God was felt to be working in many ways, seemingly meant that all the conditions for salvation had been met. God had created a desire, a curiosity, which attracted multitudes; simultaneously his spirit was making possible the realization of personal repentance (with the orthodox alternative of a sizzling hell made clear) and return to God, through Jesus Christ. The unprecedented size of the services simply relegated Calvinistic talk of particular election to the background; the immediate, convincing effectiveness of the revival spectacle pushed an emphasis on personal volition to the forefront.[51]

Using every technique known to their profession, the ministers urged their listeners to consider the terrors of hell and then imagine the glories of heaven. The willing crowd, their emotions buoyed by the scene around them, was easily swayed. In the swell of the sounds, sights, and numbers assaulting their imagination, God seemed quite evidently to be at hand. This then was to them an unprecedented opportunity to find security, avoid eternal torment, and gain everlasting glory. Even those who had never been devout were aware of the claims of religion, which, in such a situation, seemed difficult to doubt. Whenever a listener would fall, overcome by his emotions, large numbers of worshipers would crowd around him, praising God and singing hymns. All this added to the clamor and confusion.

Everything acting together—the size of the crowd, the noise of simultaneous sermons and hymns, assorted shouts, cries, groans, and praises, the exhaustion brought on by continual services, the summer heat—simply overwhelmed the participants with their beliefs in providential omnipotence. The event itself generated further acceptance of its authenticity as heaven-sent, and this attitude further contributed to the frenzied commotion. In a very real sense, given the outlook of most of those in attendance, the camp meeting revival typified by Cane Ridge became a self-authenticating work of God.

[51] David Rice, in *A Sermon on the Present Revival of Religion, &c., in this Country: Preached at the Opening of the Kentucky Synod* (Lexington, Ky., 1803), p. 32, discussing the theology of revival sermons, said: "Sometimes there is in our discourses, a strange heterogeneous mixture of antinomianism, arminianism, and I may add, calvinism: calvinism, perhaps in the beginning, antinomianism in the middle, and arminianism at the end of a sermon."

Remarkable in the daytime, the almost incomprehensibility of the Cane Ridge revival was enormously magnified in the darkness. As a contemporary described it in awe:

> At night, the whole scene was awfully sublime. The ranges of tents, the fires, reflecting light amidst the branches of the towering trees; the candles and lamps illuminating the encampment; hundreds moving to and fro, with lights or torches, like Gideon's army; the preaching, praying, singing and shouting, all heard at once, rushing from different parts of the ground, like the sound of many waters, was enough to swallow up all the powers of contemplation. Sinners falling, and shrieks and cries for mercy awakened in the mind a lively apprehension of that scene, when the awful sound will be heard, "arise ye dead and come to Judgement." [52]

Cane Ridge also saw several attendant exercises which came to distinguish particularly the Kentucky phase of the revival. Many participants, in the midst of the totality of revival phenomena, seemed to have lost control of their emotions. Considering themselves in the very presence of God, many felt so remorseful for their sins (the horrors of which were usually intensified by the ministers) that they fell apparently senseless to the ground. Others who, perhaps, were seeking a sense of assurance that they were being saved, unconsciously generated a series of physical "exercises" as evidence of their conviction and justification.

These exercises, whatever their exact psychological motivation,[53] were of six distinct varieties, commonly called the falling exercise, the rolling exercise, the "jerks," the barking exercise, the dancing exercise, and the laughing and singing exercises. The latter revival symptoms, as their names suggest, were simply uncontrollable singing, dancing, and laughing, generally performed with a countenance of joy and peace. The common

[52] Armenius, "Account of the Work of God," p. 273.

[53] Theodore X. Barber has suggested that there is little difference between what is commonly called "hypnotism" and simply a "high level of suggestibility" which is activated by strong "motivational" instructions. Under such conditions, he writes, most people will act, feel, and "forget" exactly as they have been led to expect properly "hypnotized" subjects to act. Many of those at camp meetings doubtless believed that true conversion would produce some kind of cataleptic state; such a condition was often felt to be substantial proof of conversion; many persons on every hand seemed to be experiencing these strange "exercises"; and the trusted ministers by implication at the very least were promoting the "wonderful work." Probably something similar to social hypnosis or intense social suggestibility can be used to explain the infamous revival scenes. See Theodore X. Barber, "Who Believes in Hypnosis?" *Psychology Today* 4 (July 1970): 20–27, 84. For an older but somewhat comparable view, see Frederick Morgan Davenport, *Primitive Traits in Religious Revivals* (New York, 1905).

falling exercise was the collapse into a semi-conscious state, after which many arose to shout praises to their God. In the rolling exercises communicants rolled around like logs, unable to control their motions. Probably the barking exercise was an exaggeration of the grunts elicited by the more common jerks. In this exercise people began a spasmodic jerking of their body and limbs, with a speed and ferocity beyond belief. Levi Purviance recalled that the first worshipers he saw thus affected were of exemplary piety: "Their heads would jerk back suddenly, frequently causing them to yelp, or make some other involuntary noise. . . . Sometimes the head would fly every way so quickly that their features could not be recognized. I have seen their heads fly back and forward so quickly that the hair of females would be made to crack like a carriage whip, but not very loud." [54]

These grossly exaggerated revival exercises, which have been cited widely to discredit the revival, were probably restricted to a comparative few. Only among some of the splinter groups that developed in Kentucky did they become ultimately respectable. Often the revival's supporters were pressured into defending them as further miraculous signs from God only because ridicule threatened to put a premature end to the revival. Except at the very start, they were never a significant factor in the camp meetings. The more extreme exercises did achieve great notoriety, and, for many hearing of them, they seemed more assuredly to presage the beginning of a new dispensation of God's activity. But at most camp meetings, shouting, crying, and falling down were the only physical responses to passionate preaching.

After the extensive revivals of 1801 and continuing in 1802, religion came to monopolize the attention and talk of a substantial portion of the population. Traveling to Lexington in October 1802, James Fishback heard "of but little else than the great revival of religion." This talk was so prevalent that as he neared the central portion of the state, he "felt much anxiety lest I should fall down when amongst them." [55] On Christmas Day of the same year a gentleman wrote back to Virginia from Frankfort, Kentucky: "It is a very comfortable thing to be in a country where religion has obtained the pre-eminent influence. That is those that have it shows it, and those that have it not wish to be considered religious for the credit it gives in the society." [56] Despite the squabbling and schisms that had arisen by 1804 in Kentucky, Francis Asbury still felt justified in calling the state, "which

[54] Purviance, *Biography of David Purviance*, p. 249.
[55] "Life and Writings of James Fishback," p. 19.
[56] Col. Arthur Campbell to Rev. Charles Cummings, December 25, 1802, in the Draper Collection, Kings Mountain Papers, Wisconsin Historical Society, on microfilm in the Tennessee State Archives, Nashville.

was a few years [ago] a dangerous frontier, . . . the centre of the western front of our [Christian] empire where we behold a second part of the new world." [57]

This unusually widespread revival fervor gave Kentucky a special image in the eyes of the faithful everywhere. Letters poured out of Kentucky, bearing the news of an apparently unprecedented flood of revival success. As these communications, along with amazed travelers, filtered back through the rest of the South, the revival began to appear in state after state. This was to be the Great Revival of the South.

[57] Asbury to Zachariah Myles, August 16, 1804, in Asbury, *Journal and Letters*, 3:299.

Chapter Six

The South Conquered

For too long "the Great Revival" has meant, to most historians, only those hysterical "holy fairs" associated with Kentucky, Cane Ridge, and simple frontiersmen who wanted their whiskey straight and their religion red-hot. It should be obvious by now that there was present a pervasive, strongly believed system of ideas about God and his dealings with men. Most emphatically, there existed a vigorous cerebral element behind the revivals that began in Kentucky. And just as the revival was not entirely emotional and physical, it certainly was a regionwide phenomenon, evoking similar beliefs, crowds, and responses in North Carolina as well as Kentucky, in Georgia as well as Tennessee. In the same manner that the awakening enthusiasm spread from Gasper River to Cane Ridge, it swept back over the entire South with amazing rapidity, even seeping into the contiguous portions of the Ohio Territory, western Pennsylvania, and Maryland. By almost instantaneously overrunning the South, the Great Revival proved itself to be more than a mere frontier aberration, suitable only to Scotch-Irish pioneers suffering from a boredom and loneliness unique to the trans-Appalachian West. This was the first revival common to the whole South, and the first in which all denominations shared simultaneously. In a very legitimate sense, this was the South's "Great Awakening."

The Cumberland region overlapped both northern Tennessee and southern Kentucky. Once the revival reached the combustion point at Gasper River, it caught the neighboring Tennessee settlements aflame when those visiting the Logan County event returned home. As in Kentucky, there had been scattered outcroppings of localized revival fervor in Tennessee before the summer of 1800. In Blount County, near the North Carolina border, Presbyterian Gideon Blackburn had carefully promoted a reawakening of religious commitment in the spring of 1800.[1] William and John McGee had been creating a spirit of religious enthusiasm in the Tennessee Cumberland district. A fiery Methodist, John Page—originally from North Carolina —had successfully stoked the previously smoldering religious zeal of the

Cumberland communities in 1799.[2] Hence Tennessee was not devoid of religious background, beliefs, or inclinations.

In mid-summer 1800 a contingent from the Shiloh congregation of William Hodge made the short trip to Gasper River, "having heard of such extraordinary things as took place in that country."[3] Upon returning to their homes in Sumner County, the stories they related shocked all hearers. The poignant admonitions of the small son of one of the witnesses especially seemed to affect listeners. The entire neighborhood was alarmed, for these accounts certainly seemed to point beyond the futile efforts of man. They decided to meet together as a congregation in the middle of the week. At this meeting some stood and described what they interpreted to be the work of God in nearby Kentucky: "Having never heard such things before," the church members were gravely affected. They joined together for social prayer, and amid the praying and excited talk of revival news, many began weeping and crying for mercy. God was at hand, they reasoned. With the sobering revival news, the work began to spread rapidly throughout the congregations.

Soon afterward a large communion service was scheduled to meet at "Robert Shaw's, on the head waters of Red river." Hundreds came, and under the urgings of William McGee and the visiting James McGready and John Rankin, many "fell down like men slain in battle."[4] This local meeting, combined with the reports from Kentucky, generated tremendous religious enthusiasm and more than a little curiosity. At a September sacramental occasion on Desha's Creek, near Shiloh, a crowd of unprecedented size appeared. Hodge, both McGees, McGready, Rankin, Page, and others of both denominations were present. Here those peculiar emotional reactions which had taken place at Gasper River reoccurred. Hodge, who by this time was experienced in such matters, wrote: "Sabbath evening exhibited the most awfully solemn scene, I ever beheld. About the centre of the camp, they were lying in heaps, and scattered all around; the sighs, groans,

[1] "Extract 65. Of a letter from the Rev. Gideon Blackburn, dated Blount County (Tennessee), Sept. 29, 1800," in Woodward, *Surprising Accounts*, pp. 160–63. Originally appeared in the *New York Missionary Magazine* 2 (1801): 237–40.

[2] John Berry McFerrin, *History of Methodism in Tennessee. From the Year 1783 to the Year 1840*, 3 vols. (Nashville, Tenn., 1874–1875), 1: 283–84, 307, 309.

[3] "Extract of a Letter from the Rev. William Hodge, of Summer [*sic*] County, State of Tennessee, to the Rev. Francis Asbury," in the *Methodist Magazine* [London] 26 (1803): 268–69; see also, "Extract of a Letter from the Rev. Mr. John Evans Findley, of Mason-County, Kentucky," ibid., p. 125; and John Carr, *Early Times in Middle Tennessee* (Nashville, Tenn., 1857; reprinted, 1958), pp. 34–35.

[4] Carr, *Early Times in Middle Tennessee*, pp. 34–35.

and prayers seemed to pierce the heavens, while the Power of God fell upon almost all present."[5]

Again the revival exercises themselves seemed to the participants to authenticate the work. So unusual that they could be explained easily only as the work of God, their acquired label served to increase the fervency of the beholders. The thought that God himself was present and at work was certainly enough to elicit the most devout and extreme professions of faith. The believers were genuinely overcome, for their faith was too strongly felt to be calmly reasoned. Just as in Kentucky, this substantive "proof" of all their ideas about providential deliverance intensified religious commitment in congregation after congregation.

In early October 1800 three Methodist ministers, Richard Whatcoat, William McKendree, and Francis Asbury, were traveling south from near Lexington, Kentucky, to the vicinity of Nashville. Along the way they heard "a strange report about religion. We were told that the Presbyterians work by new rules; that they make their people cry and fall down."[6] On the nineteenth the three preached in Nashville; the next day they were asked to participate in a large sacramental meeting being held by the Presbyterians on Drake Creek. At least five Presbyterian ministers were there. Several thousand people were in attendance, and Asbury spoke from the preaching stand under a grove of tall beech trees. This was his first camp meeting, but he knew no such term to designate it; he only remarked that here "heaven smiled."[7]

From these initial revival meetings in the summer and autumn of 1800 the movement proliferated until, by the next summer, settlements across Tennessee were reporting awakenings. A letter of October 1801 recounted that Presbyterians, Methodists, and Baptists were uniting "in the common cause"; crowds as large as 10,000 were frequent; persons under conviction were exercised in the "most remarkable manner."[8] During the summer Asbury had been receiving letters describing the miraculous work, and on his fall tour he himself attended a "camp meeting" (here, for the first

[5] "Extract of a Letter from William Hodge," *Methodist Magazine* [London] 26 (1803): 269–70.

[6] "Memoirs of the Rev. Richard Whatcoat," in P. P. Sandford, *Memoirs of Mr. Wesley's Missionaries to America* (New York, 1843), p. 373.

[7] Ibid.; and for Asbury's remarks, see Asbury, *Journal and Letters*, 2:257. This was the meeting as "Montgomery's Meeting-House" (on Drake Creek) which McGready mentioned, in McGready, "Narrative of the Commencement of the Revival," p. xv.

[8] "Extract of a Letter to the Publisher, from Tennessee, dated October 10, 1801," *New York Missionary Magazine* 3 (1802): 38–39.

time, October 17, 1802, Asbury used the term) in the easternmost part of Tennessee. Two days later he recorded that, in the past year, the Methodists had added three thousand members in the Western District alone.[9]

With their built-in beliefs of how God would eventually effect deliverance from the apathetic religious decline of the 1790s, worshipers were eagerly receptive. Any indication of providential activity fed their hopes for reformation. In such an atmosphere of expectancy, the religious news emanating from the revival center in the Cumberland region generated successive awakenings throughout the state. James Gallaher tells how the movement entered his community in eastern Tennessee some 250 miles from Nashville. When the news first began arriving,

> A deep solemnity prevailed [through] the entire community, filling the minds of old and young with awe and reverence in view of God and his holy gospel. I remember . . . the unparalleled impression in our neighborhood. We had assembled in the house of worship. Each man and woman seemed to realize the sentiment of the patriarch: "Surely the Lord is in this place." Rev. Mr. Dobbins . . . preached a sermon. The attention was profound. During the sermon two young men . . . began to tremble. . . . The people felt that the great Master of assemblies was among them. They knew that this was that mighty power of God of which they had heard among the Churches in Kentucky.[10]

In similar fashion the camp meeting revivals leaped over the mountains to the seaboard states, beginning in North Carolina.

The peculiar tenets of the belief system characteristic of the three major southern denominations were widely accepted in North Carolina. The Methodists, Presbyterians, and Baptists had long worked there, and had readied the people for a revival. Letters and personal accounts had already begun filtering back by the end of 1800, and by early 1801 such evangelical leaders as Francis Asbury were often reading to congregations letters describing the apparent new dispensation. It took little time for this news to take effect: by February 1801 Asbury could detect a difference and happily confided to his Journal that "the minds of the people are strangely changed."[11]

As the accounts of the extensive work in Kentucky reached the former congregations of McGready and William Hodge, their old friends were

[9] Asbury, *Journal and Letters*, 2:303, 362, and 365; 3:221–22.

[10] R. N. Price, *Holston Methodism from Its Origin to the Present Time*, 5 vols. (Nashville, Tenn., 1912), 1:338–39, quoting James Gallaher, *Western Sketch Book*.

[11] Asbury, *Journal and Letters*, 2:284.

animated with a strong desire to experience such an awakening as they heard described in the West. It seems the happy news only made the religious condition in North Carolina seem worse. A falling away made more obvious, followed by an intensification of prayer, fasting, and expectation preceded the appearance of camp meetings. In August of 1801 a communion service was appointed for the Cross Roads church, in McGready's old county, Orange. The regular minister, William Paisley—who had been educated at Caldwell's Academy and ordained in 1794, when McGready was a dominant personality in the Orange Presbytery—and his associates led the congregation in special prayer. Over the weekend the people, though serious and attentive, were not moved to any special degree. On Monday Paisley rather despondently arose to dismiss the meeting, but his disappointment at the failure of anything to happen overcame him and he sat down without saying a word.[12]

The congregation sat in embarrassed silence. Abruptly a young visitor from Tennessee sprang to his feet—he had just finished telling the people of what was transpiring in the West before Paisley decided to conclude the prolonged service. Suddenly he threw his hands upward and shouted: "Stand still and see the salvation of God!" This unexpected, precipitate action somehow seems to have stunned the audience into a reconsideration of his message: "In a few moments the silence was broken by sobs, groans and cries, rising commingled from all parts of the house. All thoughts of dismissing the congregation at once vanished. The remainder of the day was spent in the exercises of prayer, exhortation, singing, personal conversation, and midnight came before the congregation could be persuaded to go to their respective homes."[13]

The following October the regular autumn communion service was scheduled for Paisley's other congregation at Hawfields. An unusually

[12] Foote, *Sketches of North Carolina*, p. 378. For Paisley's background, see Herbert Snipes Turner's monograph, *Church in the Old Fields: Hawfields Presbyterian Church and Community in North Carolina* (Chapel Hill, N. C., 1962), pp. 103–5.

[13] Foote, *Sketches of North Carolina*, pp. 378–79. Paul Henkel, a German-Lutheran minister in the North Carolina piedmont, has left a corroborative though unfavorable account of the beginning of the revival in the vicinity of the Cross Roads church. According to his diary, two young Presbyterians fresh from the Kentucky revival challenged their North Carolina brethren with astonishing reports of the "wonderful progress in Cumberland." Henkel continued: "Accordingly they gave assurance that the work would soon begin in this region. This created a great sensation among the people and aroused great expectation." A full-fledged revival soon broke out. Homer M. Keever, ed., "A Lutheran Preacher's Account of the 1801–02 Revival in North Carolina," *Methodist History* 7 (October 1968):41–42.

large crowd was present, including many from the Cross Roads church. Most of the people were there as a direct result of the reports of extraordinary happenings at the August meeting. From great distances people came in their wagons and encamped in the vicinity. They were, in the words of Foote, "full of expectation, some wondering, and some seeking their salvation." The hopeful were amply rewarded, for this five-day meeting developed into North Carolina's first camp meeting[14] and in the ensuing commotion of prayer and preaching, many persons found the comfort they sought. Meeting at about this time, the Synod of the Carolinas noted that while there was still a prevalent coldness and indifference, they had great reason to be thankful, for in several pockets of revivalism within the state, God had evidently "begun to pour out his Spirit, in an eminent degree."[15] This interpretation of events multiplied the awakening enthusiasm and instilled greater reverence among more nominal churchgoers in regions as yet untouched.

Among the Baptists of North Carolina's Kehukee Association the revival also entered on the coattails of Kentucky news. The association had long been concerned over the depressed state of religion and for years had promoted prayer-meetings throughout its churches. They devoutly expected their prayers to be answered someday.[16] There were some indications in 1800 of an impending revival, but at the convocation of the association in 1801, the chain reaction again occurred. Elder Lemuel Burkitt had just returned from a tour of Kentucky and Tennessee. Speaking before the associational gathering of representatives from each of the Kehukee churches, he gave an account of the phenomenal outbreak in the West. His words were charged with emotion—six thousand, he said, had recently been converted beyond the mountains, and the supernatural work showed no signs of abating. This was the catalyst needed to activate that scheme of deliverance so long promoted by prayers and fasts. "The desirable news seemed to take such an uncommon effect on the people, that numbers were crying out for mercy, and many praising and glorifying God. Such a Kehukee Association we had never before seen. The ministers all seemed alive in the work of the Lord, and every Christian present in rapturous desire, was ready to cry, *Thy kingdom come*. The ministers and delegates carried the sacred flame home to their churches, and the fire began to kindle in the greatest part of the churches, and the work increased."[17]

[14] Foote, *Sketches of North Carolina*, p. 379.

[15] Synod of the Carolinas, "Minutes," October 9, 1801, Ms 2 : 94, in the library of the Union Theological Seminary in Virginia, Richmond.

[16] Burkitt and Read, *History of the Kehukee Baptist Association*, pp. 138–40.

[17] Ibid., p. 141.

In church after church attendance rose greatly. People cried, shouted, fell down. So desperate were many to secure their salvation that they called out in agony, " *'What shall we do to be saved.'* " Professors and doubters, young and old were struck by this new feeling. In the large meetings that followed, group singing was especially effective in bringing the congregation to the edge of conversion. Then the ministers would walk among the excited masses, shaking hands, relating their own experiences, and pleading with the hesitant to place their total reliance upon God. This intense personal pastoral attention was reputed to be enormously successful.[18]

Another method pioneered in the Baptist churches of the Kehukee Association was a definite forerunner of the "anxious bench," widely used thirty years later in the revivals of Charles G. Finney and his contemporaries. Near the close of the exercises, the ministers asked those who still felt condemned in the eyes of God but were anxious to receive salvation to come down near the preaching stage. The evangelists intensified their prayers for these, and supposedly the sight of friends and neighbors leaving their seats and walking down to the pulpit made others more serious and intent. And those who had overcome their hesitation to present themselves in front of everyone for special prayer now felt that failure to live up to their new convictions would be a public disgrace.[19] These techniques, combined with the huge crowds, the roar of many voices, the flickering torches throwing their eerie shadows across the strange revival landscape, resulted in a large ingathering by the Baptist churches of North Carolina.

Throughout 1802 and 1803, the revival rampaged across North Carolina with all the force and fury of its Kentucky parent. In almost every section of the state, there were meetings marked by extraordinarily large crowds, cooperating ministers of various denominations, hundreds falling, shouting, convulsing, finding security in apparent salvation. There are abundant records proving that all the characteristics of the Cane Ridge camp meeting were present here.[20] As Richard Furman wrote to a prom-

---

[18] Ibid., pp. 144-45.

[19] Ibid., pp. 145–46. Benedict, *A General History of the Baptist Denomination,* 2:108, describes the North Carolina situation, though he evidently means 1801 instead of 1800: "that astonishing work which had been prevailing a short time in Kentucky and other parts, made a sudden and unexpected entrance among them, and was attended with most of the new and unusual appearances, which in many places it assumed. This work was not confined to the Baptists, but prevailed, at the same time, amongst the Methodists and Presbyterians."

[20] See, for example, James Hall, *A Narrative of a Most Extraordinary Work of Religion in North Carolina* (Philadelphia, 1802); Matthew H. Moore, *Sketches of the Pioneers of Methodism in North Carolina and Virginia* (Nashville, Tenn.,

inent Baptist leader in Philadelphia, "The Revival, or religious Stir, in N. Carolina, I understand, continues and Increases: They have had several Meetings, lately, quite in the Kentucky Stile." [21] And a Virginia Presbyterian leader reported after a visit to North Carolina: "I have seen strange things since I came to this state; a revival of religion after the manner of that in Tennessee and Kentucky. It is, indeed, a very extraordinary work, and I rejoice much that I have seen it." [22]

Perhaps of the almost innumerable camp meetings described, the one conducted in late March 1802 in Mecklenburg County was typical. The site was about a dozen miles southeast of the present city of Charlotte, near the South Carolina border. The encampment was on a large, gently sloping hill, half encircled at the bottom by a creek—ideal for large crowds. By early Friday morning, March 27, 1802, men began pitching tents for their families and clearing a large central area on the hillside for the meeting ground. In the center they erected a preaching scaffold, from which seventeen ministers of varied denominations would soon be speaking. By Friday evening several thousand people had assembled, and the services began with a prayer and the text "Surely this is the house of God, this is the gate of heaven!" Throughout most of the night the work progressed, with all the clamor and excitement of Gasper River repeated. "The novelty of the scene," wrote a witness, "and the fervour of the devotion, which seemed

---

1884), which reprints many contemporary letters; Foote, *Sketches of North Carolina*, wherein Hall is reprinted along with additional information; Lee, *A Short History of the Methodists*, p. 287 and passim; John Witherspoon to Charles Pettigrew, August 5, 1802, in the Pettigrew Papers; William Ormond, "Journal," September 28–November 1, 1802, typescript in Duke University Library, Durham, N. C.; and various letters interspersed through the *Georgia Analytical Repository*, the *Western Missionary Magazine*, and the *New York Missionary Magazine*. Several important accounts are in Dow, ed., *Extracts from Original Letters, to the Methodist Bishops*. Of course, Asbury's *Journal* often relates the revival news in North Carolina, as do the various local denominational studies. An extremely valuable account has been left by the Lutheran Paul Henkel, as cited above.

These camp meeting revivals have been partially treated in Guion Griffis Johnson, "Revival Movements in Ante-Bellum North Carolina," *North Carolina Historical Review* 10 (January 1933); 21–43, and "The Camp Meeting in Ante-Bellum North Carolina," ibid., 10 (April 1933):95–110; and Durward T. Stokes, "Religious Denominations in North Carolina and the Great Revival" (M. A. thesis, University of North Carolina, 1965).

[21] Furman to William Rogers, April 22, 1802, Richard Furman Papers, South Caroliniana Collection, University of South Carolina, Columbia, S. C.

[22] "Extract of a letter from the Rev. Moses Hoge to the Rev. Dr. Green, dated Mecklenburg (N. C.), April 24, 1802," *Western Missionary Magazine* 1 (1803): 103.

to be kindled up in almost every mind, so arrested the attention of the multitude, that but few in this assembly closed their eyes in sleep the whole of this memorable night."[23]

In addition to carriages, 160 wagons were counted at this large camp meeting. Allowing four square feet per person, it was computed that at least 5,000 were in attendance. On Saturday and Sunday several hundred in the congregation fell to the ground and felt they received pardon. At Monday noon "there were about 100 persons down on the ground, the greater part of whom were shouting aloud." The vastness of the meeting multiplied the effect of hard-hitting revivalist sermons. One participant asked, "In the immediate presence of the adorable Jehovah, in the presence of God. . . . In this situation who would not worship; who would not adore?"[24] Here, obviously, was the frontier camp meeting, with all its theological and emotional trappings, transplanted to the older states of the coastal South. Even though the general revival declined after 1805, as late as 1809 there were advertisements for interdenominational camp meetings planned in central North Carolina.[25]

Traveling through South Carolina in January of 1801, Francis Asbury found that reading accounts of the news he was receiving from the Cumberland area, along with assorted other revival accounts, greatly invigorated both fellow preachers and their congregations. So he continued to relate to his audiences the startling stories of how God was working in the West.[26] In the spring of 1802 appearances started changing in the state. Quite expectedly, the revival impetus in South Carolina began in that portion nearest the region of southeast North Carolina where camp meetings were already being held as early as March 1802. Again the reports from one state precipitated similar meetings in the other. The upcountry of South Carolina was to be the stage of most of the state's revival activity. For one thing, here most of the people were small farmers, not as preoccupied with

[23] John Brown to Rev. Dr. Wm. Hollinshead, April 13, 1802, reprinted in the *New York Missionary Magazine* 3 (1802): 181. This letter describes the meeting in detail, pp. 181–82.

[24] Ibid., p. 182.

[25] See the "Religious Intelligence" of the *Raleigh Register and North-Carolina State Gazette*, Thursday, September 7, 1809. Cf. Ebenezer Pettigrew to James Iredell, August 6, 1806, describing an emotional camp meeting in Washington County; Pettigrew Papers. Margaret Burr DesChamps discusses this lingering of the eastern camp meetings in an excellent study, "The Presbyterian Church in the South Atlantic States, 1801–1861" (Ph.D. diss., Emory University, 1952).

[26] Asbury to Daniel Hitt, January 30, 1801, in Asbury, *Journal and Letters*, 3: 197–98; and in his *Journal*, October 18 and 20, 1801, 2: 310.

politics, markets, and slavery as the large planters crowding the sea island districts. And here too the evangelistic Separate Baptist heritage was strongest, for the Charleston region was the citadel of the erstwhile Particular (now Regular) Baptists and what remained of the Episcopal faith.

Just a month after the camp meeting conducted in Mecklenburg County, North Carolina, the new revival fervor appeared in South Carolina at Lancaster, only thirty miles away. A witness reported that upwards of 12,000 attended this mid-April meeting, and the scenes which stunned the mind, he wrote, "baffle all description." "It appears to me, that God is affording the world, in this age of degeneracy and infidelity, a testimony of the truth and efficacy of the gospel, addressed to our senses; little inferior to that which he gave the world on the day of Pentecost. . . . This work . . . presents a demonstrative proof of the power of the gospel, and thereby prepares the way for access to the heart."[27]

The next month, May 1802, a group of eleven Presbyterian, four Baptist, and three Methodist ministers conducted a huge revival meeting on the border of the two Carolinas, at Waxhaws (halfway between Charlotte and Lancaster). Thousands were in attendance, and here South Carolina encountered the first outbreak of "those bodily affections, which have been before experienced at Kentucky, North-Carolina, and at other places, where the extraordinary revivals in religion within this year or two have taken place."[28] These phenomena seemed only to increase the worshipful attitudes among those present. The faithful found that which they had long desired—a vigorous renewal of religious dedication. And one witness reported that of all those present, the very ones who had come the greatest distance—and hence the ones probably most dedicated, faithful, and hopeful—were in far greater proportion afflicted with the strange revival exercises.[29]

Another spectacular camp meeting worthy of notice occurred near the present city of Spartanburg during the first week of July. This area was some sixty-five miles from the previous camp meetings near Charlotte and Lancaster, but, besides the accounts sprinkling in from that region, Asbury had journeyed through the Spartanburg vicinity in the fall of 1801, reading to his congregations from James McGready's narrative of Logan County.[30]

[27] "Extract of a Letter from the Rev. John Couser, dated Lancaster, South Carolina, April 21, 1802," in the *Methodist Magazine* [London] 26 (1803): 131–32.

[28] "A Letter from Dr. Furman of Charleston, to Dr. Rippon of London. Charleston, 11th August, 1802," in Benedict, *A General History of the Baptist Denomination*, 2:169.

[29] Ibid., p. 170.

[30] Asbury, *Journal and Letters*, 2:310.

As Mark Moore, a Methodist minister, wrote him fourteen months later, "the account you brought us, together with various circulating ones, revived our hopes, and we waited with anxious expectation of having a gracious visitation."[31] The other denominations undoubtedly had heard of this revival too, for on July 2, 1802, ministers of each of the three major groups met near Spartanburg in a valley near the Tyger River. A congregation estimated to be not less than 5,000 gathered, and before the fervent preaching and roar of song and prayer, several hundred fell to the ground. The noise "rent the air, and was reverberated by the surrounding hills."[32]

The revival tempo increased in South Carolina, and hardly a week passed in which there was not a camp meeting somewhere in the upper portion of the state. Near the end of July over 200 wagons and 5,000 persons were reported at a meeting in the westernmost county of the state.[33] These religious stirrings were generally confined to the more recently settled, less densely populated western half of South Carolina. Richard Furman, a Baptist leader from Charleston, who although eminently orthodox nevertheless appreciated heartfelt religion, wistfully wrote to an associate, "The Revival in the Back and Middle Country is a blessed Visitation from on high: God grant it may be extended to the Sea Coast: that you, that we, and Thousands more may partake in its Blessedness and Joy."[34] In the locations where they were successful, Asbury in January 1803 could claim that in the preceding year, the Methodists had gained 3,371 new members.[35] Even

[31] Mark Moore to [Asbury?], December 28, 1802, reprinted in Dow, ed., *Extracts from Original Letters, to the Methodist Bishops*, p. 30.

[32] Ibid., p. 31; and "Extract of a Letter, Dated July 7, 1802," *Georgia Analytical Repository* 1 (July–August 1802): 87-92.

[33] "Extract of a Letter from a Gentleman in Pendleton District, to his Friend in this City, dated July 30, 1802," in *New York Missionary Magazine* 3 (1802): 310-11. There is much documentation for the camp meetings which covered the upper counties of the state. For example, see Lee, *A Short History of the Methodists*, pp. 286-87; "Extract of a letter from the Rev. L. Floyd, Missionary, employed by the Congregational Society of the State of South Carolina . . ." in *Connecticut Evangelical Magazine* 3 (February 1803): 314-15; Benedict, *A General History of the Baptist Denomination*, 2: 165–67; Shipp, *History of Methodism in South Carolina*, pp. 273, 398–400; Edmund Botsford to John Roberts, November 24, 1802, and Botsford to Richard Furman, June 11, 1803, in Edmund Botsford Papers; Robert Wilson to "Aunt," April 17, 1803, in L. C. Glenn Collection; various entries in Asbury's *Journal;* and assorted letters reprinted in the *Georgia Analytical Repository.*

[34] Furman to Edmund Botsford, October 12, 1802, in Richard Furman Papers, South Carolina Baptist Historical Society, Furman University.

[35] Asbury, *Journal and Letters*, 2: 375.

after this particular revival movement had spent itself in 1805 or 1806, South Carolina—with the other southern states—continued to have regular camp meetings for over a century.

At the end of 1800 the Reverend Stith Mead was appointed presiding elder of the Georgia District Methodists. Mead regularly conducted services throughout a circuit between Augusta and Macon. He was a long distance from the revival center in Kentucky, but on January 20, 1801, he received an informative letter from Asbury—evidently Mead already had some indications of the spiritual storm in the West. Asbury warmly related the news from Cumberland, along with reports of revivals in other parts of the nation. The work seemed to have no end: "God hath given us hundreds in 1800, why not thousands in 1801, yea, why not a million if," asked Asbury, "we had faith. 'Lord increase our faith.' "[36]

With such admonitions in mind, Mead toured his new territory and found but few examples of genuine piety. Undoubtedly the Cumberland reports made his own neighborhood seem more depressed by contrast. The first quarterly meeting he attended in the state met in mid-July 1801; representatives, both lay and clerical, from all the nearby Methodist churches were present. Mead deftly led them through an inquiry into the state of religion in their individual churches. On the Saturday evening of the two-day services he asked one of his fellow ministers, " 'How long is it since the last revival in your neighbourhood?' He replied, 'It is yet to begin.' As we were conversing together with [still another minister], about the nature of revivals, and the distance between the times of a general out-pouring of the Spirit,—we concluded, that the favourable period was now arrived, and I exhorted them to look for it."[37]

The very next morning, during the administration of the Lord's Supper, several of the more faithful members (these "advanced Christians," as Mead called them, apparently believed that God was beginning to effect his long anticipated deliverance) became strongly moved. Their "loud lamentations and streaming eyes" so affected many of the younger members that they fell to the floor. From this date throughout Mead's district in central Georgia numbers were "awakened" and fell prostrate on the floor, or laid on the pews, crying, moaning, begging for mercy.[38] Again

[36] Asbury to Mead, January 20, 1801, in ibid., 3:196.
[37] "From Mr. Stith Mead, to the Rev. Dr. Coke . . . May 11, 1802," in the *Methodist Magazine* [London] 26 (1803):521.
[38] Ibid., pp. 521–23.

the revival fervor spread, for these accounts gravely affected others in the vicinity. Another local revival area had caught fire in Elbert County,[39] just across the boundary from the upper region of South Carolina that was most prone to camp meetings. Accounts of these proceedings raced through the Georgia farming country "like fire in dry stubble."

In December 1801 Asbury made a trip through Mead's district, and on several occasions he read from the explosive letter of James McGready which over and over Asbury had found would invigorate the sagging energy of depressed churches.[40] Here in Georgia McGready's communiqué simply reinforced the already vigorous efforts of the ministerial forces. To this date, however, no real camp meeting had yet appeared in the state—only a greatly increased enthusiasm for religious services. But just as in the other states to the north and west, the next half decade exhibited unprecedented revival scenes everywhere in Georgia, except in the immediate vicinity of Savannah.

In a long letter probably addressed to Asbury, Mead detailed the multiplicity of actual camp meetings held throughout Georgia in the latter part of 1802 and the early months of 1803. An intensification of religious interest and enthusiasm was a prerequisite for camp meetings, for a large proportion of the normally indifferent church members—along with many who claimed no allegiance to any church—had to indicate desire for one of these interdenominational gatherings before the local ministers would promote one. Also, only an unusual degree of concern about religion would draw the necessary crowds. Yet once a camp meeting was held, it generated so much curiosity and abnormal religious devotion that other revival meetings occurred almost spontaneously. By the summer of 1802, these conditions had been met in Georgia.

The first multidenominational camp meeting Mead attended was held at Rehoboth Chapel, Warren County (in the center of Mead's district), beginning Friday, October 8, 1802.[41] A plot of land nearly a quarter mile long was cleared, and two preaching stands were erected. A congregation numbered at 7,000 gathered in the clearing and heard relays of twenty-six ministers—eighteen Methodists, three Presbyterians, and five Baptists.

[39] "From the Rev. Moses Black, Georgia, Elbert-County, Dec. 24, 1802," in ibid., pp. 418–19; and "Extract 27. From a respectable Minister of the Gospel, in the upper part of Georgia, to his friend in Savannah, dated Nov. 17, 1801," in Woodward, *Surprising Accounts*, pp. 54-55.

[40] Asbury, *Journal and Letters*, 2: 316–17.

[41] "Mead to [?], Georgia. April 21st, 1803," in Dow, ed., *Extracts from Original Letters, to the Methodist Bishops*, pp. 38-39.

Especially on Sunday the audience was enthusiastic, but the falling and shouting increased toward the close of the meeting on Tuesday. In this Cane Ridge-like setting, Mead conservatively estimated that more than one hundred were converted. As in every revival report, the number actually said to be converted seems minuscule when compared to the size of the congregation. Yet most of those who attended, excepting many of the young people, had already been converted—and the revival only reinvigorated their faith. A major role of the revival was to stir indifferent backsliders to renewed activity. Church attendance multiplied more dramatically than the membership increased.

During the following months camp meetings were held with remarkable frequency and effect. On October 14–15, 1802, Mead attended a camp meeting sponsored by the local Presbyterians, and on October 23–25 he preached at another huge assembly attended by ministers of all three denominations. At a camp meeting held in early November judged to be almost a mile in circumference there were reported to be 10,000 in the audience; among the twenty-five ministers was even one Episcopalian. By the close of these services many were still so physically shaken that they had to be placed in some of the more than 250 wagons present and taken home. During the winter months the meetings decreased, but despite the February cold, more than 3,000 appeared at a camp meeting in Hancock County, between Macon and Augusta.[42] The revival in Georgia reached its height between the summers of 1802 and 1804, but camp meetings continued for many years. They became an institutionalized feature of Georgia religion.

The religious situation in Virginia was spotty and difficult to characterize during the two years from the revival's first appearance across the mountains in Kentucky until it came to maturity in the Old Dominion. Throughout 1800 and 1801 there were occasional local revivals, fomented by a single church or denomination, but they never amounted to much. In their immediate vicinity they increased the hopes and expectations for an extensive,

[42] Ibid., pp. 39–41. The famous and eccentric Methodist evangelist Lorenzo Dow witnessed his first camp meeting in Georgia in 1803; see Dow, *History of Cosmopolite; or, The Four Volumes of Lorenzo's Journal, Concentrated in One* (New York, 1814), pp. 170–71. For further evidence on Georgia revivals, see Lee, *A Short History of the Methodists*, pp. 292-93; "Extract of a Letter, from the upper part of the state, dated July 15th, 1802," in *Georgia Analytical Repository* 1 (July–August 1802): 74; and "Revival of Religion at Black Creek," in ibid. (September–October 1802): 124–25; Asbury, *Journal and Letters*, 2: 415, and 3: 229–30; and John Melish, *Travels in the United States of America, in the Years 1806, 1807, and 1809*, 2 vols. (Philadelphia, 1812), 1: 36–37.

general revival such as the ones held in Kentucky and Tennessee. In the many areas of Virginia which failed to experience a transitory revival the decline seemed even more critical. Baptist H. Tolar, writing to the prominent Massachusetts Baptist Isaac Backus in 1801, noted little immediate prospect of resurgence in his neighborhood, but expressed his hopes: "May the many revivals begun in different States of this Union, spread, till the earth shall be full of the knowledge of the Lord."[43] These conditions at home, combined with the enticing news from Kentucky, were preparing the way for a Virginia revival.

During the first six months of 1802 there seems to have been a gradual increase in the number of Virginia churches undergoing a revival of religion. For example, the Roanoke Baptist Association in south-central Virginia had been concerned about its lukewarm membership since the late 1790s. In 1797 it had appointed a group of four men to travel among the association's churches in an attempt to stir them to invigorated service. On the belief that revived ministers created revived churches, the association formulated a program to bolster their ministers' enthusiasm. These efforts resulted in a rebirth of religious commitment, and by the spring of 1802 (by which time the revivals to the south and west were common knowledge) the membership of some of their churches had more than doubled. By May 1802 the association had baptized almost 1,350 new converts, and the revival was still continuing.[44]

At the close of 1801 a group of ministers representing the three major denominations met in Bedford County. They had come to a special Christmas meeting, hoping somehow to unite so as to promote more effectively a resurgence of religious vitality. The meeting was marked by unusual harmony, and in its aftermath there developed successively larger interdenominational meetings. From these revival services a hundred were reportedly converted to religion in Bedford County alone, and their awakened zeal rapidly spread beyond county lines. Soon there were accounts of revivals in

[43] Tolar to Backus, August 8, 1801, reprinted in Alvah Hovey, *A Memoir of the Life and Times of The Rev. Isaac Backus* (Boston, 1859), pp. 296–97. My discussion of the Virginia situation is based on such sources as Jonathan Jackson to F. Asbury, August 20, 1800, in Moore, *Pioneers of Methodism in North Carolina and Virginia*, p. 304; Asbury, *Journal and Letters*, 2:249–50, 307 and 3:225; Isaac Backus, *An Abridgement of the Church History of New England, . . . With a Concise Account of the Baptists in the Southern Parts of America* (Boston, 1804), pp. 241–42; and John Lee to Jesse Lee, September 5, 1801, in Jesse Lee, *A Short Account of the Life and Death of the Rev. John Lee, A Methodist Minister in the United States of America* (Baltimore, Md., 1805), pp. 168–69.

[44] Semple, *A History of the Baptists in Virginia*, pp. 237–39.

Albemarle and Rockbridge counties;[45] Baptists, Methodists, and Presbyterians were sharing in these ever more frequent revivals.

In the southeast section of the state, Methodist itinerant William Ormond in April 1802 attended a large outdoor religious meeting. Several Baptist ministers cooperated with the nine Methodists, and many among the congregation of this primitive Virginia camp meeting seemingly were converted.[46] The magnitude, fervor, and technique of the western revivals were beginning to appear in the Old Dominion. In the words of the Hanover Presbytery which met April 17, 1802: "In some places God has been pleased to revive his work. . . . In other places the attention of people to the importance of Religion seems to be increasing, whilst the hopes of the few remaining pious are considerably revived. These favorable appearances . . . afford encouragement for all the lovers of Jesus . . . to be importunate at the Throne of Grace for an outpouring of the Spirit, and a revival of his work in a more extensive degree."[47]

After June the revival ferment spread, but Virginia did not experience the Great Revival in all its power until after the winter of 1802–1803. In July of 1802 Ormond again attended a huge outdoor meeting in southern Virginia which had all the characteristics of its Kentucky forebears. At least a dozen ministers participated, and, under the pressure of their messages, as well as the awesome spectacle made visible by torchlight, hundreds fell to the ground, exclaiming to God their repentance. These clamorous revivals continued far into the night.[48] From wagons and tents came the prayers of the penitent—again the camp meeting was effecting mass conversion.

Throughout the "Southside" of Virginia the Methodists especially en-

[45] Archibald Alexander to Nathan Strong, January 25, 1802, in the *Connecticut Evangelical Magazine* 2 (March 1802): 354; "Extract of a Letter from a Respectable Clergyman in Virginia, to one of the Editors, dated November 19, 1802," in ibid. 3 (January 1803): 278–79; "From the Rev. Daniel Hall, Presiding Elder of the Richmond District, Virginia, to the Rev. Dr. Coke, Sept. 23, 1802," *Methodist Magazine* [London] 26 (1803): 371–72; and "Extract 60. Of a Letter from the Rev. Drury Lacy . . . January 22, 1802, to Mr. Robert Ralston . . . ," in Dow, ed., *Extracts from Original Letters, to the Methodist Bishops*, pp. 130–34.

[46] William Ormond, "Journal," April 17–18, 1802. A week later Asbury reported "a general revival" on Virginia's Eastern Shore. Asbury, *Journal and Letters*, 2: 335. Carlos R. Allen, Jr., "The Great Revival in Virginia, 1783–1812" (M.A. thesis, University of Virginia, 1948), an able study, does not discuss these camp meetings, or any before 1803.

[47] Hanover Presbytery, "Minutes," April 17, 1802, Ms vol. 4:91–92, photocopy in Union Theological Seminary in Virginia, Richmond.

[48] Ormond, "Journal," July 22–26, 1802, pp. 50–52.

joyed revival success: at Merritt's Chapel, Salem, Ellis' Meeting House, Lloyd's Chapel, the work went on. Reports poured in of memorable meetings to the north in Rockingham County, across the Blue Ridge in the Valley.[49] This Rockingham revival, like its counterparts in other southern states, engendered far-flung imitation. As the Methodist itinerant Philip Bruce wrote Bishop Asbury, "The postmen carried the news to New Town [northeast of Richmond], while Brother Samuel Mitchell was there, and it gave them such a spring in that barren place that when my information came away about fifty souls had happily found redemption . . . and the prospect was growing in that quarter of the vineyard, as our old Steadies had caught the flame."[50] From Bedford County, just east of the mountains between Roanoke and Lynchburg, Sarah Callaway wrote to her brother in Pittsylvania County that the only news worthy of notice was the "grate talk of religion in this neighbouhood [*sic*] and the neighbourhood of new london."[51]

Two hundred miles to the northwest, in the present state of West Virginia adjacent to the Ohio and Pennsylvania lines, a Presbyterian minister was reporting welcome news. During the summer, he wrote, there had been an unusual "stir" in his congregation, and—significantly—a "raised expectation among the people." In late September, during a communion service, most of the churchgoers spent the whole night in religious celebration, and the strange exercises were "in the same manner, as in the states of Kentucky, Tenesee, and the Carolinas." Two weeks later, because of the increased interest, another sacramental occasion was appointed. To this came ten ministers and "not less than 10,000" people in countless wagons, bringing their provisions and encamping for four days. Hundreds fell, "cries and groans" rose from among the people.[52] Hence by late 1802, the camp meeting revival had been introduced in Virginia from the southeastern to northwestern extremes. Yet the following two years were to see

[49] Lee, *A Short History of the Methodists*, pp. 287-88; and Asbury, *Journal and Letters*, 2: 360-62, and 3: 250.

[50] Bruce to Asbury, December 12, 1802, reprinted in Moore, *Pioneers of Methodism*, pp. 189-90. The Rockingham meeting had large crowds, multiple preachers, overnight services in the open air, people come from afar by wagon, falling down—all the attributes of the camp meeting. See James Ward to [?], October 23, 1802, in Dow, ed., *Extracts from Original Letters, to the Methodist Bishops*, pp. 70-72.

[51] Sarah Callaway to Henry G. Callaway, August 19, 1802, in the Pocket Plantation Manuscripts, Alderman Library, University of Virginia, Charlottesville, Va.

[52] "Extract from a letter from the Rev. James Hughs, dated West Liberty, Ohio County, Virg., Nov. 9, 1802, to Rev. Stephen West, of Stockbridge, Mass.," in the *Connecticut Evangelical Magazine* 3 (February 1803): 315-17.

this revival ceremony really flower only among the Methodists of the Old Dominion.

Until 1802, both the Baptists and Presbyterians of Virginia had prospered with the Methodists in a universal religious awakening. After 1803, for reasons not entirely clear, the Methodists seem to have drawn those most enthusiastic from the other denominations and they alone conducted large-scale camp meetings.[53] Uniquely in Virginia the revival news from other states, and the general feeling that this must be the time appointed by God for deliverance from the decade-long depression, to some extent resulted in revivals confined to individual churches. Denominational lines seem to have been firmer in Virginia than in the neighboring states to the south and west. Most of the Baptists north of the James River were of unevangelical Regular (formerly Particular) Baptist heritage, less disposed to the mass revivalism of the camp meeting. Most Virginia Presbyterians, taught by Hampden-Sydney and Liberty Hall graduates, shunned the revival emotionalism accepted by Presbyterians like McGready. And by 1803 the camp meeting had, among a growing number of people, become associated with unchecked "Methodist enthusiasm."

In those states where all groups were already involved in camp meetings, this newly acquired reputation was not the severe limiting factor that it was in Virginia. Here, as in coastal South Carolina and Georgia, the unsavory repute accorded the mass conversion technique restrained the "respectable" denominations from taking part. By this date evidence suggests that even the Baptists in Virginia had achieved more status than the Methodists.[54] Since the Methodists with their elaborately effective system of itinerants appeared to be making great use of the camp meeting, the Presby-

---

[53] Allen, Jr., "The Great Revival in Virginia," pp. 71ff., notes the Methodist dominance but does not explain it. He does offer many descriptions of their camp meetings after 1803.

[54] See, for example, Robert B. Semple's comment, in his *History of the Baptists in Virginia*, p. 39, describing Baptists in the 1790's: "Their preachers were become much more correct in their manner of preaching: A great many odd tones, disgusting whoops and awkward gestures, were disused: In their matter also, they had more of sound sense and strong reasoning. Their zeal was less mixed with enthusiasm, and their piety became more rational. They were much more numerous, and of course, in the eyes of the world, more respectable. Besides, they were joined by persons of much greater weight, in civil society: Their congregations became more numerous, than those of any other Christian sect . . . . This could not, but influence their manners and spirit, more or less." The revivalistic Separate Baptists had never penetrated much north of the James River, and a great many of these evangelists, unable to preach without pay and eke out a living from Virginia's worn-out soil, had migrated to Kentucky.

terians and Baptists evidently decided to withdraw and leave the emotional excesses to the Methodists. For whatever reason, the Methodists alone in 1803, 1804, and 1805 enjoyed almost a monopoly of the camp meeting in Virginia.

In the spring of 1802, when William Ormond first attended in southern Virginia gigantic outdoor meetings, the name "camp meeting" had not yet come into use. Sometime in late 1802 the phrase was coined and adopted throughout the South. In Virginia especially this appellation, with its connotations of practically inevitable revival success, seemed to add a special element of noteworthiness to the outdoor meetings which had been conducted with increasing regularity since early 1802. The services so named gained additional support and participants. Indeed, in Virginia where there were many churchgoers who vaguely remembered the revivals of 1787–1789, the use of the phrase "camp meeting" appeared to give the current movement a greater degree of novelty—an element significant in the propagation of the revival across the South. This image of uniqueness was a boon to Virginia Methodists, but a mark of reproach to the Presbyterians and Baptists of rising status.

The first "camp meeting" held by that name in southeastern Virginia met in Brunswick County, May 27–30, 1803.[55] Just as it had rapidly diffused in the other southern states, this Methodist camp meeting revival leaped from location to location. The reputation for exaggerated emotionalism which the camp meeting had acquired since its origin in Kentucky meant that at this comparatively late date it received greater opposition from the more decorous denominations. As an old Methodist leader described to Asbury the beginning of the camp meetings in Virginia:

> The thought of people encamping on the ground, living in Tents for three or four days, and carrying provisions for themselves and their horses, met with a variety of objections from all sorts of people.
> Great numbers of different characters attend on the occasions. Here are a mixed multitude of different ages, sentiments, and designs: some hearing for Life the Word of God, some looking on, and others walking to and fro. Here you may see various exercises in the congregation; some praying, some weeping, some rejoicing, some scoffing and blaspheming.[56]

[55] Lee, *A Short History of the Methodists*, pp. 292–95.

[56] Edward Dromgoole to Asbury, December 20, 1805, in the Edward Dromgoole Papers, Southern Historical Collection, University of North Carolina, Chapel Hill, N. C. In this general vicinity Presbyterians were experiencing revivals in their churches, but were not conducting or attending the Kentucky-style meetings. See Drury Lacy to Ashbel Green, October 6, 1804, in the Gratz Collection.

Despite the objections of the fastidious, the camp meetings continued unabated, spreading across southern Virginia in 1803, 1804, and 1805. In early 1804 eccentric Lorenzo Dow, who claimed to have been carried to heaven in a cyclone at the age of thirteen, conducted revival meetings throughout the area.[57] As an indication of the prevalence of the revival, Stith Mead, who had been relocated in Virginia, wrote a long letter giving details of twenty-three camp meetings he had attended between March 1804 and April 1805 at which over one thousand were supposedly converted. The disapproval of more urbane denominations could not slow the burgeoning Methodist revival. "Persecution," Mead confidently concluded, "has raged in proportion to the revival; but hitherto the Lord has helped us."[58]

Thus from an auspicious beginning one summer day in distant Logan County, June 1800, the camp meeting revival had swept back across the South. It retraced the routes by which its promoters in Kentucky had come west, and from North Carolina the seemingly miraculous new revival technique was disseminated throughout the length and breadth of the southern states. Yet as the movement developed, opposition gradually arose. At first in Kentucky even the most orthodox Presbyterians thought the revival exercises were a special dispensation from God, but as the novelty wore off and the convulsions grew more extreme, many turned against the camp meeting.[59] This change was too slow to stay the development of the revival in most states, but by the time it came to fruition in Virginia, the disrepute limited popular participation. Though here and there in the Carolinas and Georgia both Presbyterians and Baptists still occasionally joined in, the camp meeting after 1803 and 1804 was quickly becoming a Methodist institution. What had begun as an almost universally acclaimed, interdenominational revival method had evolved into a controversial trademark of Methodist extremism. Yet along this path from near unanimous approval to opprobrium literally thousands in each denomination had been moved to a sincere conversion experience. Herein lies the recurring saga of mass revivalism.

[57] Dow, *History of Cosmopolite*, pp. 201–2.

[58] Mead to [Asbury?], in Dow, ed., *Extracts from Original Letters, to the Methodist Bishops*, pp. 59–61. For other camp meetings in Virginia, see Henry Smith, *Recollections and Reflections of an Old Itinerant* (New York, 1848), pp. 105–10.

[59] For example, read John Lyle's diary from his first encounter with the camp meeting through to his efforts to counter the extremes of Barton W. Stone and Richard McNemar. Lyle, "Diary, June 1801–July 1803."

Chapter Seven

The Changing Revival Image

When after a long decade of religious decline the camp meetings first came to the fore, they were almost universally greeted as the welcome vanguard of God's returning mercy. Within several years, however, some of the more orthodox clergy began to withdraw their approval, while others, still more rigid, declared the revival and its excesses to be nothing more than the demonic delusions of an ignorant people. In the face of such criticism, many of the undaunted supporters of pietistic religion strove mightily to defend their "work of God" from the verbal slurs of those they considered hypocritical nominalists and cocksure deists. After a barrage of attacks and counterattacks had marred the pristine reputation of the camp meeting revival, most Baptists and Presbyterians gradually disassociated themselves from the movement they had once so actively desired and praised. Yet the zealous Methodists, quick to recognize the efficacy of the mass meeting as a spur to conversion, seized upon the camp meeting for their own and purposefully turned it into a revival technique. As such it was to spread eventually throughout the entire nation.

The almost unbelievable successes of the full-blown revival effected another intellectual development. Evangelical theology had always included a recognition of a prophesied "Day of Judgment" and "Second Coming of Christ." But almost never did any southern evangelist before the revival presume to predict when this anticipated event would occur. Seemingly none dared conjecture as to how or when the last days foretold in the scriptural record would begin. After the outbursts of 1801, however, all these biblical prophecies, these promises concerning the end of time, suddenly surfaced. It appeared to many that the miraculous developments of this exalted era presaged even greater days to come. Events which were thought to be unparalleled in the annals of church history now seemed afoot, and many imagined this second Pentecost to be the vanguard of the final dispensation when God would bring history to an auspicious close. In this exalted view, the Great Revival had triggered the epoch of the millennium. Quite obviously, then, the revival through its changing images mirrored the religious complexity of early nineteenth century southern society.

The very titles of the contemporary pamphlets published to extol the spiritual news indicate how people marveled at the revival occurrences: *Surprising Accounts of the Revival of Religion in the United States* (1802); *Gospel News, or A Brief Account of the Revival of Religion in Kentucky, and Several Other Parts of the United States* (1801); *Glad Tidings; or, An Account of the State of Religion, within . . . the Presbyterian Church* (1804); and *Increase of Piety, or the Revival of Religion in the United States of America* (1802). Cast as they were against a dismal decade of deism and indifference, the unusual fervor of the camp meetings seemed all the more remarkable. This feeling of genuine uniqueness elicited the widespread conviction that God was working his miraculous deliverance. Behind this general idea lay the myriad impressions that the revival represented a creative display of providential interference in the lives of men.

In 1801 the Reverend Moses Hoge, a Virginia Presbyterian, sent a copy of a letter he had received from Kentucky to a prominent colleague in Philadelphia. "The revivals of religion in this country are really novel in our church," noted the unnamed Kentuckian, who proceeded to describe ecstasies and spasms shocking to educated ears. Yet he concluded—and apparently Hoge concurred—that "As to the work in general there can be no question but it is of God." [1] Another letter from Kentucky, dated March 19, 1801, proclaimed, "The spirit of God appears in powerful operation, among all denominations of Christians." [2] The emotional convolutions and physical contortions of Gasper River and Cane Ridge were not, in the expanse of history, authentically unique—even to the South. But time and religious introspection can dim the memory. At least in the rhetoric of participants, the revivals exhibited unparalleled scenes. "Indeed," remembered a Methodist itinerant, "this strange work appears to have taken every turn to baffle the conjectures and philosophizing of those who were unwilling to acknowledge it was the work of God." [3]

This was the consensus of southern evangelicals when the movement was in its infancy. The fury, the frenzy, the extremes of the revival were intended, according to this view, for a certain purpose. God was using this instrumentality to awaken hardened and indifferent sinners to the precariousness of their unregenerate condition. As Barton W. Stone concluded his

[1] "Extract 26. Of a letter, from the Rev. Moses Hoge, of Shepherd's Town, to the Rev. Dr. Ashbel Green, of this city, dated Sept. 10, 1801," in Woodward, *Surprising Accounts*, pp. 53–54.

[2] "Extract 22. Of a letter from a gentleman in Washington (Ken.) to his Son in this city, dated March 19, 1801," in ibid., pp. 46–47.

[3] Strickland, ed., *Autobiography of Rev. James B. Finley*, p. 376.

discussion of the Cane Ridge spectacle: "So low had religion sunk, and such carelessness universally had prevailed, that I have thought that nothing common could have arrested the attention of the world; therefore these uncommon agitations were sent for this purpose."[4] Given the pervasive belief in God's ability and willingness to intervene in the affairs of men, Stone's interpretation was so general as to contribute vastly to the proliferation of the revival. The pietistic set of mind enabled believers to incorporate whatever took place into a hypothetical scheme of redemption manipulated by their creator.

Falling down, the jerks, and other uncommon spasms were considered to be new revelations of the Spirit. It was argued that the "sensible feelings" of conviction and conversion were effected by this immediate "miraculous outpouring."[5] "The design of Divine Providence, in this work," conjectured a Presbyterian in South Carolina, "appears to be to convince the world, that there is a truth and power in the Christian religion, by addressing the external senses with an undeniable testimony. And so soon as this truth is fully and sufficiently known to the world, I think these extraordinary exercises will undoubtedly disappear."[6]

Such resolute evangelicals seem to have recognized in their explanations of the revival phenomena that more was at stake than simple exposition of God's manner of work. To the faithful, the revival scenes themselves justified increased trust in divine providence, but many of the clergy knew these same reports would arouse doubt in the minds of some. Skeptics far removed from the arena of God's apparent miracle-working would be unconvinced by a mere retelling of revival spectacles. They might only have confirmed their worst suspicions of religion.

For these potential doubters, as well as for any subconscious hesitations on their own part, numerous participants felt called upon to justify the particular extremes to which God had gone in order to jolt hardened sinners into awareness. Unprovoked defensive overtones often appeared before any written or organized attacks upon the revival itself. The Reverend John King, in a letter to the *New York Missionary Magazine* for 1802, sought to preclude any wrongheaded attacks upon the western revivals. (Just the week before, King had submitted to the magazine a descriptive letter he had received from Robert Patterson of Kentucky.) He carefully warned that distant readers should not suppose the strange religious practices to be the result of "design, or contrivance." Rather, "They appear to have been

---

[4] Stone, *Autobiography*, p. 158.

[5] "Life of James Fishback," pp. 7–8, Fishback Collection.

[6] John Brown to Rev. Dr. Wm. Hollinshead, April 3, 1802, in *New York Missionary Magazine* 3 (1802): 182.

involuntary, as well as extraordinary, and to have arisen from special causes. They were not expected to continue; nor considered as characteristic of the ordinary state of religion; but peculiar to such an awakening season, which might be a mean[s] of reforming, and bringing many into the church, and would soon settle in a solid and rational piety, and love of sacred order." [7]

And what if, wrote a Kentucky correspondent in December 1801, there were some irregularities—"so it was in 1776 among the whigs, in their enthusiasm for liberty." In every human activity there is a margin for error, but he submitted that "if only the 10th person convicted is truly converted, it is a great work." [8] Judged by the biblical standard of knowing a tree by its fruit, this wave of southern revivals was found legitimate. A South Carolina minister recalled the effect of Peter's preaching on the day of Pentecost, and the falling of the converted jailer at Philippi, then approved the present outpouring, for "the principle fruit of this work is a holy upright life." [9] "Indeed," wrote the Reverend George Baxter, president of Washington Academy (formerly Liberty Hall and later Washington and Lee University), "I found Kentucky the most moral place I had ever been in . . . a religious awe seemed to pervade the country." [10]

In account after account contemporaries thus interpreted the revival with its excited congregations as the special work of God, an obviously miraculous example of providential deliverance. They defended its extremes as necessary, temporary, and harmless. But primarily and overwhelmingly those who witnessed the revival basked in happiness and glorious anticipation. It would be easy to overintellectualize their response—most just were thankful. "[T]he work of God has been wonderful in Kentuckey the last year," wrote one,[11] and another marveled, "It may be truly said, the Lord is doing great things for us." [12] "Hell is trembling, and satan's kingdom falling," wrote a South Carolina Methodist, "the sacred flame . . . is extending far and wide." [13] In the fall of 1802, as Bishop Asbury made his rounds amidst

[7] Ibid., pp. 124-25.

[8] "Letter from a Kentucky Presbyterian minister to a friend in Pennsylvania, December 8, 1801," in ibid., p. 83.

[9] Robert Wilson to his "Aunt," April 17, 1803, in the L. C. Glenn Collection.

[10] "Extract 57. Of a letter from the Rev. G. Baxter, Principal of Washington Academy to the Rev. Dr. Archibald Alexander, Prince Edward, dated January 1, 1802 . . .," in Woodward, *Surprising Accounts*, p. 106.

[11] Philip Gatch to Edward Dromgoole, February 18, 1802, in the Dromgoole Papers.

[12] "Extract of a Letter from a gentleman to his friend at the city of Washington, dated Lexington, March 8, 1801," in [Anonymous], *Gospel News*, p. 3.

[13] James Jenkins to [Asbury?], June 30, 1802, in Dow, ed., *Extracts from Original Letters, to the Methodist Bishops*, p. 20.

continued news of personal awakenings, he confided to his journal: "Sweet peace fills my mind; and glorious prospects of Zion's prosperity cheer my heart."[14] His career had spanned American Methodist history from its faltering beginning to crowned success.

By the close of 1801 an exuberant optimism characterized the statements of most southern ministers—in marked contrast to the troubled concern that had reigned in the years before. Not uncommon were conjectures about the deeper significance of their eventful era. For example, one minister wondered why God chose this particular time to inaugurate his work and why he had used such uncommon means: "It may be to bring about some great event, or design of Providence, for purposes which we can neither conceive, nor comprehend."[15]

Of growing importance by 1802 was a rising undercurrent of opposition to the revival. For what was probably a significant majority in the South, the revival retained its symbol as a miracle throughout the decade. But after the initial period of awed surprise, when even potential critics held their peace, outspoken observers began to attack the later phases. The faithful, readying the battle lines between the opposing views, represented their recalcitrant opponents as sinful cavilers. As Robert Patterson of Lexington wrote: "Notwithstanding that all our ministers, and a vast number of the most respectable and sensible people, in the country, acknowledge, that it is the wonderful work of God; and is marvellously manifested to us; yet there are people so hardened, that they either cannot or will not acknowledge the work to be of God, but represent it in an unfavourable view."[16]

The gradual shift of more conservative (that is, traditionally Calvinist) Baptist and Presbyterian ministerial opinion away from the revival may be documented chronologically. For example, the Reverend Edmund Botsford of the tidewater region of South Carolina was a former Regular Baptist and close friend of Richard Furman. Within four months after the camp meeting began in his state, he had received numerous descriptive letters and heard several glowing personal accounts. From these early and enthusiastic reports, he cautiously concluded in early August 1802 "That God is certainly bringing many souls out of darkness into light, & from ye [the] bondage of sin into ye glorious liberty of ye sons of God." Yet Botsford was quite circumspect toward the physical extremes which his more evan-

[14] Asbury, *Journal and Letters*, 2: 362.

[15] "Extract of a Letter from a Gent. in Pendleton District [S. C.], to his friend in [Charleston], July 30, 1802," in *New York Missionary Magazine* 3 (1802): 313.

[16] "Extract 20. Extract of a letter from Colonel Robert Patterson, of Lexington (Ken.), to the Rev. Doctor John King, September 25, 1801," in Woodward, *Surprising Accounts*, p. 37.

gelical brethren seemingly endorsed. He noted that while he did not approve of irregularities, he recognized that since the "Land was overrun with Infidelity it seems as if some thing extraordinary was necessary to arouse people from such a state—the fiery zeal will by & by subside."[17]

About three months later, Botsford and a colleague visited a camp meeting and were pleasantly surprised. Botsford wrote to a friend that he saw neither disorder nor "raving," only "good sound preaching, pathetic exhortations & fervent prayers." Despite his prudence, this rather aristocratic Baptist minister admitted that he "got some engagement of Soul, such as I have not had for several years, which I am now endeavouring to communicate to my townsmen."[18]

Botsford's approval, however, was short-lived. As the revival spread across the upper region of South Carolina, it became obvious that the camp meeting thrived best under the tutelage of the less-educated, more emotional Methodist itinerants, former Separate Baptists, and New Side Presbyterians. They evidently prospered only among the poorer semiliterates of the piedmont—not among the wealthier, more orderly "respectables" of the Sea Island district. Given this social background, the strange and uncontrolled exercises continued beyond the time the religious conservatives considered necessary to awaken men to God's efforts. It seemed to them that clerical rabble-rousers were appropriating revival emotion for their own sectarian benefit. In a letter to like-minded Richard Furman, Botsford in 1803 criticized camp meetings run by all Methodists. Disorder was rampant; many fell "some say, on purpose." Happy not to have been present, Botsford wrote from respected hearsay. His informant recounted that upon the whole, "it was a noisy clamarous meeting, & he believes no one who is fond of order could approve of it."[19] Thus a conservative tidewater Baptist had come full circle, and in his estimation the revival had changed from an extraordinary work of God to the disorderly work of fanatical Methodists.

In Kentucky the judgment of John Lyle, a moderate Presbyterian divine educated at Virginia's Liberty Hall, followed a somewhat analogous path from approval to discountenance. First hearing of the Cumberland commotion from Barton W. Stone, Lyle was taken by surprise. After a brief pause he concluded, in mid-June 1801 that "the Lord was doing terrible things in righteousness with a kind design that the nations might see and fear and flow together. That perhaps the falling down in distress &c &c

[17] Botsford to Rev. John M. Roberts, August 1, 1802, in Botsford Letters.
[18] Ibid., November 24, 1802.
[19] Botsford to Furman, June 11, 1803, Botsford Letters.

might answer instead of ancient miracles to arouse the attention of a sleeping world & convince deists and gainsayers."[20] With a rather cautious optimism Lyle entered into the work, but he grew more wary of the spiritual excesses lest they disparage the genuine work of God. Nevertheless he willingly preached at camp meetings and exulted in the numerous converts won to Jesus Christ.

The dangers of emotionalism soon intruded upon Lyle's troubled conscience. In late June 1801 James Bradford—brother of the Episcopal editor of the *Kentucky Gazette*—along with a doubting cohort, attempted to disrupt the revival by ridiculing the agitations. Lyle defended the meetings, minimizing the attendant confusion. Several days later, in his sermon to a large gathering, the moderate Presbyterian attempted to calm down the extremists. Unchecked enthusiasm, he warned, "like a worm destroyed the beauty of a revival & would ere long discredit the work of God."[21] A month later the inner dynamism of the revival emphasized again to Lyle the need for caution. In early August he heard Richard McNemar preach. McNemar and Stone, with several other enthusiastic revivalists, had already begun their leftward shift in theology and emphasis which ultimately produced the "Christian" and Shaker schisms. Such doctrinal wandering frightened Lyle for what it could do to Presbyterian unity. "I expect," he wrote in his diary with a feeling of desperation, "the conduct of these hot-headed men & the effect of their doctrine will separate the Church of Christ & quench this revival."[22]

Subsequently Lyle grew increasingly conscious of the deleterious effects of unchecked emotionalism not only to outside critics but even to the genuine believers—"bodily agitations," he felt in September 1801 could become habitual and too easily evoked, eventually to be only the "sport of lesser passions."[23] The following August he carefully warned against disorders; the next summer he preached against irregularities. He had begun to speak out in refutation of the doctrinal innovations propounded by Stone, McNemar, and other schismatics.[24] Lyle never really turned against the revival, never denied its good effects. He sincerely believed that the profoundly novel commotions had been sent by God for specific and temporary shock value, but they were being misused by artful men. The camp meeting, with its exercises had, he came to feel, outlived its gospel usefulness. Instead of

---

[20] Lyle, "Diary," June 14, 1801, p. 1.
[21] Ibid., p. 7. The *Kentucky Gazette* never deigned to mention the revival.
[22] Ibid., pp. 9–10.
[23] Ibid., p. 20.
[24] Ibid., pp. 16, 25, 31, 42, 43, 46-49, 50.

modern-day miracles, he slowly began to view the attention-stirring agitations as destructive nuisances. Though emerging as a critic of revival extremes, he never became an opponent of the revival as such.[25]

Still another example of the revival's shifting reputation is offered in a letter by the Reverend John King, of Franklin County, Pennsylvania, to Ashbel Green of Philadelphia. King based his report upon correspondence from the awakened area and conversations with recently returned visitors. His opinion illustrates the common belief that sinful man could corrupt and misapply even the heaven-sent methods of conversion.

> It appears that the power of God has been eminently displayed in the beginning and progress of the work, in the West, & much good has been done; yet as few things, in the management of men, escape some tintures of their imperfection, it is to be feared that this sacred work also, may, on some accounts, suffer a little in its reputation. It may be, that the extraordinary affection of being *struck down*, in such a manner as is common with them, is held in so high account as the effect of divine grace, & a sure sign of *becoming a subject of the work* (a common phrase) that ways & means may be used to excite the powers of sympathy, in order to promote it.[26]

King was not alone in this belief. William C. Davis, of Lincoln County, North Carolina, felt deeply that it was easy "for poor weak mortals to abuse the best of blessings." Given the widespread belief in divine omnipotence and providential deliverance, most southern evangelicals were "ready to take all things for granted," only provided it was somehow associated with the revival and "exercised" persons. Davis feared that this indulgence would lead to enormous extravagance, and this in turn would topple the legitimate revival "by its own weight." Whereas even those ministers cautious of excess usually restrained themselves to prevent a premature disruption of the work, Davis felt that hesitation to criticize might end the revival: "I am afraid the work will eventually be stopped by the too great zeal & wild sallies of its own votaries. . . . I hope God will give us prudence."[27] He campaigned against the extravagances in order to prolong the awakening.

As the element of surprise vanished, the camp meeting exercises, which once seemed to authenticate the revival, gained more opponents. The Charleston Baptist Association in 1803 warned its members of blind zeal

[25] For example, see Fishback's account of how Lyle admonished him to be careful in strictures against the revival, in "Life of James Fishback," Fishback Collection.

[26] King to Green, May 4, 1802, in the Gratz Collection.

[27] Wm. C. Davis to Robert Patterson, April 3, 1803, in the Patterson Mss, Shane Collection.

and exercises caused "merely by enthusiasm."[28] In North Carolina a strict Presbyterian recently arrived from Scotland attacked the whole revival as a "work of the Devil."[29] But the most sustained and vitriolic attack of the entire period was penned in 1802 by a Presbyterian minister of Lexington— the noted Adam Rankin of the hymnology dispute. The newspaper advertisement for his stinging rebuke, entitled *A Review of the Noted Revival in Kentucky, Commenced in the Year of our Lord, 1801,* marked the only mention of revivalism in the contemporary Kentucky press. Here is an indication of how the upper-class urbanites in Lexington viewed the spiritual brushfire encircling their secular citadel.[30]

By this date Rankin had turned against his fellow Kentucky Presbyterians, and they, in turn, had effectively removed him from the Presbyterian Church. Yet the cantankerous Rankin was no easy man to dismiss; rather than leave the area, he had gathered around him a small group of supporters and claimed allegiance to the hyperconservative Associate Reformed Presbyterian Church, which was still closely allied with the Scottish organization. Rankin was one of those cast-iron individuals who gives credence to the stereotype of ministerial rigidity. He had long fought the steady intrusion of nonbiblical singing, but here, in the form of opposition to revival enthusiasm, he found his greatest cause. Rankin justified his imminent attack: "For as there never was a greater enemy to Christ, than a false Christ, nor to true religion, than a false religion: there cannot be a better friend to either, than he who detects the fallacies of both, and exposes their meritricious dress to the hooting of ridicule."[31]

From this beginning Rankin proceeded to blast the awakening in a sanctimonious tone of unrelieved sarcasm. Such interdenominational cooperation, he wrote, implied an indifference to doctrine. Huge mass meetings were the playground of the basest passions. The unusual agitations, adolescent exhortations, and ecstatic trances, which to the evangelicals proved the legitimacy of the work, meant exactly the opposite to Rankin. The maelstrom of emotion, he argued, was nothing more than a delusion.

The impact of Rankin's diatribe was probably not substantial. Those

[28] Charleston [S. C.] Baptist Association Minutes, "Circular Letter for November, 1803," pp. 6-7, on microfilm in the library of the Historical Commission, Southern Baptist Convention, Nashville, Tenn.

[29] Orange Presbytery, "Minutes," April 9, 1803.

[30] *Kentucky Gazette*, July 2, 1802. See also Michaux, *Travels to the Westward of the Allegany Mountains,* p. 243.

[31] Adam Rankin, *A Review of the Noted Revival in Kentucky Commenced in the Year of our Lord, 1801* ([Lexington, Ky.], 1802; 2d ed., 1803), "Introduction," p. [3].

who would agree with it felt little rapport with the revival in the first place. For the vast multitudes involved in the revivals, hope and faith had already convinced them that the revival was legitimate. The same may be said of a later exposé published in Pennsylvania in 1804.[32] Nevertheless, defenders of the revival soon had their view represented when David Thomas, a popular Baptist minister lately from Virginia, published a pious rebuttal to Rankin, *The Observer Trying the Great Reformation in This State and Proving It to Have Been Originally a Work of Divine Power*. . . . He denied Rankin's charges of immorality, said the emotional agitations were peripheral to the main work, and compared the revival favorably with other "extraordinary reformations of religion, either in Europe or America."[33] Similarly a detailed refutation of the critical Pennsylvania pamphlet was soon given to the public by the Reverend Thomas L. Birch.[34]

Much more influential in dampening the revival enthusiasm were the numerous moderating sermons preached by such ministers as John Lyle. In state after state, by 1803, the Baptists and Presbyterians had begun to disassociate themselves from religious extremes. Certainly this conservative reaction effected the late-developing revival in Virginia. In many cases these were men who genuinely believed the movement as a whole was the work of God, but had come to doubt the continued necessity of extraordinary measures. The Baptists probably pulled away first, for even in the midst of their revival support, they never consented to general communion. They would meet, worship, shout, and fall with the Presbyterians and Methodists, but refused to share the sacrament with advocates of infant baptism. In later years, after Baptists and Presbyterians no longer shared in camp meetings with anything approaching their early enthusiasm, their historians wrote condescendingly of the revival. These accounts often concealed their previous participation in camp meetings, now considered both extravagant and gauche.

[32] [John Cree, John Anderson, William Wilson, Thomas Alison, E. Henderson], *Evils of the Work Now Prevailing in the United States of America, Under the Name of A Revival of Religion; Shewn by A Comparison of that Work, As It Is Represented by Its Friends and Promoters, With the Word of God* (Washington, Pa., 1804) is more moderate than Rankin's work, but the intent was similar.

[33] *The Observer Trying the Great Reformation in This State and Proving It to Have Been Originally a Work of Divine Power* . . . (Lexington, Ky., 1802), p. 21 and passim.

[34] *Letters Addressed to the Revs. Messrs. John Cree, John Anderson, William Wilson, and Thomas Allison . . . in Answer to their Pamphlet, Entitled Evils of the Work Now Prevailing in the United States Under the Name of a Revival of Religion* (Washington, Pa., 1805).

The inner dynamism of the awakening created a rupture in the existing Presbyterian Church. While the zealous Methodists gradually moved to appropriate the camp meeting as their own special device, the western Presbyterian Church split wide apart. The liberal, revival-oriented wing broke away from orthodoxy, and although many eventually returned, a sizable segment jointed two new denominations, the moderate Cumberland Presbyterian Church and the more radical Stoneite (named for Barton W. Stone) or "Christian" movement. The most extreme, fanatical revival participants were drawn into the Shaker camp, where their fanciful doctrines and unorthodox practices earned them the hostility of all other parties. This denominational fission did more to end the Kentucky phase of the Great Revival than all the pamphlets combined, and it left the camp meeting primarily the property of the Methodists.

These disruptions were the dangers which the revered Presbyterian, David Rice, had warned of in 1803 and lamented in 1805 and 1808. He was convinced that "the present stir in the land, is a real revival of the christian religion." [35] He disapproved of the theological laxity, the lack of emphasis on humility, temperance, and brotherly love, and the dangerous procedure of licensing many untrained ministers. Too great a stress on bodily exercises and continued meditation on the arrival of the millennium, wrote Rice, did not profit the cause of religion. Worldliness and materialism still controlled too many people for Christians to accept without reservation the wildest millennial dreams. By 1805 the elderly Rice bewailed the passing of the revival. Popular theology, he testified, had descended from Calvinism to Arminianism, and from there to universalism, and so on down the ladder of error to the pits of atheism. [36] A revival was perpetuated not by eschatological speculation but by routine "living more constantly by faith in Christ." [37] Denominational discord, Rice warned, would be the price of unregulated revival enthusiasm in all its forms.

The grandiose visions of an approaching new age which Rice cautioned against were another product of the revival's symbolic meaning.

---

[35] Rice, *A Sermon on the Present Revival of Religion*, p. 23.

[36] Rice, *An Epistle to the Citizens of Kentucky, Professing Christianity; Especially Those That Are, or Have Been, Denominated Presbyterians* (1805), in Bishop, *An Outline of the History of the Church in the State of Kentucky*, pp. 329–31. See also Rice's *A Second Epistle to the Citizens of Kentucky, Professing the Christian Religion*, in ibid., esp. pp. 367–69, and 375.

[37] Ibid. Another spokesman stated that too great a dependence upon "feeling" rather than scripture had led to the deterioration of doctrine. See [Anonymous], *Two Letters Written by a Gentlemen [sic] to his Friend in Kentucky* (Lexington, Ky., [1804]), p. 19.

Millennial theology as such has an immensely complex history predating the Great Revival by centuries. Based on careful biblical exegesis, it deals with the future metamorphosis of the world from the arena of sin and sorrow to the glorious kingdom of God on earth.[38] An intricate and esoteric field of study, millenarian scholarship had been primarily the province of scholastics. Eminent clergymen such as Jonathan Edwards and Timothy Dwight delved into the subject and produced significant essays. Less learned ministers spent little time meditating upon such complex matters. This was certainly true in the South. Even the most illiterate Baptist and Methodist ministers had vague concepts about the long foretold Second Coming, but they preached penitence and faith, not prophecy. Eschatology was simply not an important, pervasive, or critical issue among the southern evangelicals before the Great Revival.

Implicit within the providential persuasion which dominated southern theology was a definite though imprecise belief in a future day of judgment when all would account for their lives before God. This was the momentous event which warranted the tremendous concern about salvation; the assurance of divine judgment underwrote evangelical Christianity. This emphasis was as old as pietistic religion. Three decades before the revivals, Francis Asbury, then an obscure Methodist itinerant, consoled himself against the criticism of his sect by writing, "But the day is coming when everyone will appear in his true colours, and be constrained to render an account of all his conduct to God."[39] Asbury, along with other ministers, often preached on the subject.[40] That such tenets were believed by laymen is illustrated in the letter of a devout father, John Callaway, to his worldly young son. The father urged him to consider the role of religion in life, "for we must all die come to Judgment & give an account of the deeds done in the body: whether they be good or evil."[41] Though it was universally expected, none claimed to know when the appointed hour of accountability would arrive. Often extraordinary scenes and marvelous reports of the

---

[38] See Ira V. Brown, "Watchers for the Second Coming: The Millenarian Tradition in America," *Mississippi Valley Historical Review* 29 (December 1952): 441–58; David E. Smith, "Millenarian Scholarship in America," *American Quarterly* 17 (Fall 1965): 535–49; Shirley J. Case, *The Millennial Hope: A Phase of War-Time Thinking* (Chicago, 1918); and Norman Cohn, *The Pursuit of the Millennium* (New York, 1957).

[39] Asbury, *Journal and Letters*, September 21, 1773, 1:94.

[40] Ibid., October 19, 1800, 2:256; and the Reverend William Burke, quoted in Redford, *The History of Methodism in Kentucky*, 1:357.

[41] John Callaway to Henry G. Callaway, February 12, 1804, in the Pocket Plantation Manuscripts.

camp meetings, interpreted as God's special efforts to effect his final plans, conjured up thoughts of that storied rendezvous with eternity. As an eyewitness wrote of the excitement of the era: "Sinners falling, and shrieks and cries for mercy awakened in the mind a lively apprehension of that scene, when the awful sound will be heard, 'arise ye dead and come to Judgment.' "[42] Perhaps the contemporary hymn-writer most accurately captured this feeling:

> Our moments are flying,
> Our time is expiring,
> We're call'd to improve it and quickly prepare
> For that awful hour
> When Jesus in power
> Will come into Judgment, all states to declare.[43]

The nearness in time of the day of judgment was irrelevant. Christians expected to have long been dead before it arrived. During the years of religious decline, men hoped only for an awakening; ministers prayed that a rousing revival would prepare thousands for that great day of judgment far in the future. The immediate issue then was regeneration and revival. No religious spokesman interpreted the gloomy 1790s as a sign foretelling a new age. Many ministers did read the religious indifference as an introduction to an eventual awakening—but there was no significant millenarian tradition in the South before 1801.

The revivals erupting in Kentucky in 1801 temporarily revolutionized thinking about the present time and the age to come. Such unrivaled success in preaching, such remarkable scenes of mass conversion, infused the faithful with a buoyant optimism. In the spiritual realm, anything now seemed possible. From this roseate attitude millennial speculations burst forth in full bloom. The rapidity of this intellectual development suggests that such views were inherent in the evangelical theology—a silent partner of providential omnipotence. Expansive revival success had set free millenarian imaginations. The image of the awakening now transcended mere numerical growth; it now pointed toward the final justification of history.

In the previous history of chiliastic thought, there had been two basic distinctions. This was between those who believed the millennium could only be inaugurated by Jesus Christ through his return to earth, and those

---

[42] Armenius, "Account of the Work of God in the Western Country," *Methodist Magazine* 2 (1819): 273.

[43] *Hymn Book* ([n.p., n.d.]), in Michaux-Randolph Papers, North Carolina State Archives, Raleigh, N. C.

who felt that the thousand year reign of the godly led up to and culminated in Jesus' second coming—hence the terms premillennial and postmillennial, the latter being dominant in America after Jonathan Edwards and the Great Awakening.[44] A subsidiary concern was whether the actual millennium would begin gradually through an evolutionary process of reform, or via an earth-shaking cataclysmic event. The recent revival successes practically removed this last concern from serious consideration, but both premillennialism and postmillennialism were evident in the southern response to the Great Revival.

Most common by far were the postmillennial beliefs that the church would triumph over wickedness and Christian principles would rule the world before Jesus Christ's second advent. The glorious scale of the ongoing revivals convinced some that the millennium had already begun, while others believed that events had been set in motion which would soon propel the world into the prophesied kingdom of God. For awestruck witnesses of the revival, it was not difficult to imagine that something extraordinary had been inaugurated. Levi Purviance recalled that in Kentucky, "the good work of reformation went on with irresistible force, and appeared like carrying every thing before it. Many were fully persuaded that the glorious Millennial Day had commenced."[45] According to a Presbyterian minister, Robert Stuart, "It was the declaration of some of the clergy, and perhaps believed, that the millennium had now commenced."[46] As a South Carolinian wrote to his minister in 1802, "The new thought of Millenium comes on well in these parts and many signs & wonders appear which testify who is at the head of the business."[47] From Georgia it was reported that when confronted with the awesomeness of a camp meeting, a Baptist minister replied, "These works appear like the last efforts of the Deity to preserve his church, and promote the cause of religion on the earth."[48] And a devout North Carolina lady wrote to her sister in 1802, describing both the revival itself and the ministerial response: "Mr. Bow-

[44] Compare with C. C. Goen, "Jonathan Edwards: A New Departure in Eschatology," *Church History* 28 (1959): 25–40; Alan Heimert, *Religion and the American Mind from the Great Awakening to the Revolution* (Cambridge, Mass., 1966); and Stow Persons, "The Cyclical Theory of History in Eighteenth Century America," *American Quarterly* 6 (Summer 1954): 147–63.

[45] Levi Purviance, *The Biography of Elder David Purviance*, p. 248.

[46] Stuart, "Reminiscences of the Presbyterian Church in Kentucky," p. 76.

[47] Alexr. Porter to John Hemphill, September 7, 1802, in the W. R., J. C., and R. R. Hemphill Papers, Duke University, Durham, N. C.

[48] "Extract from a letter dated July 7, 1802 [from Ebenezer H. Cummins]," *Georgia Analytical Repository* 1 (July–August 1802): 93.

man says he has no doubt but 'twill spread all over the Country for he believes the Melinium begun." [49] Through such views the Great Revival was seen as the inaugural movement in the beginning of the millennium.

A more widely expressed postmillennial belief interpreted present affairs to be the final events preparatory to the beginning of the millennium. From this view the reign of the saints for a thousand years could not begin before the gospel had been spread to all peoples, the Jews and Catholics had become good Protestants, and the majority of people had become practicing Christians. Certainly God would be behind this transformation preliminary to the millennium, and Jesus Christ's return would follow the conclusion of the ten-century epoch of saintly domination. It was comparatively easy to see the seemingly irresistible revivals as the vanguard of this era. And this outlook may have increased the evangelical zeal as it enlarged the expectation of many southern pietists. As the Reverend David Thomas in Kentucky wrote in reply to Adam Rankin's denunciation of the revival: "And why may it not be considered as a prelude of greater things to be done in time to come? Why not as a preliminary essay toward the introduction of that rosy morning, when the sun of righteousness shall arise with healing in his wings, and cover the earth with the knowledge of the Lord, as the water covers the sea." [50]

Rejoicing in the recent awakening in Georgia, Methodist pioneer Stith Mead wrote to Bishop Coke across the Atlantic: "O that this may be the ushering in of a glorious Millennium! May the Jews and Heathens be quickly christianized, and all brought to know the Lord." [51] The 1804 circular letter of the Georgia Baptist Association reviewed the pleasing accounts of religious prosperity and concluded that "our king is pushing his conquest into various parts of the world *gloriously*. THESE, we view only as preludes to the *latter-day-glory*." [52] "Ride on, blessed Redeemer," wrote an ecstatic Francis Asbury in the spring of 1802, "until all the states and nations of the earth are subdued unto thy sacred sway." [53] The year before a young English newcomer to Kentucky simply described to his relatives in the old country what he saw and heard: "some prophesey that the Millenium or Christ's Kingdom is about to take place on Earth others that the world is to be

---

[49] A. Smith to "Sister Polly" [Mrs. William Williamson], May 31, 1802, in the Williamson Papers, Shane Collection.

[50] Thomas, *The Observer Trying the Great Reformation*, pp. 33-34.

[51] "From Stith Mead, to the Rev. Dr. Coke. May 11, 1802," *Methodist Magazine* [London] 25 (1802): 523.

[52] Quoted in Mercer, *History of the Georgia Baptist Association*, p. 157.

[53] Asbury, *Journal and Letters*, May 23, 1802, 2: 340.

Barton W. Stone
*Courtesy of the Disciples of Christ
Historical Society, Nashville, Tenn.*

A New England camp meeting, similar to later Methodist revivals in the South From James Young, *A History of the Most Interesting Events in the Rise and Progress of Methodism* (New Haven, Conn., 1831)

reformed as soon as the English & French Nations leave of[f] murdering one another."[54]

The South's two religious magazines, both founded after the revival, picked up this theme. The *Georgia Analytical Repository*, edited in Savannah by the Reverend Henry Holcombe, printed letters mentioning millennial hopes and in the spring of 1803 published an article, "Analysis of Prophecy," which conjectured that people were "living in the *last days*," when God was working "to prepare the righteous remnant of the church for the Kingdom of CHRIST."[55] In similar fashion the preface of the *Virginia Religious Magazine*, a Presbyterian organ, referred to the benign era then beginning: "According to the best interpreters of the prophecies in the sacred scriptures, the time, probably, draws nigh, when 'the kingdoms of this world are to become the kingdoms of our God, and of his Christ.' " It was precisely because the age had such miraculous potential that the journal was founded, for such magazines can "lead the mind to a saving knowledge" of Jesus Christ, and rightly should be "considered as valuable instruments for promoting the interests of Christianity." God was evidently at work across the face of the land—great religious harvests were being reaped, in preparation for the millennium. "To be the humble means of hastening that desirable period, is, we trust, the sincere desire of this publication."[56] Thus the Great Revival, for many evangelical supporters, transcended a mere religious resurgence, and was a wonderful introduction to the glorious culmination of all history—and as such it was a powerful evangelical stimulant.

These extravagant hopes, of course, were soon dashed. The camp meeting revival, though it swept across the South with amazing force and result, did not banish sin and dispute. This failure of millennial expectations brought disrepute, and the latterday accounts of the revival often ridiculed or berated the chiliastic dreams.[57] But even those at the time who, after the revival began producing schismatics, doubted that the millennium had arrived or was arriving, did not deny the theory of millenarian expectation;

[54] H. Anderson to Thom. Jackson, in England, September 10, 1801, Ms in the Library of the Kentucky Historical Society, Frankfort, Ky.

[55] "Analysis of Prophecy," *Georgia Analytical Repository* 1 (March–April 1803): 266. The editor says (p. 270) that the article is extracted from "Brief Commentaries Upon Such Parts of the Revelation and Other Prophecies as Immediately Refer to the Present Times," published by S. Gosnel.

[56] "Preface," *Virginia Religious Magazine* 1 (October 1804): v, vi, and viii.

[57] For example, read Stuart, "Reminiscences of the Presbyterian Church in Kentucky"; Davidson, *History of the Presbyterian Church in Kentucky*; and both of David Rice's *Epistles to the Citizens of Kentucky* (1805 and 1808).

they only denied its application to the present time. For example, David Rice in his sermon of 1803 reviewing the revival did not think the "latter-day-glory" was approaching. The actual coming was hidden in God's mystery, he wrote, but nevertheless he doubted that the time was "*very near*." He based this conclusion not on contrary theological interpretation but on the failure of present-day Christians to effect the necessary conditions. There was too much "pride, self-confidence, and censoriousness" among the disputing denominations; drinking in excess was still prevalent; even Christians were too worldly and devoted to luxury; there were not enough evangelical preachers with international aspirations to promote the worldwide Christianization introductory to the millennium.[58] Yet the implication was that when Christians were sincere and devout and put aside their worldly interests, then they could begin the work of ushering in the millennium. To effect these reforms was something the churches should work for.

Such postmillennial ideas, stimulated and partially validated by the short-term successes of the Great Revival, had significant implications for the southern evangelical mind. Certainly the belief that the church would be perfected and made universal before the Second Coming infused a greater degree of hope and justified increased activity among the faithful. It promoted a sense of optimism, for Christians had biblical and experiential assurance that through the aid of Providence the ideals of their catholic faith would eventually win their way around the world. Revivalism, missionaries, religious publications, the active reform of individuals, all had an enlarged role in bringing on the future glory.

Postmillennial views even lent themselves to a linear, progressive view of history. With this concept it became easier to place the American past and future in the grand scheme of time. In a Fourth of July sermon in 1802, Richard Furman began with the cyclical theory of history common to the enlightenment; he spoke then of the United States where, if men would be virtuous, Christian, and wise enough to choose the correct leaders, an almost unblemished millennial future lay ahead. Providential deliverance had secured American independence, implying that the nation was "orginally designed as asylum for religion and liberty." Possessing a republican government which sponsored freedom and upheld Protestantism, the United States, provided its citizens remained moral, could break loose from the chains of past history and inaugurate the millennium. The "advantages" the nation possessed, wrote Furman, "encourage us to look forward, with pleasing hopes, to a day when America will be the praise of the whole earth; and shall participate, largely, in the fulfillment of those sacred

[58] Rice, *A Sermon on the Present Revival of Religion*, pp. 37–39.

prophecies which have foretold the glory of Messiah's kingdom: when 'there shall be abundance of peace;' 'when God shall build the cities,' and 'cause them to be spread abroad;' when 'righteousness shall dwell in the fruitful field, and the wilderness shall rejoice and blossom as the rose.' "[59] Hence God had prepared this land for a great mission, to lead the world into the millennium. This was to be America's manifest destiny.

For only a comparatively small number of believers did postmillennialism remain a compelling issue more than a very few years. Doubtless most of those momentarily caught up in the heady aura of revival success continued to desire constant reform aimed toward that expected day when worldly wickedness would be eradicated. A lasting sentiment for evangelism, for suppression of vice, and for increased Christian unity—the primary aim of the "Christian" movement which developed from the revival era— was grounded on ideas implicit in millennialism. Yet there was a small segment of revival participants in Kentucky for whom the awakening season signaled the beginning of a radical new departure in eschatology. Either for reasons of temperament or training, or perhaps both, an enthusiastic group interpreted the seemingly momentous occasion of God's intervention as the foreshadowing of Jesus Christ's imminent return. Man had no arduous task of international Christianization and reform to complete; only Jesus through his miraculous advent could effect this superhuman transformation. Those subscribing to these premillennial views were among the most affected of all revival participants. It was they who suffered—or enjoyed—trances, prophetic dreams, heavenly visions.[60] And their particular expectation swept them into the Shaker camp when three missionaries of the "United Society of Believers" arrived in Kentucky in the spring of 1805.

John Rankin, Matthew Houston, and John Dunlavy were among

[59] Furman, *America's Deliverance and Duty. A Sermon Preached at the Baptist Church, in Charleston, South-Carolina, on the Fourth Day of July, 1802* (Charleston, S. C., 1802), p. 14, and passim, esp. p. 19. See also Persons, "The Cyclical View of History," passim. Such views in the South were given great stimulus by the revival. It had been widely recognized before that God played a leading role in the American Revolution. The relationships between the millennium and American mission were discussed relatively often in the states north of Virginia, where eschatology had more students. The emphasis on virtue and against divisive "partyism" common to millennial sermons had secular implications. It in part explains the similar emphasis in popular political rhetoric pointed out by John R. Howe, Jr., in his article, "Republican Thought and the Political Violence of the 1790's," *American Quarterly* 19 (Summer 1967): 147–65.

[60] More than a few of the sources cited in Chapter 5 mention these revival extremes. For example, see M'Nemar, *The Kentucky Revival*, pp. 66-68; Cartwright, *Autobiography*, pp. 51-53; and Stone, *Autobiography*, p. 187.

those overwhelmed by premillennial anticipations, but it was Richard Mc-Nemar who preeminently represented this viewpoint. McNemar was an attractive and talented minister who began shifting from Presbyterian orthodoxy almost as soon as the camp meetings began.[61] He is best known for his *Kentucky Revival*, published in 1807, a volume which portrays the revival as the vanguard of Jesus Christ's early return. In a letter written at the time the revival reached his section of Kentucky in early 1801, McNemar exulted, "The master is come indeed, to our almost hopeless gospel-trodden congregation." He admonished his correspondents to "cry aloud and spare not, the Lord is at hand, and verily he is a God that heareth prayer. Tell our dear friends in Washington [Kentucky] to arise, and trim their lamps. Behold the bridegroom cometh!"[62] Yet it was in the words of a hymn which he wrote in 1801, "A Pure Church Anticipated," that McNemar most clearly displayed his fervent premillennialism.

> The glorious day, is drawing nigh,
>   When Zion's light shall come;
> She shall arise and shine on high,
>   Bright as the morning sun.
> The north and south their sons resign,
>   And earth's foundations bend;
> Adorn'd as a bride Jerusalem,
>   All glorious shall descend.
>
> The king who wears the glorious crown,
>   The azure flaming bow,
> The Holy City shall bring down,
>   To bless the saints below:
> Descending with such melting strains,
>   Jehovah's name adore;
> Such shouts thro earth's extensive plains,
>   Were never heard before.
>
> Let Satan rage and boast no more
>   Nor think his reign is long;

[61] John Lyle argued with McNemar in a futile attempt to stem his theological creativity. Alan Heimert, in his influential *Religion and the American Mind*, wrongly interprets McNemar as a postmillennialist, and from Heimert's work one gets the erroneous impression that McNemar was typical of those involved in the Kentucky revivals. Heimert also seriously misreads McNemar's relation to republican government and Jeffersonianism. For a sketch and description of McNemar, see John MacLean, *The Life and Labors of Richard McNemar* (Franklin, Ohio, 1905), pp. 3–6.

[62] "Extract 43. Of a letter from the Rev. Mr. Richard M'Namar [*sic*], dated Cabin Creek, Kentucky, March 22, 1801, to his friend at Washington, Kentucky," in [Anonymous], *Increase of Piety, or the Revival of Religion in the United States of America* (Philadelphia, 1802), pp. 97–98.

> The saints tho feeble, weak and poor,
> Their great Redeemer's strong; . . .
>
> The crystal stream comes down from heav'n,
> It issues from the throne;
> The floods of strife away are driv'n—
> The church becomes but one;
> That peaceful union they shall know;
> And live upon his love,
> And shout and sing His praise below,
> As angels do above.[63]

It is not surprising then, that when the Shakers appeared with their belief that through the person of Mother Ann Lee, Jesus Christ's second coming had been effected, and the millennium thus already begun, McNemar along with others quickly fell into their mode of thought. It was as a prominent Shaker advocate that McNemar in 1807 wrote his tract, *The Kentucky Revival*. As a spokesman of the "Millennial Church," he presented the revival in a glorious image: "far from esteeming the Kentucky Revival a day of small things, we believe it was nothing less than an *introduction* to that work of *final redemption*, which God had promised, in the latter days." [64] He continued,

> The *Kentucky Revival*, from the beginning, spoke better things. . . . It was not . . . that faith, in the promise, which puts heaven at a distance; nor merely preaching about the kingdom. . . . It was a near prospect of the true kingdom of God, into which many were determined to press, at the expense of all that they held dear upon earth. The late revival was not sent to RE-FORM the churches. It did not come with a piece of new cloth to patch the old garment, to mend up the old hope with some new experience; but to prepare the way for that kingdom of God, in which all things are new.[65]

Just as God sent the revival, wrote McNemar, so he dispatched three Shaker missionaries from New York, and they transferred *"the testimony of Jesus Christ"* to the subjects of the western revival. Jesus Christ had returned, the missionaries preached, in the person of Ann Lee, and now those convinced could, by following the "way" presented by the "United Society of Believers," enter into the final salvation and redemption of the world.[66] Hence for McNemar and other revivalists who turned Shaker, the Great Revival had become the open sesame for the millennium.

[63] Quoted in MacLean, *Life of Richard McNemar*, pp. 18–19.
[64] M'Nemar, *The Kentucky Revival*, p. 3.
[65] Ibid., p. 5.
[66] Ibid., pp. 80–83, and passim.

The image of the revival had proved to be neither static nor simple. Moving from the work of God to the work of the devil, it inspired evangelists and it motivated energetic supporters of orthodoxy to rebuttal. How a Presbyterian responded intellectually to the revival determined, in large part, his eventual affiliation with either the Presbyterian, Cumberland Presbyterian, or "Christian" Church. It was felt to be the beginning of the millennium concluding with Jesus Christ's return, or the event preliminary to the millennium. For still others it represented the absolute fulfillment of history, promising a millennial epoch coming after Jesus Christ's advent in his female counterpart. Thus the Great Revival triggered a chain reaction of responses, proving anew the complexity and pervasiveness of the southern evangelical cast of mind.

Chapter Eight

Homiletics & Hymnology

"As to the Idea of sermonizing," scribbled a Methodist itinerant in 1803, "I thought but little about it. It concerned me but little, the Idea was to go out and call Sinners to come to Christ, that they might be saved from Sin here, and saved in heaven for ever here-after."[1] Calling sinners to Jesus Christ was certainly the end toward which all homiletics was aimed, but this is not to say that all, or even most, evangelical ministers gave as little thought to their message as James Watts apparently did. In the scholarly mind the revivalist preacher often occupies a despised and ridiculed position. It would be fatuous to argue that the southern ministers of the Baptist, Methodist, and Presbyterian churches, as a type, were genuinely sophisticated, rational, and erudite defenders of their faith. Even so, the ministers possessed these traits to a remarkable degree. They desired intellectual assent to their propositions.

An emphasis on emotions, it is true, was widely used to gain the potential convert's attention and emotive consent. As such, emotionalism performed a necessary and extremely successful role in the ministerial efforts toward evangelization. Frequently, however, the emotional harangues which travelers have noted time and again were not part of the body of the sermon. Indeed, they were often in the form of a fervent application, affixed by the minister to the end of his more orderly address. In many cases, these passionate calls to conversion were separate talks delivered either by a specialist in exhortation or another minister called upon to enforce the previous message on the minds of the listeners. This division of labor made it possible for congregations to hear first an orderly and well-structured sermon, buttressed by biblical quotation and even historical or literary allusions, then to be urged passionately to accept Jesus Christ or imitate his life. The preachers hoped this would produce a combination of warmed hearts and filled heads. Among a populace predominantly illiterate, religious hymns proved another way of imparting doctrinal tenets. Chanted, sung, and memorized, these simple tunes served to reinforce the messages presented in a sermon context. The zeal of the revival season and the surprising sophistication of the theology both preached and accepted attest to the success of these methods.

Few today would deny that to read the sermons of a Henry Holcombe, a George Reed, a John McCue, a Henry Pattillo, or a James McGready is to stalk boredom. Beyond this, though, one gains an appreciation for the art of preaching and writing sermons as practiced by southern ministers during the time of the Great Revival. The normal method was to find a biblical text and from it develop the entire sermon. Taking the essential idea from the quoted verse, the minister would then briefly define his purpose in the form of three or four main points. After this short introduction and overview, he would return to the first point and develop it, meanwhile enumerating and explaining several subsidiary points. In such outline form each of the original ideas was expanded.

Neither the ministers of the popular churches nor their congregations divided their modes of thought into divergent types, civil or political and religious. The instructions of the Methodist *Book of Discipline* on preaching could have served as useful advice for an aspiring politician merely by exchanging the candidate's name for Jesus Christ's. "What is the best general method of Preaching?" the *Discipline* asked rhetorically: "1. To convince: 2. To offer Christ: 3. To invite: 4. To build up: And to do this in some measure in every sermon."[2] Such a schema characterized most evangelical preaching. The first part of this plan was the least emotional; the third part, the most. Reason, logic, analogy were applied to the task of persuading and convincing the nonbeliever to have faith in the miracles and promises of Jesus Christ. Enlightened reason was most abstractly employed when the minister addressed so-called deists. Henry Holcombe thus introduced a sermon: "I shall attempt, on merely rational grounds, to prove that Christ, as he affirms, is honoured of God. I take nothing for granted, but that a God exists, and is an intelligent and designing agent who created, and who governs the world."[3] From such a beginning Holcombe, in overtones of both Pascal and Descartes, argued for confidence in the Christian pageant of salvation.

---

[1] Watts, "Diary," p. 7, Ms in Alderman Library, University of Virginia, Charlottesville, Va.

[2] Methodist Episcopal Church, *A Form of Discipline, For the Ministers, Preachers, and Members of the Methodist Episcopal Church in America*, 5th ed. (New York, 1789), pp. 18–19.

[3] Holcombe, *Primitive Theology, In a Series of Lectures* (Philadelphia, 1822), p. [13].

Yet the overwhelming majority of ministers, in most of their sermons, were not addressing literate and philosophical deists. Instead, their listeners usually shared a belief in God's truth, his omnipotence, his justice, and his inspired message presented in the visible form of the Bible. With this kind of understanding at hand, the preachers used reason of a different sort. Less abstract, it moved from accepted point to accepted point, each firmly rooted in the bedrock of scriptural text, until the speaker could effect an affirmation of faith. Everything had to be grounded in the Bible, and from this enormous quarry of quotation, elaborate plans of action were chiseled.

Just as the enlightened philosopher reasoned from axioms of natural law, the pious churchmen proceeded from axioms of received faith. The evangelical ministers did not resort to base emotionalism, superstitious fears, or exaggerated mysticism to persuade their listeners. Instead, they argued from texts of accepted truth. So few doubted the general authenticity of scripture and revelation that the record of sermons shows slight concern with the complexities of epistemology. To have shown such a concern would have required a degree of sophistication alien to the vast majority within the church both in the South and elsewhere.

When the evangelical clergy moved from the persuasive to the exhortatory section of their sermons, their tempo often increased. It was here that ministerial powers to move their listeners were tested; here the manipulation of emotions was a common, though honest and respected tool. There was nothing fraudulent in their intentions. Ardent and fiery discourse most often revealed warm conviction, not calculating deceit. Much of the emotive content of the sermons was not aimed at forcing the sinner in the audience to come to God in fear. Rather, it was evidenced when the deeply religious ministers described the moving panorama of Jesus Christ's spiritual agony and physical suffering. Such a momentously poignant story of suffering and love, guilt and forgiveness, elicited the innermost feelings from the faithful both behind and in front of the pulpit. Yet this sincere emotion was far removed from fear; instead it reflected the incomprehensible love of God for man which the evangelical ministers found to be the central thrust of the New Testament. By presenting to their congregations this verbal Passion Play, the fervent clergymen offered Jesus Christ in the most effective, least demagogic way—as the loving son of a caring and forgiving father.

The conventional salvation scheme of Christianity, represented in such form, permitted wide-ranging opportunities for the role of persuasion. Exhibiting the enormous love and mercy of Jesus Christ's suffering and sacrifice, ministers could urge unbelievers to faith by stressing their comparatively easy role in the whole epic of redemption. All the unbeliever had to do was accept Jesus Christ's mediatorial role.[4] Explicit or implicit in almost every sermon was the overarching love of God for sinful man. Necessarily emotion was required to express, in however primitive form, this view of a benevolent God.

Fear of God, then, was not the exclusive revivalistic emphasis. Yet the same minister who in one sermon could portray God's forgiving love could in another stress the frightful precariousness of a sinner's position. However, the widespread understanding of God's benevolence tempered this terrifying theology. In many instances, fear was used to shake congregations away from their indifference. This kind of sermon was often followed by an invitation, emphasizing providential kindness and compassion. McGready, for example, could expound the limitless mercy of God through Jesus Christ in one instance: "no case is too desperate, too hopeless, for the almighty goodness of Christ Jesus, our Lord. . . . Though your crimes were more numerous, and infinitely more provoking than all the sins that have been pardoned from the beginning of the world to the present day, yet Jesus bids you welcome."[5] He could also, without being inconsistent, prod those outside the church with fear in an effort to awaken them to the mercy made abundant by Jesus Christ: "[The minister] must use every possible means to alarm and awaken Christless sinners from their security, and bring them to a sense of their danger and guilt. . . . He must convince the awakened sinner that the vengeance of God pursues him every moment while out of Christ—that there is no safety a hair's breadth short of a sound conversion."[6]

It was this juxtaposing of fear and anxiety with love and security that made evangelical preaching so convincingly effective. Often different ministers offered the contrasting but interlinked messages, and which preceded the other seems to have been unimportant. The result—conversion—was the same. For example, Barton W. Stone, who led the meeting at Cane Ridge in 1801, recalled in his anecdotal autobiography that memorable day in 1791 when he experienced conversion. This event began in February, when Stone visited in Virginia and heard a fire and damnation sermon from McGready, himself a guest of the Reverend John Blair Smith of Hampden-Sydney College. McGready "thundered divine anathemas" against those

[4] McGready, *Posthumous Works*, 1: 34, 36–37, 48–49, and passim, and 2: 237–38. In this last passage McGready says, "God's love for his people is from everlasting to everlasting; but there is no manifestation of it known or conceivable to us, that is to be compared to this [the crucifixion]."

[5] Ibid., 1: 47–48.

[6] Ibid., pp. 316 and 318.

in an unconverted state, making uncomfortably real "the horrors of hell." [7]
For unexplained reasons McGready at this particular time failed to press
home the accompanying love of God. As a result, after the meeting, Stone
remained in a "gloomy state"—aware of his separation, guilt, and danger,
but ignorant of God's willingness to forgive. Several weeks later he heard
a sermon given by William Hodge, an early McGready convert. Hodge
completed the evangelical message. Stone wrote: "His text I shall never
forget, 'God is love.' With much animation, and with many tears he spoke
of the Love of God to sinners, and of what that love had done for sinners.
My heart warmed with love for that lovely character described. . . . I
yielded and sunk at his feet a willing subject." [8]

Although one could not be frightened into heaven, the pietistic ministers believed one could be scared away from hell. "Conviction of sin is
necessary & with out it no sinner will come to Christ," wrote a South
Carolina minister, "but conviction is not conversion tho it is perhaps often
mistaken for it." [9] Each of the three denominations under discussion held
that "we are justified by faith only." This faith, which even the Methodists
believed was ignited in the individual soul only at God's command, required
the recognition of divine love. "Let us remember," preached a Virginia
Methodist in the 1790s, that "all is a *free gift*. He *gave* his Son; he *gives*
all things with him.—The gospel allows no place for merit of our own in
any respect. There was no moving cause in us, unless our misery may be
deemed such. Our deliverance, in its rise, progress, & accomplishment, must
be ascribed to grace alone." [10]

It is this two-pronged, mutually dependent attack of love and fear
upon the sinner's unbelief that explains much of the widespread upper-
class and educated opposition to revivalistic preaching. In times of religious
apathy and feared collapse, when congregations seemed particularly indifferent to the necessity of what the zealous termed "vital piety," the proportion of terrifying theology increased. Indeed, a Methodist itinerant in North
Carolina noted in his diary that a "good friend seemed concerned that I
preached so little terror." The feeling of crisis which dominated clerical

---

[7] Stone, *Autobiography,* pp. 122–23.

[8] Ibid., pp. 123–24. Stone may have been unduly harsh on McGready because
although McGready had pioneered the revival and in a sense promoted the movement
culminating both in the Cumberland Church and Stone's Christian denomination,
McGready himself later hesitated and returned to the orthodox Presbyterian fold.

[9] William Williamson to John and Lucy Benford, December 18, 1796, in the
Williamson Papers, Shane Collection.

[10] Reed, "Sermon," Reed Papers.

[11] Norman, "Diary," August 9, 1800, Stephen B. Weeks Collection.

cares during the 1790s augmented the evangelists' sense of urgency. Along with the sensitive introspection, jeremiads, and prayer societies went an invigorated effort to pry open the consciousness of backsliders and the unconverted. This has been the element of evangelical preaching which has gained the disfavor of those removed from pietistic urgings of the heart.

Once the revival was underway, with its marvels apparently authenticating what ministers had preached all along, the felt urgency did not diminish. Now was even more certainly the time to reevaluate one's relationship with God. The propitiousness of the revival season, when to faithful minds Jesus Christ's sacrifice seemed so relevant, brought forth a greater effort on the part of revival ministers to frighten people out of their complacency into a consideration of divine benevolence. At a time when revival successes symbolized God's mercy and love, the verbal emphasis on action-provoking terror momentarily increased. Thus the awakening season produced sermons of slightly different accent. Yet the concomitant importance of God's love as revealed through Jesus' Passion was always implicit when not overtly expressed.

Much of the admonition common to evangelical preaching was either reserved for a follow-up speaker or added to the main thematic sermon as an obvious addendum. Herein were pressed with redoubled vigor the main points of the sermon, as well as the broad tenets of pietistic religion. The practice of having a separate exhorter allowed the people to hear more specialized sermons. The change in speakers alone probably increased the attention of the congregation. As early as 1789 the Methodist bishop Thomas Coke observed: "There is a custom peculiar to the *American* Preachers, which is this: If there be more Preachers than one in a congregation, the Preachers that have not preached, give each of them a warm exhortation. And as far as I can judge by external effects wrought on the congregation . . . more good has been done in most instances by the exhortations than by the sermon: more souls have been awakened and converted to God." [12]

Two years later William Hill, a Presbyterian minister on a preaching tour through Virginia, noted such practices on an interdenominational scale. "Mr. [John] Lyle preached at a meeting house near Capt. Harristows, I then exhorted—& was followed by exhortation from a Mr. Blanton a methodist, & a Mr. Hall a baptist." [13] In the midst of a camp meeting ten years after this in North Carolina, according to the Reverend Eli Caruthers,

[12] Coke, *Extracts of the Journals of the Rev. Dr. Coke's Five Visits to America* (London, 1793), pp. 112–13.

[13] Hill, *Journal*, June 8, 1791, p. 72.

there was present a Hagert (or Tagart) possessed of a "very strong but melodious" voice. "'As he was 'gifted,' or fluent in prayer & excelled in exhortation, he seldom preached; for it was soon agreed among them that they wd. do the preaching & that he should still follow the sermon with an address to the unconverted. Almost as soon as he began to speak fresh indications of increased excitement began to appear and by the time he had spoken from five to ten minutes that vast crowd was in a perfect uproar."[14]

On still other occasions the minister who preached the sermon moved into moments of exhortation as the situation demanded. An early authority on the Baptist pioneers of Kentucky wrote that their ministers "felt themselves at perfect liberty, at any time, to leave the theme of their discourse, and pass into a strain of exhortation to the people, if they thought they could be more useful in so doing."[15] Neither was it unusual for a minister himself to reserve the urgent, pressing portion of his sermon for the very end, after he had outlined God's love and man's position. In such a rousing conclusion even the calmer clergy often attained lofty heights of enthusiasm. This latter portion of their address, toward which all the preceding had often been aimed, was usually left to the discretion of the circumstances. According to his apparent effectiveness and the needs of the congregation, the able minister appropriately shaped the application in which the truths and warnings of the entire evangelical tradition were put to practical test. For this reason, as the editor of James McGready's works explained, the exact content of such revivalistic summations is unpreserved. "Many of the sermons, even to the ordinary reader, will seem to close abruptly, owing to an omission of the author in writing out the application—that being a part he almost uniformly delivered extemporaneously, and according to the circumstances of his audience."[16]

The composition and understanding of their congregations made such sermon techniques remarkably effective during the era of the Great Revival. Due to a proliferation of churches, ministers, and religious organizations following the Revolution, and spurred by small local revivals in the late 1780s and early 1790s, the basic doctrines of the evangelical churches became rather generally known (though often incomplete and technically inaccurate) throughout the South. A simple awareness of religious beliefs in itself does not make for a vigorous church life, and this was represented

[14] Caruthers, "Richard Hugg King," p. 28.

[15] James E. Welch, "Early Preachers of Kentucky," *Christian Repository* 5 (May 1856): 292. For a scholarly account of this subject for one state, see Jerry L. Tarver, "Exhortation among the Early Virginia Baptists," *Virginia Baptist Register* 5 (1966): 228–36.

[16] McGready, *Posthumous Works*, 1: iv.

in the widespread indifference faced by the clergy at the close of the eighteenth century. Nevertheless, the prevalent comprehension of divine omnipotence allowed the clergy to generate a near universal trust in providential deliverance. After all, the average people in an age before the general dissemination of scientific knowledge had few ways besides superstition to explain the unexpected and unpredictable in life.[17]

Possessing this conception of a benevolent God, most southerners inhabited an intellectual world responsive to the theological teachings and emphases of pietistic ministers. Furthermore, the realities of life for most people in the South prepared them emotionally for the evangelical warnings. The common mode of terror used in exhortations was to remind listeners of the uncertainties, the ephemerality of their life. For most people life was often quite literally short, nasty, and brutish. This was not just a frontier condition, but almost the normal rural one. One cannot read the correspondence of contemporaries without being absolutely overwhelmed by the prevailing sickness, suffering, and death. Clerical warnings emphasizing this painful reality struck a sensitive vein in the emotional life of the people. Exhortation was effective because it was so frightfully relevant.

It is significant that Michael Gaffney of comfortable residence in Charleston, South Carolina, found the upland region of the state in late 1800 so inhospitable to delicate habits. Yet the people he described there, between Spartanburg, South Carolina, and Charlotte, North Carolina, only two years later were most centrally involved in the camp meeting and revival movement. This was how life was on the eve of the Great Revival in a typical region:

> Left Charleston on the 11th of December 1800—without giving it one parting look. Nothing material happened on the journey. The country for about one hundred and fifty miles from Charleston is extremely low and unhealthy. The people looked yellow, poor, and sickly. Some of them lived the most miserably I ever saw any poor people live. We arrived at our new home in six days [near what is now Gaffney, S.C.]. I expected to see a fine country but was surprised to find it poor, sandy, rocky and hilly. The people are poor. Their dress generally is a hunting shirt and trousers of course cotton yarn. Every farmer or planter is his own shoemaker, tanner, carpenter, brazier, and in fact, everything else. Everything comes by the farmer or his family. It is the business of the wife and daughter to pick cotton and have it brought home, pick it from the seed, spin it, weave it and make it ready for your back. Some of the girls make

[17] The implications of this statement are based upon Bronislaw Malinowski's discussion of religious origins in his *Magic, Science and Religion and Other Essays* (Glencoe, Ill., 1948), passim, and Norbeck, *Religion in Primitive Society*, pp. 128–29.

very handsome cloth. The women in this country live the poorest lives of any people in the world. It is directly opposite to Charleston; here they must do everything from cooking to plowing and after that they have no more life in them than Indian squaws.[18]

For people in such circumstances, exhortation brought into focus their physically precarious position. They literally never knew what the next day would bring. Pressed by drudgery, disease, monotony, and exhaustion, thousands throughout the South found immense attraction in the glorious release offered by ministerial descriptions of redemption and heaven. This societal condition aided immeasurably the efforts of evangelical clergy. Pounding away with their twin emphases of divine love and retribution, revivalists reaped a rich harvest of burdened souls.[19] Quite obviously this combination of human conditions and accepted religious beliefs, when met by the intensification of fervor and faith characterstic of the Great Revival, was an easily combustible field for evangelicalism. The dynamic revival movement thrived on the plight and comprehension of plain folk in the Old South.

Undoubtedly there existed excesses in preaching techniques. After all, the Methodist and Baptist ministers were drawn from the common people and had little formal training. Most had learned by doing; for them, whatever preaching ability they possessed was as a result of natural talent. Often they were schooled in homiletics simply by talking first to small informal groups, then by accompanying a minister. They were finally ordained primarily on the basis of their piety and preaching successes.[20] Not unusual at all was Andrew Broaddus, a Virginia Baptist who began his career in 1789. According to his biographer, Broaddus "commenced preaching the gospel without a diploma—without a library—without theological instruction; but he had what was better than all these—a deep and experimental sense of the truth, power, and preciousness of the gospel—a heart glowing with zeal in the cause of Christ."[21]

[18] Michael Gaffney, "Journal, 1797–1854," pp. 23ff., typescript in the South Caroliniana Collection, University of South Carolina, Columbia, S. C.

[19] See Joseph Thomas, *The Life of the Pilgrim Joseph Thomas, Containing an Accurate Account of His Trials, Travels, and Gospel Labors, Up to the Present Time* (Winchester, Va., 1817), pp. 13–14.

[20] For example, follow Peter Cartwright's early career, as recorded in his *Autobiography*, pp. 78–79. See also Wesley M. Gewehr, "Some Factors in the Expansion of Frontier Methodism, 1800–1811," *Journal of Religion* 8 (January 1928): 106–11.

[21] J. B. Jeter, *The Sermons and Other Writings of the Rev. Andrew Broaddus, With a Memoir of His Life* (New York, 1852), p. 14.

The Presbyterian ministers generally had better training and came from more affluent backgrounds; even so, most of them, like McGready and his colleagues, were educated at small, primitive, backwoods "log colleges." Often these were little more than the homes of ordained ministers.[22] To a growing extent by the 1790s, clergymen, particularly in the South, represented the culture, needs, demands, and failures of the common people who ultimately maintained the churches.[23]

The primary criterion for prospective ministers was a conversion experience. Repeatedly representatives of each denomination emphasized the prerequisite importance of conversion for preaching. McGready was precise on this requirement: "It is necessary that all ministers of the gospel should be savingly converted, experimentally acquainted with the work of regeneration in their own souls."[24]

By far the greatest stress on formal education, or at least on having a working knowledge of the classics, was maintained by the Presbyterian Church. Nevertheless, in locations and times when the pressing need for devout ministers outdistanced the trained supply, even the orthodox Presbyterians lowered their standards. For them too on occasion, practiced piety was more important than sterile learning. For example, the Hanover Presbytery in Virginia, more than a decade before the Great Revival, found itself forced to dispense with the educational requirements when a former Methodist minister, William Moore, applied for ordination. After reviewing their needs and his abilities, the convened members of the presbytery gave the following reason for accepting into their fold this man ignorant of Latin: "Because in the present state of religion in our Churches, men of liberal education & real piety cannot be obtained in sufficient numbers to supply the pressing demand of the people for the word & ordinances. On these accounts in an extraordinary case such as the present, the Pby. thought it proper to recede from the General rule adopted by our church, which requires its ministers to possess a classical education."[25] Yet even with such

[22] Cf. William Warren Sweet, "The Rise of Theological Schools in America," *Church History* 6 (September 1937): 260–74.

[23] For the implications of this fact in the decades ahead, consult Sidney E. Mead, "The Rise of the Evangelical Conception of the Ministry in America: 1607–1850," in *The Ministry in Historical Perspective*, ed. H. Richard Niebuhr and Daniel D. Williams (New York, 1956), pp. 207–49; and especially Hofstadter, *Anti-Intellectualism in America*, part 2, "The Religion of the Heart," pp. 55–141.

[24] McGready, *Posthumous Works*, 1: 312–13. See also William Fristoe, *A Concise History of the Ketocton Baptist Association: Wherein a Description Is Given of Her Constitution, Progress, and Increase* (Staunton, Va., 1808), p. 37.

[25] Hanover Presbytery, "Minutes," October 16, 1789.

exceptions, which were not uncommon, the Presbyterian fondness for educated ministers forced them to fall behind the Methodists and Baptists in the evangelization of the South. In the aftermath of the Great Revival the issue of education also contributed to a schism in the Presbyterian Church in Kentucky.

Given the emphasis placed on conversion, the meager training of the clergy, their deeply felt urgency both about the crisis in religion before the revival and then the signal opportunity presented by the ongoing awakening, perhaps ministerial excesses and fanatical sermons were inevitable. In addition, the real indifference to religion which characterized the decade before 1800 emphasized to the faithful the need for unusually strong, arousing preaching. The deep conviction of many ministers catapulted them into emotional tirades when they were confronting the apathy of the unconverted. Very significantly, the average educational level and sophistication of their listeners were not such as to temper any emotions that might be expressed. Indeed, for most congregational members, emotional responses were perhaps their best developed means of comprehension and communication. Considering all factors, it is perhaps understandable that feeling occasionally prevailed over reason. More remarkable than the evangelical excesses, however, was the extent to which theological ideas were accepted and preached throughout the South.

Revival hymnology provided an extraordinarily effective means of popularizing and disseminating complex theological doctrines. During these years a large percentage of worshipers were illiterate and hence could not read their creeds if their particular denomination had one. All Methodists and probably the majority of Baptists professed nothing but the Bible. Neither the Baptists nor the Methodists used a liturgy, and at this time practicality and reality forced many Presbyterian churches to do without. In this situation, singing complemented sermonizing in teaching and enforcing religious precepts.[26]

The genius of revival hymns was that they reduced doctrine to melodic and easily memorized lines. Often the minister would read one line at a time to the congregation, and they would respond in rhythm. Religious attitudes were thereby effortlessly ingrained. Simple refrains and choruses were used interchangeably with many different songs. As crowd participation multiplied, a simple refrain was increasingly used after each line spoken by the minister. Then, after two lines and two refrains would follow a

---

[26] There is a good discussion of Methodist hymnology in Gewehr, "Expansion of Frontier Methodism," pp. 113–16.

popular chorus. In this manner different ministers with new lines could still effectively lead their audiences in simple song.[27] But singing proved to be too popular, especially among the Baptists and Methodists, to be left to such primitive methods. Very early there began to appear numerous printed pocket-size hymnbooks. It was here that the songs were standardized, and ministers (and whoever else in the field that could read) found a common expression of the general evangelical beliefs. So very few could read musical notation that these early songsters contained only the printed words. More than one observer has discovered, with David Singer, that in these pocket hymnals we may gain "the best insight into the popularization of sophisticated religious concepts."[28]

The Methodist *Book of Discipline* outlined for ministers the way to get the optimum results from hymns. It warned against slow hymns which might lead to formality, against too much singing, and against innovation. "Sing no hymns of your own composing," it said, and "Recommend our tune-book." Proof of the importance of hymns was the recommendations to "Exhort every person in the congregation to sing, not one in ten only," and to make sure they learn the words. One should not introduce new tunes "till they are perfect in the old." The paramount role of teaching was indicated, however, in the advice to interrupt their singing often, and ask them: "Now! Do you know what you said last? Did you speak no more than you felt?"[29] By such pedagogical drilling, evangelical concepts were pressed home to the consciousness of the faithful.

The hymns contained in the contemporary Methodist, Baptist, and Presbyterian pocket-hymnals were arranged almost in the form of correspondence courses in theology. Appropriate songs were listed under headings like "Awakening and Inviting," "Providence," "Penitential," "The Holy Spirit," and "Praying for a Blessing." The messages presented in those of either of the three denominations were remarkably similar and indicate how closely they shared beliefs at this time. Frequently the same anonymous songs would appear in the hymnbooks of the different churches, and each drew heavily from the writings of the great English evangelists such as

---

[27] Most of the above is based on George Pullen Jackson, *White and Negro Spirituals: Their Life Span and Kinship* (New York, 1943), pp. 82–86.

[28] "God and Man in Baptist Hymnals, 1784–1844," *Midcontinent American Studies Journal* 9 (Fall 1968) : 14. See also Ralph H. Gabriel, "Evangelical Religion and Popular Romanticism in Early Nineteenth Century America," *Church History* 19 (March 1950) : 38–39; and John Norman Sims, "The Hymnody of the Camp Meeting Tradition" (D.S.M. diss., Union Theological Seminary, 1960).

[29] Methodist Episcopal Church, *Discipline*, pp. 17–18.

Philip Doddridge, Charles Wesley, and Isaac Watts.[30] Widely and enthusiastically used, these hymns as the repositories of popular theology will be cited in the later account of evangelical doctrines preached and believed.

Rhythmic, poetical, and not infrequently epigrammatic, revival hymns invited group participation. Usually accompanied by clapping and stomping, these songs gave vigor and enthusiasm to many meetings. This was welcome relief from the sleepy sermons of the almost forgotten prewar Anglican Church and its successor, the Episcopal. The monotony and physical exhaustion that marked rural life were forgotten in the enthusiasm of religious communion. This involvement, both mental and emotional, prepared the way for evangelical preaching.

Over and over observers noted the relationship between singing and revivalism. Describing the emergence of the Great Revival among the Kehukee Association in North Carolina, the Baptist authors wrote, "*Singing* was attended with a great blessing. . . . At every meeting, before the minister began to preach, the congregation was melodiously entertained with numbers singing delightfully, while all the congregation seemed in lively exercises. Nothing seemed to engage the attention of the people more . . . [than] these melodious songs. . . . [Singing] proved a blessing in this revival."[31]

There are numerous similar accounts linking hymns with the revival, and some, like the Reverend John Evans Findley of Kentucky, remarked that the "falling down of multitudes, and their crying out . . . happened under the singing of Watts' Psalms and Hymns, more frequently than under the preaching of the word."[32] Robert Davidson, a Presbyterian writing

[30] Among the hymnals consulted were the following: [Thomas Coke and Francis Asbury, introduction], *A Pocket Hymn-Book, Designed As a Constant Companion for the Pious. Collected From Various Authors*, 9th ed. (Philadelphia, 1790); Lorenzo Dow, comp., *A Collection of Spiritual Songs, Used at the Camp-Meetings, in the Great Revival in the United States of America* (London and Dublin, [minor differences in text]); John Rippon, *A Selection of Hymns from the Best Authors, Intended to be an Appendix to Dr. Watts' Psalms and Hymns* (Philadelphia, 1802); Isaac Watts, *Hymns and Spiritual Songs in Three Books. . . . Corrected, and Accommodated to the Use of the Church of Christ in America*, bound with Watts, *The Psalms of David* (Norwich, Conn., 1793); and *Hymn Book* ([n.p., n.d.]), in the Michaux-Randolph Papers. The English evangelical movement is discussed briefly in John T. McNeill, *Modern Christian Movements* (New York, 1968), chapt. 3.

[31] Burkitt and Read, *A Concise History of the Kehukee Association*, pp. 144–45.

[32] "Extract of a Letter from the Rev. Mr. John Evans Findley, of Mason-County, Kentucky," *Methodist Magazine* [London] 26 (1803): 126. Many accounts, such as John Lyle's "Diary" and M'Nemar's *The Kentucky Revival*, refer to the "fine singing extac[ies]."

some forty years afterward, probably best summarized the evident role of revivalistic singing. He is speaking here only of Methodist hymns, but his characterization is accurate for evangelical hymnology in general:

> It is to the Methodists [that] these measures ["extravagant irregularities and enthusiastic fantasies"] are to be traced. . . . They succeeded in introducing their own stirring hymns, familiarly, though incorrectly, entitled "Wesley's Hymns;" and as books were scarce, the few that were attainable were cut up, and the leaves distributed, so that all in turn might learn them by heart. By those who have ever reflected how great are the effects of music, and how probable it is that the ballads of a nation exert more influence than their law, this will be acknowledged to have been of itself a potent engine to give predominance to the Methodists, and to disseminate their peculiar sentiments.[33]

Thus in various ways the people of the South were both instructed in theology and admonished to recognize their present position. The different homiletic techniques stored their heads with doctrine, warmed their hearts with zeal, and invited them to participate in communal worship. Through clear, organized sermons, complicated theological systems were worked out with surprising rigor. Simple, engaging songs helped further spread and explain the general conception of Providence, prayer, grace, and redemption. Apathy was shattered and indifference disturbed by fervent exhortations. Interwoven throughout the sermon or confined to a fervent conclusion, applied by a single minister or by several, self-consciously provoking exhortations had one intention—to move people closer to God. The minister's role had become primarily one of activism, more concerned with gaining new converts than counseling old ones. Evangelization had captured the ministerial profession. The resulting emphasis on individual spiritual welfare largely shaped the religious history of the region. Technique and circumstance, beliefs and emphases, intertwined and interworking, helped to produce both the religious mind of the South and its consummation in the Great Revival of 1801 through 1805. Sermon and song had prepared the providential persuasion which underlay the awakening.

[33] Davidson, *History of the Presbyterian Church in Kentucky*, pp. 140–41.

Chapter Nine

A Theology of Individualism

In practically every aspect, the fundamental emphasis of the popular churches in the South was individualistic. For neither Baptist, Methodist, nor Presbyterian did the idea of the church mean a universal institutionalized body. Instead, whenever they spoke of the church, they meant the local congregation, or, in the most abstract sense, they sometimes used this phrase to refer to that mystical body of individual believers known only by God. This localized, individual ecclesiology was intimately related to the prevalent evangelical theology. The brunt of the preaching and teaching was exerted to break down the barriers of personal indifference. The ministers' aim was immediate conviction and conversion. For this goal they had no overarching purpose beyond the development of individual Christians. Though they recognized that the final result of effective preaching would be the approximation of a Christianized social order, this was not their self-conceived role. Rather, the ministers representing the three popular denominations of the South were devoted to awakening individual souls to a dependence upon God. The communal thrust was subordinated to the personal.

A corollary to this theology of individual conversion was a vigorous emphasis on sanctification, or Christian perfectionism. Necessarily the more those committed to Christianity pressed toward an "imitation of Christ," the society they in part composed would be purified. Private perfectionism would produce social improvement. This personal, inward, pietistic theology has characterized the dominant religious beliefs in the South since at least the Great Revival itself.

Before the American Revolution, pietistic religion in the region below the Potomac was on the defensive. With disestablishment and democratization came a surge of religion catering to those masses filling the hinterlands removed from commercialism, education, and entrenched political power. This popular religion of the South had its faltering beginnings in prerevolutionary Virginia and North Carolina. The autonomous Presbyterian, Baptist, and Methodist revivals of the 1750s, 1760s, and 1770s, combined with the simultaneous, though largely independent revivals of the late 1780s, almost imperceptibly built up to the great explosion of revivalism after 1800.

In the tidal wave of supposedly irrepressible religious progress that followed, the mold of pietistic evangelicalism was indelibly stamped on the South. After this a more rational, more societally oriented theology never found a significant role in the drama of southern Protestantism.

Until the Revolutionary destruction of the fragile Anglican establishment, the triune contingent of dissenter churches was in an insecure position.[1] For these zealous groups the grandiose concept of the church had connotations of a less than ideal establishment with its legal exclusiveness. Partly in reaction and partly from theology, the Baptists and Presbyterians, along with the Methodists (who were the evangelical arm of the Anglican Church), came to share a new idea of what the Christian Church was. Not an international institution like the Roman Church, not a state-upheld institution like the repressive Church of England; instead the true church was a voluntary society of converted believers for whom institutional identity was irrelevant. The individual's relationship to God, not denomination, was fundamental.

Robert Hastings Nichols observed several decades ago that this manner of church had its roots in the Great Awakening, if not earlier, and he showed that such religious thinkers as Jonathan Edwards were primarily interested in the local congregation.[2] Certainly the Puritan belief in a church based on the covenant of grace carries these implications, along with the emphatic communal emphasis of the Bay Colony founders. Moreover, as Nichols pointed out, the seemingly ubiquitous John Locke in his *Letter Concerning Toleration* expressed a view of the church which in many ways defined the highest ideals of the American religious structure. "A church I take to be," wrote Locke, "a voluntary society of men, joining themselves together of their own accord in order to [*sic*] the public worship of God, in such a manner as they judge acceptable to him, and effectual to the salvation of their souls."[3] This notion of the church as a group in special relationship to God undefined by state or institution was inherent (though often submerged) in the Calvinistic strain of Christianity. Moreover, the totally personal aspect of being in a state of justification was common to Methodist

---

[1] Here for reasons of convenience rather than exactitude, I am terming the Methodist Church a dissenter group. This it was in fact if not in organization before 1784.

[2] "The influence of the American Environment on the Conception of the Church in American Protestantism," *Church History* 11 (September 1942) : 181–92.

[3] Quoted in ibid., p. 188, from *The Works of John Locke, In Ten Volumes*, 11th ed. (London, 1812), 6 : 13.

belief as well. Possessing an otherworldly comprehension of the union of believers, those Presbyterians, Baptists, and especially Methodists who found themselves in the South faced with a ruling religious institution—however ineffective—that equated church and state, had special reason to define the church in voluntaristic terms.

Richard Furman, for example, in "A Sermon on the Constitution and Order of the Christian Church" (1789), defined the true church as a group of individual saints, known with certainty only by God. In particular, he argued, "That the Church of Christ is not National is apparent from this that Christ has promised his Presence to two or three met in his Name."[4] Here, in the local congregation, was to be found that voluntary society of believers who constituted the gospel church. It had long seemed blatantly obvious that the institutionalized church as it had existed in the colonial South contained many members who never had intimated any converting knowledge of God. Hence there were practical and theological reasons for the dissenters' position on disestablishment, for, as the prominent Baptist Elder John Leland wrote, they believed "that pure Christianity would gain much by such a dissolution."[5] Francis Asbury, upon confronting an opposing establishment in Connecticut in 1794, repeated these views when he wrote bitterly of "ecclesiastical chains" and "iron walls of prejudice."[6]

From this understanding of the church developed the peculiarly American concept of denominationalism. Sidney E. Mead has aptly defined this organizational term: "a voluntary association of like-hearted and like-minded individuals, who are united on the basis of common beliefs for the purpose of accomplishing tangible and defined objectives."[7] Following the complete disestablishment of the Anglican Church in the South, all religious groups were thrown upon their own resources. As a voluntary society of converted believers, each denomination was forced to use persuasion to maintain its position and hopefully augment its membership. Such a religious body could grow only by converting individuals.

[4] Richard Furman, "A Sermon on the Constitution and Order of the Christian Church, Preached before the Charleston Association of Baptist Churches, 1789," Ms in South Caroliniana Collection, University of South Carolina, Columbia, S. C.

[5] John Leland, "An Oration, Delivered at Cheshire, July 5, 1802, On the Celebration of Independence: Containing Seventeen Sketches, and Seventeen Wishes," in Leland, *The Life and Writings*, p. 264. Leland had been a pioneer defender of religious freedom in Virginia until 1791; then, having found success, he moved to Massachusetts and continued his struggle till death a half-century later.

[6] Asbury, *Journal and Letters*, August 10, 1794, 2:22.

[7] Mead, "Denominationalism: The Shape of Protestantism in America," *Church History* 23 (December 1954): 291.

This emphasis on suasion changed the primary role of the minister from that of counseling and performance of ritual to that of evangelization. The minister now had one central concern—to convert unbelievers and hence increase the local church congregation. Such congregations often united into associations, synods, or conferences, but their aim was no higher than encouraging the evangelical efforts of the individual congregations. The outlook of the popular southern churches was personal, provincial, and noninstitutional.

Closely related to the clerical concern with local affairs and individual conversions was what Lefferts A. Loetscher has termed "at least the shadow of catholicity."[8] If institutional identification was less important than being one of the invisible saints of God, if being converted was the primary requirement for joining a denominaton, then was not the fact of conversion more important than the denominational label? The evangelicals joined in an emphatic yes! As Henry Pattillo of North Carolina, a noted liberal Presbyterian, preached in 1788: "Though the people of CHRIST are divided in name, yet they are one in will and affections. Their will is to do, and submit to, the will of GOD in all things; their wish and endeavour is, to be holy; and their affections are set on things above: they love each other too, notwithstanding their different names, and would love more if they were better acquainted."[9] This mutual love was perhaps more theoretical than practiced, but even such a denominational devotee as Asbury could remark, in the midst of religious depression in 1790, "Glory be to God for what religion there is still to be found amongst all sects and denominations of people!"[10]

The vague, often unexpressed feeling of unity was based upon widely shared theological beliefs. Conversion, each denomination held, was ultimately effected by God's spirit and grace. Salvation was entirely unearned— it was the free gift of a merciful God to those who had been led to repent of their sins and put their faith in him. This being the measure of redemption, a certain unity existed among all those who had experienced conversion. Far more significant at the highest level of spirituality than human classifications was this special communion of individuals with God. "In that awful day," warned revivalist James McGready, "when the universe, assembled, must appear before the judge of the quick and dead, the question brethren, will not be, Were you a Presbyterian—a Seceder—a Covenanter—a Baptist

[8] "The Problem of Christian Unity in Early Nineteenth-Century America," *Church History* 32 (March 1963): 7.

[9] Pattillo, "The Divisions among Christians," in *Sermons*, p. 51.

[10] Asbury, *Journal and Letters*, March 29, 1790, 1:630.

—or a Methodist; but, Did you experience the new birth? Did you accept of Christ and his salvation as set forth in the gospel?"[11]

A common accent upon personal conversion characterized the three popular southern denominations, and this emphasis also provided a thread of Christian unity. The primary thrust of the theology of each denomination concerned experiential conversion; hence, most of the doctrinal ideas of the three groups were almost exactly the same. The differences were primarily ones of tone and organization. The Baptists were zealous in their support of believer baptism by immersion, the Presbyterians were often extremely rigid in their allegiance to the Westminster Creed, and the Methodists sometimes made a creed of having none. But the shared beliefs outweighed the differences. Often denominational bickering looked like theological or semantic shadow-boxing. Their emphasis upon voluntary support made each group dependent upon persuasion for additional members—with differences minor and competition keen for converts, small points had to be magnified. This explains why, for example, Methodists and Baptists could be at each other's throats during periods of intense rivalry, and yet unite in shared purpose when widespread apathy or deism threatened. In like manner, all denominations cooperated in the prerevival prayer societies and in camp meetings. Success produced thousands of converts, and it was in this comfortable time of competition for allegiance that most group rivalries erupted. We must look beyond the small epicycles of denominational differences if we are to see the huge centrality of their shared beliefs.

The emphasis on a voluntary union of converts was largely the dissenter response to an institutionalized church whose members often seemed anything but converted and voluntary. The result was an intense individualization, both of the idea of the church and the ministerial role. The deeply personal matter of one's relationship to God was now the central issue. Yet within this resultant provincial and noncommunal religious attitude there lay a catholic principle. If the paramount issue was conversion, then all those who shared this experience in some way were members of a vast spiritual community. In the South the revolutionary heritage of dissent, the widely scattered pattern of settlement, the central issue of revivalistic preaching, all combined to maintain the southern evangelical mind within a narrowly individual, pietistic, inward mold. But the essential unity of a conversion-centered theology so shaped the course of religious development in the South that the popular denominations can be viewed as one large synthesis of evangelical pietism. This basic unity of southern religion—practical, pro-

---

[11] McGready, *Posthumous Works*, 2 : 71.

vincial, individualistic—makes it possible for one to discuss the religious mind of the Old South.

Denominational religion in the nation as a whole has shared this characteristic of unity—so much so that in 1846 Robert Baird could classify all American religion as either evangelical or nonevangelical. Winthrop S. Hudson has defined this ecumenical concept of denominationalism into which the structure of American Protestantism is divided:

> It implies that the group referred to is but one member, called or *denominated* by a particular name, of a larger group—the Church [i.e., the body of converted believers]—to which all denominations belong. The basic contention of the denominational theory of the Church is that the true Church is not to be identified exclusively with any single ecclesiastical structure. No denomination claims to represent the whole Church of Christ. No denomination claims that all other churches are false churches. Each denomination is regarded as constituting a different "mode" of expressing in the outward forms of worship and organization that larger life of the Church in which they all share.[12]

Southern evangelism was somewhat distinct in its firm individual orientation, as opposed to the more communal emphasis of mainstream American Protestantism which resulted in numerous reform efforts, voluntary societies, and ultimately the social gospel. The southern churches that were to determine the region's religious attitudes had balked at the idea that church, state, and society were conterminous. From their experience with an exclusive establishment they had erected a wall of separation between church and state. The local church attempted to oversee the social behavior of its own members, but no societal coercion was implied. It was left for the churches in the Midwest and Northeast, with their stronger Puritan heritage of example, to develop the "evangelical united front" for national communal reform efforts.[13] The long-lasting Congregational establishment

---

[12] *American Protestantism* (Chicago, 1961), p. 34.

[13] Other scholars have shown that a different relationship existed between religion and society in the Northeast and Midwest. These patterns are described, for example, in Clifford S. Griffin, *Their Brothers' Keepers: Moral Stewardship in the United States, 1800–1865* (New Brunswick, N. J., 1960), and Charles I. Foster, *An Errand of Mercy: The Evangelical United Front, 1790–1837* (Chapel Hill, N. C., 1960). Quite obviously I do not see in the South the more pervasive societal emphasis of popular religion that T. Scott Miyakaya portrayed for the Midwest in his *Protestants and Pioneers: Individualism and Conformity on the American Frontier* (Chicago, 1964). As for early New England, Perry Miller has written: "There was, it is true, a strong element of individualism in the Puritan creed. . . . But at the same time, the Puritan philosophy demanded that in society all men, at least all regenerate men, be

in Massachusetts and Connecticut served as the command post for this activity. These endeavors were not a manifestation of southern religion.

Central to the popular southern notion of the church was a common set of beliefs which stressed the pivotal importance of personal conversion. Conversion was set in a teleological context wherein God was the supreme moral governor of the created universe. In this image God was infinitely perfect, "of spotless purity and immaculate holiness."[14] As such he could not even tacitly countenance anything or anyone less than holy. Sin was treason against him and what he stood for. By universal evangelical assumption, the unconverted person was endlessly sinful and separated from God by virtue of the absolute moral standard. Understandably then, for God to have accepted a sinner on his own merits would have been flagrantly unjust. There was no possible way for infinite goodness to compromise with human failings. The seriousness of man's sinfulness was beyond his comprehension—McGready spoke of the "unfathomable oceanlike wickedness even of the best heart."[15] Henry Holcombe, Georgia Baptist minister, later wrote than man's nature was "radically depraved, and utterly destitute of moral goodness."[16] This "corruption of the nature of every man," as the Methodist *Discipline* referred to it,[17] left God in a hypothetical quandary. The evangelicals' God was moral, just, and sinless—how could depraved man be reunited with him without God's justice being prostituted?

The commonly accepted idea of God posited him with another necessary attribute—infinite love and mercy. Man was helpless, and his sinful nature could not be minimized. Some method had to be devised whereby the universal standard of justice would be observed, and yet man's due punishment be assumed by another. "Every fallen soul by sinning,/Merits everlasting pain," stated the Baptist hymn,[18] and somehow this penalty had to be paid. The faithful trusted that there was a "remedy in Christ" for this seeming impasse for man. Escape from eternal punishment was provided for in the Christian "plan of salvation, by which God can be just

marshaled into one united array. The lone horseman, the single trapper, the solitary hunter was not a figure of the Puritan frontier; Puritans moved in groups and towns, settled in whole communities, and maintained firm goverment over all units. . . . they thought of [society] not as an aggregation of individuals but as an organism, functioning for a definite purpose"; "Puritan State and Puritan Society," in Miller, *Errand into the Wilderness*, p. 143.

[14] McGready, *Posthumous Works*, 1: 5.
[15] Ibid., 2:63.
[16] Holcombe, *Primitive Theology*, p. 116.
[17] Methodist Episcopal Church, *Discipline*, p. 5.
[18] Rippon, *A Selection of Hymns*, number LXV.

and justify the ungodly sinner trusting in Jesus."[19] Jesus Christ was the hero in this scheme of deliverance. Co-equal with God in holiness and perfection, he took upon his own shoulders the collective sin and punishment of each potential convert. In this manner, the faithful believed, Jesus Christ paid the price for sin and imputed his own unblemished righteousness to those for whose sin he died. Hence through Jesus Christ God provided a way in which sin could justly be atoned for and men could have an escape from the universal finality of death.

This idea of man's position, whereby he in life was stranded somewhere between God and a hell of eternal punishment, was accepted in detail by the proponents of evangelical Protestantism in the South, as elsewhere in the nation. Furthermore, the Baptists, Methodists, and Presbyterians all held depraved man to be in a state of absolute dependence upon God for aid in salvation. Man could not by his own free will turn aside from his sinful condition. God had to initiate within man the faith that recognized Jesus Christ. That this was a general belief common to Methodists as well as Presbyterians, Separate Baptists as well as Regulars, is indicated by their doctrinal statements. On this extremely important theological point, each denomination was in total agreement. According to the Methodist Book of Discipline on free will: "The condition of man after the fall of Adam is such, that he cannot turn and prepare himself by his own natural strength and works to faith, and calling upon God: Wherefore we have no power to do good works pleasant and acceptable to God, without the grace of God by Christ . . . [enabling], that we may have a good will, and working with us, when we have that good will."[20] The Presbyterians in their Confession of Faith argued almost the same thing: "Man, by his fall into a state of sin, hath wholly lost all ability of will to any spiritual good accompanying salvation: so as a natural man being altogether averse from that which is good, and dead in sin, is not able, by his own strength, to convert himself, or to prepare himself thereunto."[21]

John Asplund, who traveled about preparing a yearbook on Baptist activities, summarized the "principles held by the Baptists in general," although he should have admitted that he spoke for those of Regular Baptist back-

[19] McGready, *Posthumous Works*, 1: 312.
[20] Methodist Episcopal Church, *Discipline*, p. 5.
[21] Presbyterian Church, U. S. A., *The Constitution of the Presbyterian Church in the United States of America, Containing the Confession of Faith, The Catechisms, And the Directory for the Worship of God: Together With the Plan of Government and Discipline, As Amended and Ratified by the General Assembly at their Sessions in May, 1805* (Philadelphia, 1815), pp. 57–58.

ground: "We believe in man's impotency to recover himself from the fallen state he is in by nature, by his own free will ability."[22] The less rigid Baptist position is exemplified in a letter from the Reverend William M. Bledsoe, writing from his western outpost in Craborchard, Kentucky, in 1790. He made clear that he and those he represented differed from "the Calvinistical antinomians on the one hand and those who on the other propagate Justifycation by works." Yet even he held that "men was created a free agent: and by transgression has fallen into a State of Intire depravation," and now only by "Virtue of [Christ's redemptive] death Light is Restored to mankind."[23]

Here was the dilemma accepted by the three dominant southern denominations: God was just and perfectly holy; man was vile and helpless. Only a transcendent catalyst beyond man's ability could effect reconciliation. In the Christian plan of salvation, it was Jesus Christ's atoning death which provided man the only way of escape from the "wages of sin." This pathway from punishment to paradise was open *only* for those who placed their ultimate trust in Jesus Christ. But man in his depraved state was unable to entertain this level of faith. Only the benevolent grace—unmerited love —of God made possible saving faith among men. The three popular denominations were in perfect accord. It is difficult to find any substantial difference in theology among the pietists.

Spokesmen of evangelical religion in the South all agreed that God had to initiate the process of repentance and faith—this was not just a rigid Presbyterian notion. Georgia Baptist Henry Holcombe emphasized that the "salvation of every sinner is *wholly* of God. . . . Salvation is not of him that willeth, . . . but of God's mercy."[24] A popular Methodist hymn, contained in the denominational "pocket hymn-book" as early as 1790, implored God:

> The gift unspeakeable impart;
> Command the light of faith to shine:
> To shine in my dark, drooping heart,
> And fill me with the life divine:
> Now bid the new creation be!
> O God, let there be faith in me.[25]

[22] John Asplund, *The Annual Register of the Baptist Denomination in North-America, to the First of November, 1790* ([n.p.], 1792), p. 53.

[23] Bledsoe to Robert Carter, May 19, 1790, in the Robert Carter Mss, Virginia Baptist Historical Society, University of Richmond.

[24] Holcombe, *The First Fruits, in a Series of Letters* (Philadelphia, 1812), p. 211; italics mine.

[25] Coke and Asbury, intro., *A Pocket Hymn-Book*, Hymn XXVII, p. 33.

James McGready preached that "Christ is the author and efficient cause of [the sinner's] deliverance."[26] Yet it was left for McGready's eminent colleague in North Carolina, Henry Pattillo, to express best the pietistic emphasis on God's motivating spirit: "the Sacred Spirit is the author and agent of this mighty change [regeneration]; so that what he does is as visible as the effects of the wind, and yet the manner of his operation is above all comprehension. This is that work of God on the soul, without which you are neither true penitents, nor true believers.—That work of God, that enlightens the mind to discern the glory and excellency of Christ's kingdom, and encourages the creature to become a willing subject of it—That work of GOD, that is the grand preparative for further happiness."[27]

Up to this point the theology of each evangelical denomination was practically identical. Most sermons, and especially those preached in the midst of a revival, were not recognizable as belonging to one denomination or another. All three of the major religious groups accepted the doctrine of "free salvation," in the sense that there was nothing man could do to merit it. None of the popular churches was universalist, believing that every man was or would be saved because Jesus Christ had died for every human sin. Instead, they believed that this all-important gift of salvation was operative only for those who were faithful, and upon those God had mysteriously sent his spirit.[28] It was here, in the differentiation between those who had received this spiritual assist and those who had not, and in whether the whole matter was inevitable because of God's omniscience, that dispute arose. Yet this was an issue reserved for relatively infrequent sermons—in most respects, Baptists, Methodists, and Presbyterians preached the same evangelical gospel.

The central emphasis of most sermons of whatever denomination was to convert individual sinners. Man's sinful nature was elaborated and placed in stark contrast to the pristine perfection of God. Ministers, in their desire to promote conversion, emphasized how simple it was to win security—all that was necessary was to trust in the God-Christ salvation plan. The minister's function was to present this plan in it clearest form and warn those outside the church of their dangerous position. God in his merciful providence would do the rest. For example, Republican Methodist itinerant William Hammett in his journal entry referred to this faith that God would use ministerial efforts to his purpose: "May the Lord water the seed soon,

[26] McGready, *Posthumous Works*, 1:92.
[27] Pattillo, *Sermons*, pp. 60–61.
[28] For example, see Methodist minister George A. Reed's sermon delivered in the 1790s; Reed Papers.

and *then* it will bear fruit." Again he remarked, "May God own the word, and give the increase." [29] God energized the word; the ministers were to spread the message. "Our Lord commissions preachers of the Gospel," wrote an effective revivalist, "and sends them to proclaim a free salvation to every guilty, crying sinner who will accept it." [30]

The issue of election was more important than all the other denominational differences combined. The doctrine "of effectual calling" was explicitly laid out in the Confession of Faith which all Presbyterians theoretically accepted. By this interpretation, God knew from the beginning of time each person who would be spiritually moved to conversion, and for such people—the "elect"—it was inevitable that some time in their life they would be presented the opportunity to make this predetermined decision. As the Confession explained it: "All those whom God hath predestinated unto life, and those only, he is pleased, in his appointed and accepted time, effectually to call, by his word and Spirit, out of that state of sin and death, in which they are by nature, to grace and salvation by Jesus Christ." [31]

As their critics argued, if all this were true, why should ministers bother to preach, for those whom God had elected would inevitably be saved. What difference did man's role make? And did not this imply that, for many, salvation was impossible not for anything they had done or neglected, but just because they had not been picked out for special favor—foreordained —by God before the world was founded? Furthermore, the doctrine of election would seem to limit sharply the number for whom salvation was possible. "So they suppose," said a Methodist of a Calvinistic Baptist association, "the number of the Elect from Eternity to be so Definitive that it cannot be added to now or deminished. If so, why did they Preach." [32] For many, the difficulties of Calvinism made orthodox Presbyterianism in particular unpalatable.

In practical preaching, however, the issue of election did not seem to limit effectiveness. For those Presbyterians of New Side, revivalistic orientation—men like James McGready and William Hodge—a moderate Calvinism was blended with energetic evangelism, and the result was spectacular success. In similar fashion, the Separate Baptists who had spread over the South thrived on a mixture of Calvinism and evangelical zeal. In their sermons, men of this mold stressed God's role in awakening in sinners the

[29] William Hammett, "Journal," May 22 and May 25, 1793, in the South Caroliniana Collection, University of South Carolina, Columbia, S. C.

[30] McGready, *Posthumous Works*, 2:256.

[31] Presbyterian Church, U. S. A., *The Constitution*, pp. 59–60.

[32] William Ormond, "Journal," September 23, 1799, typescript, p. 28.

regenerating faith. The minister led unbelievers to a recognition of their depraved state, but this awareness was not in itself redemptive. "It is very true," wrote James McGready on this precise point, "that no man can see Christ or behold his glory until that God, who at first commanded light to shine out of darkness, shines into his heart by the enlightening influences of his Spirit, and gives him the light of the knowledge of the glory of God, in the face of Jesus: yet [and this is crucially important] the word of divine revelation, is the medium through which Christ is seen, and his amiable excellencies discovered." [33]

In other words, God had to activate the faith, but in some way he did this through the message of the Bible as preached by ministers. Even though, in an ultimate sense, neither the potential converts nor the minister was in control of events, both played a necessary role in the conversion process: the minister by presenting the message and the unbeliever by accepting it. Hereby the "sinner" received regenerating and saving faith. [34] As Pattillo argued, predestination and election did indeed call for preaching, good works, hope, and virtuous living. [35] The theory of election did not, in this evangelical view, leave man with no responsibilities.

It should be clear that the issues of election and predestination, for all their controversial value in times of denominational competition, were not really significant factors in the realm of everyday evangelical preaching. Because this peculiar Calvinistic concept was only a small matter in the entire Christian scheme of salvation, it was often submerged in the totality of the theology. Since all three denominations shared the same essential beliefs in God's perfection, man's imperfection, and the role of grace and the spirit, slight technical differences were irrelevant when Christianity was faced with apparent apathy and infidelity. The rigid Regular Baptists could, without much difficulty, merge with the more evangelical Separates before the Great Revival in every state but Kentucky because their shared beliefs vastly overshadowed minor theological subtleties. In the midst of revival successes in Kentucky, even the most doctrinaire Baptists found merger to be most acceptable. Camp meetings across the South drew all groups together, and for a short while Presbyterians preached with Methodists without discord or inconsistency.

As a matter of record, Presbyterians caught up in the revival tended either to avoid their traditional denominational doctrines or dilute them

[33] McGready, *Posthumous Works*, 2: 191.

[34] See, for example, ibid., 1: 119–20; Pattillo, *Sermons*, pp. 93–97; and Rippon, *A Selection of Hymns*, numbers LXXII, CVII, and CVIII.

[35] Pattillo, *Sermons*, pp. 150–51, 154–55, 159, 164, 170–74, and passim.

almost past recognition. For example, except for a few who soon left the church, they never explicitly denied that only a limited elect would achieve salvation, but in practice they talked in expansive terms that an outright universalist would have been hard pressed to match. McGready spoke of "the pardon of millions of rebellious sinners," and of those "innumerable millions" who would be saved—vast hordes, "to an exceeding great number, like sand by the sea shore!" [36] Such quantities would imply that the defender of predestination when pressed would in effect admit that there was no limit upon salvation with regard to any particular individual.

Even Henry Holcombe, a representative Calvinist Baptist, said "the saved" will be as "innumerable as the stars of heaven." It is no surprise, then, that smug Methodist Peter Cartwright could say of the Presbyterians —the stereotyped Calvinists—in Kentucky: "in this revival they, almost to a man, gave up these points of high Calvinism, and preached a free salvation to all mankind." [37]

This homogenizing of beliefs was doubly important, for not only did it greatly augment the existent Christian unity, but in promoting a mode of Presbyterianism which deemphasized the creedal importance of election and predestination, it prepared the way for the eventual Kentucky schisms. This implied modification of Calvinism produced a more evangelical Baptist faith, and, in addition, it offered a beginning to the "Christian" movement. With the Presbyterian emphasis on election being qualified in the midst of what appeared an obvious outpouring of God's awakening grace, Barton W. Stone, schismatic leader, could accurately describe the theology being preached as follows: "At the commencement of the present revival, preachers in general, who were truly engaged in it, omitted the doctrines of Election and Reprobation [i.e., that some are foreordained to damnation], as explained in the confession of faith, and proclaimed a free salvation to all men thro' the blood of the Lamb. They held forth the promises of the Gospel in their purity and simplicity, without the contradictory explanations and double meanings, which scholastic divines have put upon them to make them agree with the doctrines of the confession." [38] Once orthodoxy was relaxed, ever so slightly, modification was inevitable. Paradoxically, unity and schism were two results of the revival.

[36] McGready, *Posthumous Works*, 1 : 37 and 113.

[37] Cartwright, *Autobiography*, p. 46.

[38] Barton W. Stone et al., *An Apology for Renouncing the Jurisdiction of the Synod of Kentucky. To which is Added, a Compendious View of the Gospel, and a Few Remarks on the Confession of Faith. By the Presbytery of Springfield* (Lexington, Ky., 1804), p. 4.

It is important to note that in this qualification of election, in practice if not in conscious theology, there was a definite shift of the Presbyterian and Baptist position toward the Arminian outlook of the Methodists. In the Wesleyan tradition, it was believed that Christ's atoning death was theoretically sufficient for all but in reality only the actual believers would realize the benefits. Absolute predestination was replaced by conditional election, wherein the individual was called upon to make the decision. For the required faith God would grant the necessary gift of grace. Hence the supreme role of God was not limited in any substantial way at all. Nevertheless, conversion had taken on a more individual, volitional aspect. The evangelical emphasis on conversion had produced this subtle change for all except the most rigid Calvinists. The all-important element of human decision had gained in significance as the minister's role had evolved from that of counselor to persuader. If the minister's purpose was to lead men to Jesus Christ, then by implication the listeners had acquired an enlarged degree of responsibility. This only made the southern evangelical emphasis on the conversion experience a more individual, more inward matter than before.

As southern evangelical religion worked out in practice, then, the personal responsibility for one's religious future was predominant. For example, James McGready pleaded with young people that now, at their age, was the best time for making the decision for faith. In later years, he argued, they would grow in hardness of heart and unbelief.[39] Certainly this kind of preaching made rigorous election seem meaningless and stressed the decision to believe.

In some very subtle way the awakening spirit of God was intimately involved in the will-to-believe process, but neither ministers nor laymen were precise. After all, these were preachers attempting to bring uneducated farmers to the brink of conversion—meticulous theological consistency was largely irrelevant. As an extremely effective Separate Baptist minister summed up the issue, "those who finally perish, are lost, not on account of Gods decree, respecting partial election . . . but on account of their unbelief."[40] Abstruse theological doctrines, in the final analysis, were less important than the individual sinner's coming to grips with his depraved position in relation to God and recognizing the escape provided by faith in Jesus Christ. Here was the central matter in the whole concept of individual conversion.

Both the prevalent idea of the church as a group of converted indi-

[39] See his sermon "The Young Invited to Come to Christ," in McGready, *Posthumous Works*, 2: 268–69
[40] John Waller to Robert Carter, April 20, 1789, in the Robert Carter Mss.

viduals joined together in a voluntary society, and the emphasis on the individual in the conversion-centered theology actually preached, accented the
personal role in religion. The individual Christian was the measure of evangelism. If the individual convert composed the true church and participated
in the beginning of his own religious life, then quite obviously evangelical
religion was almost wholly an individual matter. This personal importance
accentuated the individualistic concern of religion in the South. Because
individuals *were* Christianity, there was no communal or societal emphasis.
Christians were called upon to make themselves more like Jesus Christ.
They were expected to reform themselves, not society in general, though of
course it was assumed that the one led to the other. The close personal introspection which preceded conversion did not cease afterwards—instead it
produced a pietistic form of evangelical religion in the South in which emphasis was placed upon the importance of Christians making themselves
better Christians. The improved heart was the essential aim.

A pietistic emphasis on attempting to attain holiness in one's personal life
was common to those most devoted in each of the three popular denominations. "Let us strongly and explicitly exhort all believers," urged the Methodist Book of Discipline, *"to go on to perfection."* [41] There was some
question as to whether the state of perfection was gained instantaneously
with conversion, or whether it had to be achieved gradually. In some meta-
physical sense, perhaps, the potentiality for perfection was attained simultaneously with the experience of conversion, but in every real and practical
sense, Christians strove daily for eventual perfection with the necessary aid
of God's spirit and grace. Although absolute sanctification would never be
reached in this life, the pietists believed that men could make great progress
toward holiness until, with death, they entered into complete perfection.
The expected reward at the end was supposedly worth all the sacrifice and
moral control along the way. [42]

It was this pietist-perfectionist emphasis that made religion, for the
faithful, much more than mere attendance at sermons, expansion of church
membership, or periodic revivals. Instead, vital religion was a daily preoccupation. True in a constricted degree during periods of decline like that of
the 1790s, the concern with day-to-day Christian living was greatly ex-

[41] Methodist Episcopal Church, *Discipline*, p. 24; italics mine.
[42] Although Methodism had always included the idea that complete sanctification
theoretically followed conversion instantly as the "second blessing," in practice this
doctrine of immediate perfection became much more common after the 1820s. Consult
Timothy L. Smith, *Revivalism and Social Reform in Mid-Nineteenth-Century America* (New York, 1957), pp. 25, 115–16.

panded during and after seasons of revivals. For thousands of converts in the Great Revival which swept the South after 1800, the pietistic desire that one's inner self be in harmony with the Christian ideal became a central concern. Here in the heart, believed the evangelical clergy, was the center of the Christian religion. "I fear religion is extinguished," wrote Bishop Asbury, "by confining it too much to church and Sunday service, and reading of sermons." [43] Drury Lacy warned a young pupil, "take care that you are not Carried away with Religion as a Science, so as to forget, that its principal design is to make the heart better." [44]

The diaries and letters of evangelical ministers repeatedly illustrate an overwhelming concern with perfectionism. [45] Sanctification was a constant topic for sermons stressing the life after conversion. Henry Holcombe insisted that as Christians, "we are to press forward, in ardour, towards the perfection of our nature, which is found in our conformity to the image of Jesus Christ." [46] It was firmly believed that God's onworking spirit would enable the faithful to transcend the temporal vanities of a materialistic and corrupt society. The Presbyterian Confession of Faith had a detailed section on "sanctification" in which the possibility of perfection was outlined. Even in the midst of a secular environment, holiness could be approximated: "They who are effectually called and regenerated, having a new heart and a new spirit created in them, are farther sanctified, really and personally, through the virtue of Christ's death and resurrection, by his word and Spirit dwelling in them: the dominion of the whole body of sin is destroyed, and the several lusts thereof are more and more weakened and mortified, and they more and more quickened and strengthened, in all saving graces, to the practice of true holiness, without which no man shall see the Lord." [47]

Historically, evangelical religion has taken a stand in opposition to excess materialism, extreme worldliness, and general secularism. This strain of pietism is generously evident among the southern proponents of evangelicalism. Over and over again revivalists warned against such idols as "the world, money, and prosperity . . . fine clothes and beautiful ornaments. . . . the BOTTLE." [48] There were also criticisms of speculation, concern with good crops rather than religion, postwar prosperity and commercialism.

[43] Asbury, *Journal and Letters*, June 18, 1791, 1:681.

[44] Lacy to William Williamson, October 1, 1791, in the Williamson Papers, Shane Collection.

[45] For example, see Stith Mead to [William Mead], June 12, 1793, Mead Letterbook, p. 28.

[46] Holcombe, "The Vitality of Faith," in *Primitive Theology*, p. 115.

[47] Presbyterian Church, U. S. A., *The Constitution*, pp. 69–70.

[48] McGready, *Posthumous Works*, 1:166–67.

Pietistic perfectionism was both a program for personal reform and improvement, and a definite critique of societal worldliness. Frequently the emphasis on dutiful sanctification resulted in a censorious repression of worldly pleasures, as in the instance reported by James McHenry while visiting a western Virginia resort in 1794: "I attended a methodist sermon yesterday and heard cardplaying and dancing condemned as damnable sins."[49]

Nevertheless, for the rough-and-ready society which existed in most regions of the South away from the centers of commerce and cultivation, the perfectionist emphasis of pietistic religion probably served a wholesome function. The pursuit of holiness offered some substitute for total engrossment in planting, trading, gossip, and politics. It challenged church members throughout the region to personal moral improvement and held out the expectation of eternal reward. Even after the threat of Indian attacks had ended in Kentucky and Tennessee, the rigors of rural society across the South, as elsewhere, furnished the people with a surfeit of hardship, boredom, sickness, and death. The promise of a better future, which could be worked toward and expected by faith, no doubt infused a new measure of hope and enthusiasm for life in the minds of many faithful churchgoers. Methodist minister George Reed typically urged perfectionism and held forth the goal in a sermon preached several times during the dismal 1790s: "The two great points to which [conversion] tends, & which it urges ye [the] soul, where it has taken place, incessantly to press after, are, *communion* with GOD, & conformity to him; &, as neither of these can be fully attained in this life, it teaches us to pant after a better; to withdraw our thoughts & affections from temporal things, and fix them on [that] eternal state, where we trust our desires shall be abundantly satisfied: & ye work begun by *grace*, shall be crowned with glory."[50] Otherworldliness—or perhaps, an extreme detachment from unpleasant reality—has been a continuing trait among evangelical southerners especially.

In a profound sense, popular religion in the South has been a personal matter, a thing of the heart. The personal conversion experience has defined the southern idea of the church, and the theological system preached and believed has rotated about one central axis: the conversion of individual sinners. This intensely personal concern with religion has produced a pietistic, inward mold of religious enthusiasm. There has existed a subtle feeling of unity among members of each denomination, for they have felt

[49] James McHenry to Peggy [Mrs. James McHenry], August 8, 1794, in the McHenry Mss, University of Virginia, Charlottesville, Va.

[50] Reed, "Sermon," [Ms not paged], Reed Papers.

themselves to be partakers of a common conversion experience. An attempted "imitation of Christ" in their personal lives has characterized the private endeavor of thousands throughout the South who subscribe to the predominant evangelical tenets. The central thrust and goals of all three popular denominations were identical. Each contributed to the peculiarly nonabstract religious frame of mind that prevailed in the South: a personal, provincial, pietistic emphasis on the work of God in the hearts of individuals. These ideas have remained basically unchanged in the South until the mid-twentieth century.

Chapter Ten

Unity & Schism

The three major denominations shared their most important doctrines. Each accepted the idea of a perfect God who was the moral governor of the universe. Man was inherently and infinitely sinful, unable by himself to effect reconciliation with God. Being merciful, God sent a deliverer, his co-equal son, Jesus Christ, who assumed the sins of mankind and died to pay the punishment due them. By believing in him, men could escape spiritual death and be reunited with God. Yet because men were so depraved, only the divine grace of God could ignite the spark of faith. This generally accepted scheme of salvation possessed subtleties which only theorists appreciated. The sophisticated explanations of election, predestination, free will, and so on were neither completely understood nor preached by most ministers, even those of the Presbyterian persuasion.

These meticulous theological points were submerged in the ecumenical blend that the huge majority of ministers preached. They emphasized both the sinful condition of men and the love of God, and they tried to present in the most persuasive form the method of salvation spelled out in the Scriptures. This necessitated an emphasis on the bare essentials of sin and faith. Each of these major denominations knew that the others believed in the identical manner of achieving salvation for men. As long as competing denominations accepted the basis of this belief, no matter what their peculiar emphases on baptism or ecclesiology might be, they remained in essential unity. They believed that together they constituted the true church, a voluntary union of believers. Arguments and disputes could and did develop within the family of evangelicals, but the challenge of a group that did not accept the shared beliefs immediately welded the Baptists, Methodists, and Presbyterians together.

Unity and schism had more to do with theology and intellectual commitment than with petulancy, emotionalism, or simple frontier individualism. The evangelical concept of unity was based upon their ideas of the church and the centrality of conversion both to the individual and the theology. A striving for increased Christian unity was one of the persistent themes in the sermons of ministerial leaders. The "Christian" movement led by Barton W. Stone came from the ecumenical heritage within the popular southern churches. Yet the evangelical theology which so emphasized the individual and his conversion experience also led to schisms.

The institutional church was very weak, and when, for one reason or another, believers felt they were inching closer to the real heart of the Christian message, they felt free to separate from their denomination, since the particular denomination of which they were members was only a practical and voluntary means of spreading the gospel. If, in their evolving view, the denomination maintained erroneous doctrines, theirs was the right to withdraw and attempt to reform the generality of Christians. To the extent that their reformed attitudes differed from the commonly accepted beliefs, they met opposition. Theological differences were at the root both of schisms and the orthodox response to divisions within the church. A theological belief system has acted as a religious gyroscope in southern society. Within the system, there has been much motion, but it has remained pointed in the original direction, resisting change. Modification has nevertheless occurred, but it has not in reality changed the emphasis of southern Protestantism. It remained individualistic, provincial, conversion-oriented, and pietistic.

From his pulpit in North Carolina, Presbyterian minister Henry Pattillo urged his fellow believers in 1787 to accept the essential unity of all Christians. "Though the people of CHRIST are divided in name," he argued, "yet they are one in will and affections." In the period sometime in the future when the final judgment day was near, there would be a perfect union of all denominations. Before then, however, Pattillo reminded the faithful that "GOD over-rules the divisions among professors, for the general good."[1] Pattillo's recognition and expression of the inherent unity of all denominations did not lessen his support of his own denomination's doctrinal peculiarities and emphases. Terming himself "a *moderate*, but settled *Calvinist*," he wished there was less prejudice against Presbyterian doctrines. Yet most disagreement was based on exaggerated rumors of Calvinist fatalism. From his own experience Pattillo believed that "christians of different denominations will always love in proportion as they cultivate acquaintance; converse freely, on the great doctrines and duties in which they agree; worship God together, and avoid controversies."[2] Christians of each denomination could learn and be spiritually uplifted by occasionally attending the services of another group. The faith preached and lived was more important than minor theological differences. "To be sound in the

[1] Pattillo, *Sermons*, p. 51.
[2] Ibid., pp. viii–ix.

faith," concluded Pattillo, "is highly desirable; but to be pious in practice, is much more excellent. Christians may differ in points of faith, without sapping foundations, or endangering their future happiness: but virtue and holiness are uniformly the same, in all ages, nations, and professions; and indispensably necessary to the christian character."[3]

Another source for the Christian unity movement paradoxically developed from the James O'Kelly schism which rent the Methodist Church in 1792. O'Kelly and a group of supporters withdrew from the Methodist ranks because they questioned the hierarchical system of government whereby a bishop had complete control over circuits and the placement of ministers. Calling for a more democratic form of church government, the O'Kelly group organized what was temporarily called the Republican Methodist Church. This name was used at first in an attempt to stigmatize the dominant Asbury Methodists as aristocratic in polity. In 1794 these Republican Methodists met in conference in Surry County, Virginia, where they discussed the question of a permanent name. The Reverend Rice Haggard stood up with a copy of the New Testament in his hand and reportedly said: "Brethren, this is a sufficient rule of faith and practice, and by it we are told that the disciples were called *Christians*, and I move that henceforth and forever the followers of Christ be known as Christians simply." The members in attendance unanimously accepted Haggard's proposal. In addition, a North Carolina minister moved that the group accept the Bible as their church's creed, and his motion was similarly adopted.[4]

This emphasis on the Bible for the Christian standard in the place of human creeds, it was thought, would enable all the faithful to unite under the more authentic name of "Christians." O'Kelly became a great promoter of denominational union under this inclusive label. In several pamphlets he tried to articulate a central theme around which all men of faith could work together more closely. All denominational peculiarities should be removed, then Christians could convert the world. O'Kelly's movement was hindered by his views on the Trinity, which were heretical to the idea accepted by all southern evangelicals. In the words of an early Methodist historian, "[O'Kelly] affirmed that instead of distinct *persons* in the Godhead, the terms Father, Son, and Holy Ghost, were only intended to represent three *offices* of one glorious and Eternal Being."[5]

[3] Ibid., p. x.

[4] W. E. MacClenny, *The Life of Rev. James O'Kelly and the Early History of the Christian Church in the South* (Raleigh, N. C., 1910), p. 116.

[5] Leroy M. Lee, *The Life and Times of the Rev. Jesse Lee* (Richmond, Va., 1848), p. 285.

From our vantage point today, this difference seems minor. But for O'Kelly's opponents who remained in the regular Methodist church, it was "an error so profound" that compromise was impossible. The great majority of those who joined in the O'Kelly schism probably did so not for his theological statements, but solely in support of his stand against the Methodist episcopacy. Others no doubt were in warm accord with his hopes to unite all Christians. This aspect of the O'Kelly division contributed later, through the writings of Haggard, to the emerging "Christian" movement in Kentucky led by Barton W. Stone. But for the immediate situation in Virginia, O'Kelly's demands that others give up their characteristic beliefs, combined with his unorthodox interpretation of the Trinity, deprived him of most of his potential support. As Francis Asbury sardonically commented in 1799: "James O'Kelly hath sent out another pamphlet, and propounded terms of union himself, for the Presbyterians, Baptists, and Methodists. The Presbyterians must give up their confession of faith. The Baptists, if they open a more charitable door, adult dipping. The Methodists must give up the episcopacy, and form of discipline; renounce the articles of their religion, and the doctrine of the Trinity. I ask in turn, what will James give up? His Unitarian errors? . . . I am now more fully satisfied than ever that his book is not worthy of an answer."[6]

Despite the neither infrequent nor gentle disputes between the popular denominations, the ministers in their moments of introspection emphasized the need for increased unity and less disagreement. James McGready warned his congregation that "*Contention* is one of the most subtle and effective engines of hell."[7] Proponents of one doctrine on such relatively minor issues as baptism by immersion or sprinkling would harshly condemn those who accepted the other side. Christian understanding and forgiveness were forgotten in the rush to support one viewpoint. McGready urged care not to make one's creeds and confessions more important than Jesus Christ.[8] Holders of another view, as long as their essential beliefs were within the circle of commonly accepted evangelical theology, were to be recognized as fellow Christians. Division would limit the effectiveness of Christians in general to spread the gospel. Unnecessary contention and dogmatic loss of perspective led only to harmful divisiveness.

Of course, the theological basis for Christian unity and the urgings of liberal-minded ministers did not guarantee that congregations would in fact fulfill ecumenical ideals. But in spite of the many instances of narrow dog-

[6] Asbury, *Journal and Letters*, August 4, 1799, 2 : 204–5.
[7] McGready, *Posthumous Works*, 1 : 284.
[8] Ibid., 2 : 39–40.

matism, backbiting, and denominational squabbles, never did members of one of the three popular groups exclude members of the other from the Christian community. In theory and practice they accepted into the body of the church those of any of the three denominations, just so long as their beliefs did not differ in any major form from the generally accepted pietistic understanding of God, man, and sin. The obvious existence of petty disputes and factional feuding prompted unity-conscious ministers to speak out in defense of their catholic principles.

The various records for this era exhibit many instances when Christian unity and cooperation were more than theory. In periods of apparent crisis, such as the decade or so preceding the Great Revival and during the awakening enthusiasm which accompanied periods of revivalism, the incidence of mutual trust and love multiplied tremendously. There are numerous instances of the various denominations sharing a single church building. The Transylvania Presbytery, meeting in Lexington, Kentucky, in the spring of 1787, decided to call a convention for the coming July at David Rice's church. In addition to the normal Presbyterian attendance, they decided in that age of religious anxiety to "invite as members of said convention the ministers of other denominations together with one member from each church under their care, for the purpose of consulting whether any effectual measures can be adopted which may tend to suppress open vice in the district." [9]

Such interdenominational cooperation was not unusual. Though each church organization remained firmly individualistic in outlook, it did not hesitate to unite in an effort to maximize the church's ability both to gain individual converts and prod persons "on toward perfection." An elaborate example of denominational unity was practiced in Bedford County, Virginia, on the eve of the Great Revival. The Bedford cooperation was similar in form to hundreds of prayer and fast societies which developed as part of the faithful's response to religious indifference. Sharing a theology which emphasized the centrality of personal conversion and the unity of all believers, the popular denominations in the South often strove for such ecumenicity as that reported by Drury Lacy, a devout Presbyterian of Bedford:

> On Christmas day 1801 about 10 Baptist preachers, an equal number of Methodists, and 6 Presbyterian ministers met at Bedford court house in this state. The subject of the meeting was to discourse freely together on the subject of our differences, and to see if we could not adopt some terms for living more friendly than we have done, and even to commune together. . . . It was mutually agreed, that the ministers of the

[9] Transylvania Presbytery, "Minutes," in Sweet, *Presbyterians*, pp. 134–35.

different denominations should exercise all good offices towards each other, and preach in each others pulpits as occasions might serve. . . . It was further agreed, that the members of the respective societies might commune with the churches of the other denominations where they found a freedom to do so. . . . [and] That the members of the different denominations would watch over each other in brotherly love.[10]

There are numerous examples of personal friendship crossing denominational lines. In 1794 Barton W. Stone, then a part-time ministerial student of the Presbyterian faith, was appointed professor of languages at a newly founded and struggling Methodist academy near Washington, Georgia.[11] Indicative of the extent to which denominational differences had mellowed in the crisis years of the 1790s, the same Methodist who was superintendent of the academy, the Reverend Hope Hull, had in the 1780s been an extremely aggressive opponent of competing denominations. His caustic attacks against Baptist Henry Holcombe and others had earned him the epithet "the Broad Axe Preacher."[12] Yet now he assented to having a potential Presbyterian minister teach in his school.

Seasons of success, like periods of stress, increased cooperation. Tales of camp meetings commonly contain glowing accounts of ministerial unity —often dozens of clergy of each denomination shared in the pandamonium of preaching and singing. Yet out of the revival also came disagreement and schism. As they so often do, men's practices frequently fell short of their expressed ideals. Yet of more importance than denominational feuding after the Great Revival was the theological impetus the revival gave to newly developing denominations. Intellectual divisions brought forth distinctly different groups of Protestants. Unity and schism were the heritage of the Great Revival.

The common evangelical emphasis on the conversion of individual sinners lent to popular religion in the South a certain catholicity, but at the same time it contained the seeds of denominational splintering. If the primary role of the minister was to lead unbelievers to faith, then issues such as educational requirements for the clergy and strict doctrinal consistency were partially irrelevant. The matter of a felt conversion was so important that some of the most impassioned ministers attempted to make the experience more understandable. They wanted to remove all doctrinal doubts and

[10] "Extract of a Letter from Drury Lacy to Robert Ralston," in Woodward, *Surprising Accounts*, pp. 130–31.

[11] Stone, *Autobiography*, p. 129.

[12] Holcombe, *First Fruits*, pp. 45–48; Leah Townsend, *South Carolina Baptists 1670–1805* (Florence, S. C., 1935), pp. 50–51; and George Gilman Smith, *History of Methodism in Georgia and Florida, from 1785 to 1865* (Macon, Ga., 1877), p. 42.

Calvinist uncertainties from this turning event in peoples' lives. Mystery and mysticism should not be roadblocks in the pathway of decision. Similarly, they thought the only valid criteria ministers should have to meet were a warm zeal and living piety. Better a preacher should be sure of his conversion than his classics. These attitudes, which in effect reiterated the centrality of producing individual conversion, were able to prosper in the evangelical churches precisely because they were so individualistic, provincial, and practical-minded. There was no close supervision of expressed doctrines —instead ministers of each persuasion preached almost the same ideas about sin and man. Particularly during the revival season itself, many ministers set aside their meager doctrinal sermons and preached only the scheme of salvation. In such a situation of isolation and independence, it is small wonder that what the orthodox would call aberrations erupted in different parts of Kentucky.

Two men who began to shift intellectually in the revival were Richard McNemar and Barton W. Stone. They soon initiated separate religious movements of significance. Little is known of McNemar's earlier career, but there is evidence that Stone had always harbored questions about Presbyterian theology. Whereas the typical minister seems to have tacitly accepted the creed and never intellectually come to grips with the sticky points of election and faith, Stone from the beginning held reservations. He recorded in his autobiography that when he was asked during ordination if he accepted the Confession of Faith, he replied "aloud, so that whole congregation might hear, 'I do, as far as I see it consistent with the word of God.' "[13] Since no objection was made, Stone was duly ordained. Like all ministers, Stone and McNemar held the Bible to be the ultimate authority, but unlike others, they proceeded to measure the creeds against this standard. Their individual examination of the Scriptures soon resulted in a departure from the more commonly accepted views.

McNemar early evidenced an unusual interpretation of the ultimate meaning of the Great Revival, for he emerged as the foremost premillennialist of the entire era. By August 1801, during the Cane Ridge excitement, John Lyle noted that both McNemar and Stone were delivering unorthodox sermons which seemed to him unintelligible. Stone and McNemar told Lyle that they were preaching the true new gospel possessed only by them. It appeared that they were arguing that the Scriptures themselves caused people to repent, and hence the gospel itself brought pardon.[14] Their doctrines reexamined the whole evangelical scheme of God as the governor

[13] Stone, *Autobiography*, p. 148. See also pp. 149–54.
[14] Lyle, "Diary," August 8, 1801, p. 9.

of the moral universe and the necessity of his spirit to plant the seed of faith. Slight differences of emphasis were overlooked by the clergy of each denomination, but Stone and McNemar represented a significant deviation from the evangelical norm. They were in effect denying the basis of the common understanding of God, man, faith, and salvation. Like a geological fault in the rock of accepted doctrines, this emerging theological difference threatened to shake down all the foundations of Presbyterianism. As such, it could not be permitted to go unchallenged.

The severe threat of nonconformity had the effect of strengthening the Presbyterian emphasis on doctrinal purity.[15] Very soon McNemar, who often preached just across the river from Kentucky in the Ohio territory, and Stone, stationed in northern Kentucky, began attracting supporters. At this point, November 1801, the Washington Presbytery (which included both a portion of Kentucky and Ohio) met and charges were brought against McNemar. Among other things, "He was accused of holding 'dangerous and pernicious' ideas, deviating from the doctrines 'contained in the Confession of Faith of the Presbyterian Church,' embracing Arminian principles, and violating the discipline of the church."[16] When asked to defend himself, McNemar revealed his strict biblicism—he would be bound by nothing but the Scriptures. Because no one came forward to substantiate the charges against McNemar, the presbytery took no action against him, other than asking him to refrain from unorthodox preaching.

The "sticklers for orthodoxy" were not yet satisfied. They seemed to have realized that many of their co-workers had not always kept to the accepted path. The present instance of McNemar's independence of the creedal theology was the most extreme and could become contagious. As apparent danger had previously united the various denominations, so the Presbyterian clergy united in their defense of orthodoxy. On October 6, 1802, the Washington Presbytery met again, in Cincinnati, at which time a lay elder arose and complained of McNemar's propagation of false doctrines. The presbytery consequently submitted McNemar to a rather intense interrogation, deciding afterwards that his views were "essentially different from Calvinism,"[17] "though clothed in such expressions and handed out in such a manner, as to keep the body of the people in the dark, and lead them

[15] Stone, *Autobiography*, pp. 166–67.

[16] William Garrett West, *Barton Warren Stone: Early American Advocate of Christian Unity* (Nashville, Tenn., 1954), p. 54. Part of my discussion of the beginnings of the "Christian" movement parallels West's excellent monograph. See also MacLean, *Life and Labors of Richard McNemar*, pp. 8–9.

[17] Barton W. Stone, *History of the Christian Church in the West* (Lexington, Ky., 1956), p. 4.

insensibly into Arminian principles; which are dangerous to the souls of men, and hostile to the interests of all true religion." [18] Unexplainably the presbytery permitted McNemar to continue preaching at the six churches he had been serving—perhaps they thought that if they went too far in their somewhat irregular handling of him, they would antagonize the fiercely individualistic though still orthodox churches.

The newly formed Synod of Kentucky convened in Lexington on September 6, 1803. The Washington Presbytery turned over to the synod their case against McNemar and against the Reverend John Thompson, who in the spring of 1803 had been suspected of McNemarian tendencies. After careful examination, the synod upheld the presbytery's charges but reproved them for allowing McNemar to continue preaching. The synod vote was split along theological lines—the six members (including Stone) who were gravitating in the pro-McNemar direction voted nay; seventeen defenders of orthodoxy voted yes, and there was one abstention. The ministers who were of the same sentiment with McNemar recognized that through the process of "Presbyterial inquisition," no deviant from the straight party line was safe. The synod, in upholding what the majority honestly felt to be the true interests of religion, threatened the dissenters' position within the denomination. "We . . . plainly saw," wrote Stone, that the synod's action "not only involved the fate of McNemar and Thompson, but equally our own. We saw the arm of ecclesiastical authority raised to crush us, and we must either sink, or step aside to avoid the blow." [19]

During a short recess of the synod, five of the dissenters, including the two accused, consulted among themselves and unanimously decided to issue "a protest against the proceeding of [the] Synod in McNemar's case, and a declaration of our independence, and of our withdrawal from their jurisdiction, but not from their communion." [20] Their letter of separation, dated September 10, 1803, put an abrupt halt to the synod's regular proceedings. The synod then formed a committee composed of James Welsh, who had voted against the suspension of McNemar but remained in the synod, Matthew Houston, Joseph Howe, and David Rice to try to reclaim the separates. During the committee's conversation with the party, Matthew Houston decided to join them in separation from the synod. Rice, Howe, and Welsh

[18] Stone et al., *An Apology*, p. 14.

[19] Stone, *History of the Christian Church*, p. 5; and Stone, *Autobiography*, p. 168. West, *Barton W. Stone*, p. 56, lists the six who voted in favor of McNemar: Robert Marshall, James Welsh, Barton W. Stone, William Robinson, David Purviance, and Malcolm Worley.

[20] Stone, *Autobiography*, p. 168; and Stone, *History of the Christian Church*, p. 6.

were unsuccessful, and the Synod of Kentucky proceeded to suspend the signees of the letter from the Presbyterian Church for teaching subversive doctrines. The synod also declared the rebels' churches to be vacant. When the dissenters realized that the synod's decision was final, they accepted suspension from the synod but defended their connection with the Presbyterian Church. In late 1803, to signify their position, they constituted themselves into an independent entity under the name of the Springfield Presbytery.

Soon after the forming of their new organization, the members of the Springfield Presbytery replied to the synod's request that they express their criticism of the Confession of Faith. In a lengthy pamphlet published in January 1804, *An Apology for Renouncing the Jurisdiction of the Synod of Kentucky*, they outlined both their interpretation of the events leading up to their suspension and their theological objections to the Confession. They were probably correct in contending that the synod in its suspension of them had not proceeded strictly according to Presbyterian church law. In keeping with the voluntaristic concept of the church accepted by pietists throughout the South, they justified their own withdrawal in terms of a contractual theory of organizational authority reminiscent of the Lockean arguments of the Declaration of Independence. Moreover, the dissenters insisted that in the final analysis, the Bible—not the Confession of Faith— was the criterion for determination of theological legitimacy. In part they used as precedence the strong biblicism and theological liberalism of Henry Pattillo.[21] But the most important portion of the *Apology* was not the historical but the theological statement written by Stone.

Writing in 1827, Stone said that the schismatics were not preaching doctrines different from the accepted beliefs until sometime after their withdrawal and during the preparation of the *Apology*. His memory appears to have been at fault, for as early as August 1801 John Lyle detected theological deviations in the sermons of both Stone and Richard McNemar.[22] Doubtlessly these two leaders of the Springfield Presbytery worked out their theology in detail after 1801, because by January 1804 Stone could present a detailed summary of their beliefs. On several significant points the New Lights, as they were now being called,[23] departed substantially from the

[21] See the first portion of Stone et al., *An Apology*, esp. pp. 27ff. There is an excellent discussion of this section of the pamphlet in West, *Barton W. Stone*, pp. 62–75.

[22] Stone, *History of the Christian Church*, pp. 27–28; and Lyle, "Diary," August 8, 1801, p. 9.

[23] According to M'Nemar, *The Kentucky Revival*, p. 29, "these adopted a very different faith, and taught, as an important truth, that the will of God was made

commonly accepted evangelical understanding of how salvation was effected.

The important theological portion of the *Apology* was entitled "Compendious View of the Gospel." With this statement the growing New Light movement became publicly and recognizably distinct from the orthodox Presbyterian Church. Like all the other southern evangelicals, Stone believed that "mankind are depraved. . . . alienated from God, and prone to evil." Yet here the similarity ended. Whereas by the common evangelical's understanding, man was too depraved to have faith without the divine intervention of God's spirit, Stone vastly elevated man's role. Despite his miserable state outside of God, Stone wrote, man does possess "rational faculties, capable of knowing and enjoying God."[24] Here, as throughout his discussion, Stone was trying to work his way out of the Calvinistic system which somehow explained that only an elect few would be able to be saved by Jesus Christ's dying for man's sins because a faith sufficient to achieve salvation was possible only for those in whom God chose to make it possible. Stone's early awareness of this theological dilemma had obviously set his mind to work when freed from all traces of presbyterial supervision. The eventual result was a totally different scheme of salvation.

After declaring that through his rational processes man was able to know God, Stone proceeded to elaborate exactly how a saving knowledge was effected. In the first place, he argued, the idea that God only loved "the *elect world*" is patently false. Quoting page after page of scriptural text as documentation, he emphasized that "the *whole world* is the object of God's love, and that Christ is given to all without exception."[25] Jesus Christ died for all men's sins; all that is necessary, Stone insisted, is that men believe in him. Simple faith alone was sufficient to produce regeneration, wherein man was reconciled with God. Saving faith began before the spirit worked in the soul—this followed after faith in the process of regeneration. Faith was engendered in the individual through the testimony of the gospel. The scriptural record, Stone wrote, is convincing in itself—it contains the message ministers should preach. "God has revealed himself to us in his word"; man through his rational capacities is able to believe and hence receive regeneration and salvation by experiencing the unveiling of the biblical message through faith. Later Stone was to deny the substitutionary plan of salvation whereby men were saved because Jesus Christ died for their sins. In his view, Jesus' death was important because it morally influenced men

---

manifest to each individual who honestly sought after it, by an inward light, which shone into the heart. Hence they received the name of *New-Lights*."

[24] Stone et al., *The Apology*, p. 62.

[25] Ibid., pp. 64–65, and 66ff.

to consider more closely the testimony given in the Bible.[26] His death did not purchase men's salvation.

Very probably few of Stone's early supporters went as far as he did in theological exploration. Many no doubt simply accepted his dictum that the sinner could believe before the intervening effort of the spirit. However one thought this faith originated in the individual, for most people it simply meant belief in Jesus Christ's atoning death and God's love. In effect, Stone sought to make the matter of salvation more understandable and less mystical, less subject to the whims of predestination. But no sooner had Stone enunciated this revolutionary concept for his western congregations than the other leaders of the Springfield Presbytery led him and their common supporters further away from the parent Presbyterian Church. The Springfield Presbytery was to be short-lived, for Richard McNemar came to the conclusion that as an institutionalized body (in the sense that they belonged to a subdivision of the Presbyterian Church) they impeded the work of God. According to two contemporary New Lights, Robert Marshall and John Thompson, McNemar—who seems at this stage to have been the preeminent schismatic—composed a platform which pronounced the termination of their existence as the Springfield Presbytery.[27] The dissenter movement led by Stone and McNemar was entering a new phase.

During the months before and after the publication of the *Apology* in January 1804, the schismatics had been searching for a new theological set of beliefs. Led away from the ideas shared by most other evangelicals by their own independence of mind, they were open both to outside influence and their own creativity. At this juncture Rice Haggard joined their movement, injecting a vigorous emphasis on Christian unity.[28] Ten years before Haggard had stood in convention and urged James O'Kelly's Republican Methodists to accept the biblical name "Christians." Haggard undoubtedly convinced McNemar, a very impressionable man, of the correctness of such ecumenical views. Shortly McNemar, who was considered by his co-workers "to possess a high degree of piety, power, and great light in religion," began urging that "our bond of union was a carnal bond—that we ought to be

[26] Ibid., pp. 63–64, 78–81, 83–89, and passim. See also Stone, *Atonement. The Substance of Two Letters Written to a Friend* (Lexington, Ky., 1805), and *An Address to the Christian Churches in Kentucky, Tennessee, & Ohio on Several Important Doctrines of Religion* (Lexington, Ky., 1821).

[27] R. Marshall and J. Thompson, *A Brief Historical Account of . . . the Christian, or as it is Commonly Called, the Newlight Church* (Cincinnati, Ohio, 1811), reprinted in Levi Purviance, *Biography of David Purviance*, p. 256.

[28] Stone, *Autobiography*, p. 172.

united by no bond but Christian love—and that this delegated body stood full in the way of Christ, and the progress of the revival; which revival would run like fire in dry stubble, if our Presbytery was out of the way."[29]

Swayed by the influence of Haggard and McNemar, the New Lights came to believe that their existence as the Springfield Presbytery "savored," in Stone's words, "of a party spirit. With the man-made creeds we threw it overboard, and took the name Christian."[30] Rather generally coming to this conclusion, the New Lights in quick fashion published an important pamphlet by Haggard, *An Address to the Different Religious Societies on the Sacred Import of the Christian Name*, and issued a somewhat facetious statement written by McNemar, "The Last Will and Testament of the Springfield Presbytery."[31] The strong emphasis on Christian unity expressed therein was to dominate the direction of the mainstream New Light movement for decades.

Haggard argued that the disciples were called Christians in the early days of their faith; moreover, he insisted that the "church of Christ is *one body*, and one name is enough for the same body." The essential unity of all Christians made denominational partyism especially pernicious because it so often led to dispute and animosity. Christians should strive to unite under one name, accept the Bible as their one Confession of Faith, "consider themselves members one of another," and profess the "religion of Jesus Christ."[32] "The Last Will and Testament" restated many of Haggard's points in almost epigrammatic fashion and without his massive scriptural documentation. In it McNemar announced the voluntary suicide of the Springfield Presbytery and left its benefactors a series of theological advices:

> *Imprimis.* We will, that this body die, be dissolved, and sink into union with the body of Christ at large; for there is but one body, and one Spirit, even as we are called in one hope of our calling. . . .
> *Item.* We will, that the people henceforth take the Bible as the only sure guide to heaven. . . .
> *Item.* We will, that preachers and people cultivate a spirit of mutual forebearance; pray more and dispute less; and while they behold the signs

[29] Marshall and Thompson, *Brief Historical Account*, p. 256.

[30] Stone, *Autobiography*, p. 172.

[31] Haggard's pamphlet (Lexington, Ky., 1804) has been conveniently reprinted, with a preface by John W. Neth, Jr., in the Disciples of Christ Historical Society series, *Footnotes to Disciple History*, Number Four (Nashville, Tenn., 1954). "The Last Will and Testament of the Springfield Presbytery" is found reprinted in Stone, *Autobiography*, pp. 172–75.

[32] Haggard, *Sacred Import of the Christian Name*, pp. 13, 15, 17, 20–21, 26, and passim.

of the times, look up and confidently expect that redemption draweth nigh.[33]

Despite the unity and forbearance thus enjoined, the six co-signers of the unusual document were not to remain together long. McNemar himself had been peculiarly oriented toward premillennial expectations since at least 1801, and his chiliastic hopes had not diminished. The schism in the party of unionists began when they seemed to be nearing greatest proselytizing success. Just as the news of the tremendous revival meetings in Kentucky had filtered back to the seaboard South, it also had reached the Shaker settlement at New Lebanon, New York. The United Society of Believers, as they called themselves, had long looked for such a western awakening because their prophetess, Mother Ann Lee, had spoken of "the opening of the gospel in the western country." [34] The Shakers believed that the millennium had begun, for Jesus Christ had returned in the female form of Ann Lee. Consequently the miraculous reports from Kentucky seemed particularly auspicious to them. As a result, the New Lebanon church in late 1804 decided to send three missionaries westward "to visit the subjects of the revival, in that country, with a view to search out the state of their minds, and open the testimony of salvation to them." John Meacham, Benjamin S. Youngs, and Issachar Bates set forth in the dead of winter, January 1, 1805, beginning their "pedistrial [*sic*] journey of more than a thousand miles." [35] Arriving about the first of March, the trio conversed with revival veterans in northern Kentucky, then crossed the Ohio River and began spreading their message in the vicinity of Springfield, Ohio, which was ripe for religious experimentation.

To those who had broken away from the Presbyterian Church and had become seekers after a new synthesis of the Christian gospel, the zealous Shaker missionaries seemed a godsend. Barton W. Stone described them as "eminently qualified for their mission. Their appearance was prepossessing, their dress was plain and neat, they were grave and unassuming at first in

[33] Stone, *Autobiography*, pp. 173–74.

[34] [Calvin Green and Seth Y. Wells], *A Summary View of the Millennial Church, or United Society of Believers, Commonly Called Shakers* (Albany, N. Y., 1823), pp. 70–71. For a general view of the Shakers and their move West, see Edward D. Andrews, *The People Called Shakers: A Search for the Perfect Society* (New York, 1953); F. Gerald Ham, "Shakerism in the Old West" (Ph.D. diss., University of Kentucky, 1962); Marguerite F. Melcher, *The Shaker Adventure* (Princeton, N. J., 1941); Julia Neal, *By Their Fruits: The Story of Shakerism in South Union, Kentucky* (Chapel Hill, N. C., 1947); and Walter B. Posey, "The Shakers Move West," *Emory University Quarterly* 17 (Spring 1962): 38–45.

[35] [Green and Wells], *A Summary View*, p. 71.

their manners, very intelligent and ready in the Scriptures, and of great boldness in their faith." [36] Moreover, the Shakers could not have chosen a better time to gain converts, for, as Stone admitted, "Some of us were verging on fanaticism; some were so disgusted at the spirit of opposition against us, and the evils of division, that they were almost led to doubt the truth of religion in toto; and some were earnestly breathing after perfection in holiness." [37] Now that the New Lights had discarded a stabilizing creed and taken the Bible for their guide, ambiguity in doctrine grew commonplace. Marshall and Thompson, who were later to leave the movement and rejoin the parent Presbyterian Church, reported that the way had been "paved for every error." [38]

Into this situation of groping for understanding of the Scriptures, zeal for perfectionism, purity, and security of one's salvation, and—at least in the case of McNemar and several others—strong millennial hopes, the Shaker missionaries had come with great promise. "They informed us," wrote Stone, "that they had heard of us in the East, and greatly rejoiced in the work of God amongst us; that as far as we had gone we were right, but we had not gone far enough into the work; that they were sent by their brethren to teach the way of God more perfectly, by obedience to which we should be led into perfect holiness." [39]

The very first person to whom the Shakers revealed their message was Malcolm Worley,[40] a New Light who as a lay member of the Kentucky Synod in 1803 had voted against the suspension of McNemar and Thompson. Worley, along with McNemar and others, had through their millennial hopes come to have "Great expectations" of "something very great, to take place in the summer of 1805." [41] Worley listened cordially to the men with their promise of fulfillment and promptly accepted their doctrines. In short time McNemar, Matthew Houston, and John Dunlavy—all prominent in the New Light movement—professed belief in the Shaker testimony which offered "actual possession of . . . salvation." [42]

Stone now seemed to recognize that complete freedom to interpret the

---

[36] Stone, *Autobiography*, p. 184.

[37] Ibid., p. 187.

[38] Marshall and Thompson, *Brief Historical Account*, p. 257.

[39] Stone, *Autobiography*, pp. 184–85.

[40] [Green and Wells], *A Summary View*, p. 71.

[41] Ibid., and M'Nemar, *The Kentucky Revival*, p. 80. The latter half of McNemar's work is a lengthy section entitled "A Brief Account of the Entrance and Progress of What the World Call Shakerism, Among the Subjects of the Late Revival in Ohio and Kentucky."

[42] M'Nemar, *The Kentucky Revival*, p. 82.

Bible could lead to theological anarchism and religious irresponsibility. As the movement which he hoped would lead to Christian unity and a rational understanding of salvation appeared to be disintegrating, Stone became the foremost opponent of the Shaker inroads. "Never," he recorded, "did I exert myself more than at this time to save the people from this vortex of ruin."[43] The New Light movement which had begun with suspension had now come to a fork in the road. McNemar and others likeminded took the left, more radical road, leaving Stone alone as the leader of the more rational group bent on effecting universal Christian unity.

The pattern for the future was now set. With those most given to theological improvisation in the Shaker camp, Stone solidified his own doctrinal system and proceeded to formulate the tenets of the eventual "Christian" denomination.[44] Although in 1810 Robert Marshall and John Thompson withdrew and rejoined the Presbyterians because they had come to believe the lack of a firm creed invited fanaticism, the Stoneite movement gained in influence and prestige. The Shaker winnowing proved to be a blessing in disguise, for the remaining Stoneites were more stable as a result. In 1832 Stone effected a union between his "Christians" and Alexander Campbell's "Disciples of Christ," who were centered more in the East. By 1850 the combined "Christian" forces claimed a membership of almost 120,000.[45] Though the history of this later phase of the Stoneite movement is beyond the purview of this study, it is significant to note that Stone's understanding of Christian unity was in terms of the southern evangelical tradition. As his foremost biographer summed up this aspect of his life, "Stone's idea of Christian unity, though advanced for his time, failed to approximate the moderate ecumenical idea of church unity, because his stress was primarily on the individual. He failed, therefore, to

[43] Stone, *Autobiography*, p. 185; and [Green and Wells], *A Summary View*, pp. 71–73. Great animosity and violence was exerted against the Shakers, reminiscent of the treatment later accorded the Mormons—and for similar reasons.

[44] This point that the Shakers drew the most extreme elements away from the mainstream "Christian" movement is also made in an excellent work by Jerald Lee Kirkpatrick, "The Effect of the Shaker Conversions on the Christian Church in Kentucky and Ohio, 1805–1810" (B.A. thesis, Texas Christian University, 1967). A copy is in the Disciples of Christ Historical Society Library, Nashville, Tenn.

[45] Daniel Dorchester, *The Problem of Religious Progress* (New York, 1881), p. 539. For accounts of the progress of the Christian movement, see West, *Barton W. Stone*, chaps. 8–14; David Edwin Harrell, Jr., *Quest for a Christian America: The Disciples of Christ and American Society to 1866* (Nashville, Tenn., 1966); and Winfred E. Garrison and Alfred T. Degroot, *The Disciples of Christ: A History* (St. Louis, Mo., 1948).

think of unity in terms of broad social groups. Certainly, the concept of institutional unity was not in his thinking."[46] Southern religion remained provincial, individualistic, and anti-institutional.

The McNemar-Stone schism had centered in northern Kentucky and southern Ohio, but the revival had serious repercussions for the Presbyterian Church in the Cumberland region of Kentucky as well. More was involved here than simple frontier emotionalism reacting to staid eastern church polity. The beginning of the rupture traced back to Old Side-New Side divisions that split the colonial Presbyterian Church in the midst of the Great Awakening. Subsequent events in southwestern Kentucky must be seen in this historical context. Even more important, the Cumberland dispute came to a head after the Kentucky Synod had become embroiled in the McNemar case. With obvious theological anarchy and improvisation at work to the north, the synod was not about to brook any kind of deviation in its southern region which might result in another schism. These factors largely determined the outcome of the Cumberland situation.

It was in this region of Kentucky that the Great Revival had begun under the forces of James McGready, William Hodge, William McGee, and John Rankin. Remarkable awakenings resulted from their efforts in 1800, and the following year their success showed few signs of diminishing. As McGready wrote in the fall of 1801 to his mentor John McMillan in Pennsylvania, "At our Sacraments, multitudes still attend from a great distance, and the work commonly goes on day and night, as it did during the summer before."[47] According to another account, "the cries of the people for more preaching were incessant"; the congregations had become so numerous and scattered that the available supply of ministers could not meet the demand.[48] McGready and his co-workers were in the prorevivalistic strain of Presbyterianism; their theological heritage could be traced back from David Caldwell and John McMillan through Samuel Davies, directly to the Pennsylvania log colleges of Great Awakening fame. True to this tradition, the Cumberland revivalists sought an expedient way to supply the ministerial shortage and prevent the revival from dying.

[46] West, *Barton W. Stone*, pp. 210–11.

[47] McGready to McMillan, November 18, 1801, Ms in the library of Pittsburgh Theological Seminary, Pittsburgh, Pa.

[48] *A Circular Letter Addressed to the Societies & Brethren of the Presbyterian Church Recently under the Care of the Council of the Late Cumberland Presbytery, In Which There Is a Correct Statement of the Origin, Progress, and Termination, of the Difference, Between the Synod of Kentucky, and the Former Presbytery of Cumberland* (Russellville, Ky., 1810), p. [2].

David Rice suggested a practical and not unprecedented solution: the local presbytery should make use of unordained "exhorters" and catechists (ministers-to-be) to perform semi-clerical roles.[49]

Four such men subsequently presented themselves at the fall meeting of the presbytery "for the service of the church." Considering the unusual needs and opportunities, the Transylvania Presbytery at this time, October 9, 1801, appointed the four—Finis Ewing, Alexander Anderson, Samuel King, and Ephraim McClean—"to the business of exhortation & catechising."[50] With this event the opposition to the revival forces again made itself felt. Upon first coming to Kentucky, McGready had encountered resistance from James Balch, of the anti-revivalistic Old Side strain of Presbyterianism. In his letter of November 1801 to John McMillan, McGready said that "the most unheard of falsehoods" were being circulated against the revival leaders. The "Balchites," he wrote, had been seeking to break up the religious services and put an end to the "blessed revival."[51] The determination of the opposition gained strength as the revival prospered.

When, at the next fall meeting of the Transylvania Presbytery, October 8, 1802, Anderson, Ewing, and King were licensed to preach after having been examined by the presbytery and petitioned by congregations to fill vacancies, five conservative members dissented from the majority decision. In addition to James Balch, these five included Thomas B. Craighead, a tenacious personal enemy of Finis Ewing.[52] Only a week after this development—and before any members present could journey to Lexington —the Synod of Kentucky held its first meeting and promptly divided the present Transylvania Presbytery into the Transylvania and Cumberland presbyteries. The newly created Cumberland Presbytery had ten ministers, equally divided between pro- and anti-revivalist factions.[53] In subsequent

[49] Ibid., and Davidson, *Presbyterian Church in Kentucky*, p. 70. Such men could not, of course, perform any sacramental functions or officially preach.

[50] Transylvania Presbytery, "Minutes," in Sweet, *Presbyterians*, p. 186. The original minutes are in the library of the Louisville Presbyterian Seminary, Louisville, Ky.

[51] McGready to McMillan, November 18, 1801, Ms in the library of the Pittsburgh Theological Seminary.

[52] Transylvania Presbytery, "Minutes," in Sweet, *Presbyterians*, pp. 187–89; Ben Melton Barrus shows the personal animosity between Ewing and Craighead in "A Study of the Factors Involved in the Origin of the Cumberland Presbyterian Church: 1800–1813" (Ph.D. diss., Vanderbilt University, 1964). Barrus, it seems, overemphasizes the educational issue and fails to study the Cumberland split in the total context of the revival.

[53] Synod of Kentucky, "Minutes," October 15, 1802, in Sweet, *Presbyterians*, p. 310.

meetings of the presbytery, the pro-revival forces of McGready attended in greater numbers, and gradually they gained the upper hand. In accord with their views, the revivalists ordained more exhorters to facilitate the spread of the gospel. At the very first meeting of the new presbytery— Balch was absent—James Haw, "formerly a regular minister in the Republican Methodist Church," was received and allowed a seat. Seeking to promote the revival, the presbytery established Methodist-like "circuits" supplied by licentiates not yet ordained as ministers.[54] To the Old Side, anti-revival Presbyterians, the situation clearly seemed to be getting out of hand.

Not a single member from the embroiled Cumberland Presbytery attended the 1803 synod meeting in Lexington. The issue was forced, however, at the next synod in 1804 held at Danville, Kentucky. Thomas B. Craighead had addressed a letter to the synod outlining the charges of the anti-revival wing of the Cumberland Presbytery.[55] He apparently warned of irregularities in licensing ministers, in ignoring educational requirements, and in accepting for ordination those who professed or implied certain reservations toward the Confession of Faith. None of these charges were really unprecedented in the Presbyterian Church. There had been other instances in which educational requirements were lifted, ministers (like Stone) had placed the Scriptures above the creed, and irregularities had crept into presbyterial functions. But these were not normal times for the Presbyterian Church in Kentucky.

The memory of the Richard McNemar affair was fresh in the minds of the synod participants. Just the year before the synod had been handed the case of McNemar's theological aberrations. Synodical investigation had only resulted in a rupture in the church. McNemar, Stone, and three others had organized an independent presbytery, published an *Apology* which contained seriously heretical beliefs, dissolved their presbytery, and at present were promoting church unity on the basis of the Bible alone—they had rejected the Confession and the church polity it outlined. The Kentucky Synod was in no mood to accept quietly another case of possible deviation. The Presbyterian Church was rapidly solidifying its position, tightening its requirements, squelching all internal subversion. "Calvinism is a complete and compact system," summed up a later spokesman of orthodoxy in Kentucky, "and, as in a well-constructed arch, every separate doctrine is a key-

[54] Cumberland Presbytery, "Minutes," April 5, 1803, in Sweet, *Presbyterians*, pp. 283–84; *A Circular Letter Addressed to the Late Cumberland Presbytery*, pp. 4–5.

[55] Synod of Kentucky, "Minutes," October 22, 1804, in Sweet, *Presbyterians*, pp. 328–29.

stone, which cannot be abstracted from without endangering the whole." [56] Finis Ewing, a central figure in the dispute, agreed that it was "only by confounding the revival with the New Light excitement—against the errors of which these good men [comprising the synod] were battling with all their might—that the anti-revivalists gained their full confidence; and when this was done, an extension of their abhorrence of the latter to the former also was the natural consequence." [57]

Frightened, perturbed, united, the orthodox center of the Kentucky Presbyterian Church thoroughly overreacted to what in reality was a minor incident in the Cumberland Presbytery. The synod immediately constituted a committee composed of five conservative members to attend the next meeting of the feuding presbytery. Only one committeeman attended, and the presbytery denounced the rather high-handed presumption of the synod in investigating them. At the next meeting of the synod in October 1805, again at Danville, another committee examined the Cumberland records and found them "extremely defective." [58] The synod proceeded to appoint still another committee, more conservative than the first, to inquire into the proceedings of the Cumberland Presbytery. A sense of urgency motivated the committee and its sponsors. "The object before the Synod was to suppress the growing irregularities in the west," so it wrote in its official defense of the occasion, "and yet save one of her Presbyteries from disruption and final ruin." [59]

Hence the synod moved with a heavy hand to quiet the possibility of another schism, and the presbytery, accustomed to local control over such matters as ordination of ministers and supervision of their theology, bucked the inquisitional attitude of the synod. The succeeding years of the continuing squabble were marked by charge and countercharge, with each side growing more self-righteously indignant at the other's obstinacy. There are no indications that in the beginning the revival party ever considered withdrawing from the synod's control. But the insistence of the synod that it had the power to dictate presbyterial matters had the effect of driving the revival leaders away from the constituted authority of the Presbyterian Church. Synodical overreaction led to extralegal committees and attempted

---

[56] Davidson, *Presbyterian Church in Kentucky*, p. 256.

[57] Cossitt, *Finis Ewing*, p. 117.

[58] Synod of Kentucky, "Minutes," October 17, 1805, in Sweet, *Presbyterians*, pp. 332–33.

[59] *A Brief History of the Rise, Progress, and Termination of the Synod of Kentucky Relative to the Late Cumberland Presbytery* (Lexington, Ky., 1823), p. 5, typescript, in library of the Historical Foundation of the Reformed and Presbyterian Churches, Montreat, N. C.

examinations. After the presbytery became defensive and refused to submit, the eventual schism was predetermined.

When it finally became obvious in 1809 that further rigidity on the part of the presbytery would lead to its destruction as a constituent of the Presbyterian Church, several of the leading revivalists, including William Hodge and James McGready, reluctantly returned to the orthodox fold. Still others refused to submit, so firm were they in their belief that the synod had drastically and dictatorially overstepped its bounds. For this group, preeminent among whom were Finis Ewing and Samuel McAdow, freedom for theological deviation was less important than the old freedom of salutary neglect in doctrinal matters. Persistent in their contention that "there are a number of ministers who are kept in the bosom of the presbyterian church, who have deviated infinitely more from the confession than we have done,"[60] the healthy remnant of the Cumberland revivalists in the New Side tradition formally broke away from the synod, declared their independence in 1810, and organized the Cumberland Presbyterian Church. In 1816 the new denomination adopted a confession of faith and a discipline. With a relaxed emphasis on educational requirements, a zealous commitment to evangelism, and a softening of the Calvinist notion of election, the Cumberland Presbyterian Church enjoyed moderate success. By 1850 its membership approximated 75,000—largely the result of orthodox overreaction to religious improvisation.[61]

So it happened that the Great Revival, which momentarily held forth great promise of Christian unity, by 1810 had resulted in three distinct schisms in the Presbyterian Church. The Stoneite "Christian Church," the Shakers' expansion into the West, and the Cumberland Presbyterian Church in part originated in the individualistic, provincial, anti-institutional character of southern evangelical religion. Practical freedom from close theological supervision created and made difficult to stop the individual nature of Presbyterianism in particular. When orthodoxy attempted to clamp down, independence was stimulated. The very factors that hinted of increased unity resulted in a further factionalization of Christianity. Yet except for the Shakers, who were just too far left of the mainstream, the

---

[60] *A Circular Letter Addressed to the Late Cumberland Presbytery*, p. 13. For a detailed account of the evolution of this church, see Posey, *Presbyterian Church in the Old Southwest*, pp. 32–38; W. B. McDonald, *History of the Cumberland Presbyterian Church* (Nashville, Tenn., 1888); Richard Beard, *Brief Biographical Sketches of Some of the Early Ministers of the Cumberland Presbyterian Church* (Nashville, Tenn., 1867); and R. V. Foster, *The Cumberland Presbyterian Church*, in *The American Church History Series*, 13 vols. (New York, 1904), Vol. 11.

[61] Dorchester, *Problem of Religious Progress*, p. 532.

various churches could still unite in the face of apparent danger. The accepted set of beliefs which admitted one to the southern church had been slightly expanded. But the Presbyterian Church, especially in Kentucky, grew much more rigid and illiberal. It intended to suffer no more losses from what it considered misapplied freedom. As a result, Presbyterianism—already the most conservative of the southern evangelical churches—became even more so.[62]

[62] Cf. Neils Henry Sonne, *Liberal Kentucky, 1780–1828* (New York, 1939), pp. 18–19, who wrote, "A tendency exists at the present time to regard the early Presbyterians of Kentucky as liberals. No greater mistake could be made. . . . The story of Kentucky Presbyterianism is the story of the ruthless destruction of every vestige of independent theological thought which might arise among the clergy." This characterization is valid after 1804 or 1805.

Chapter Eleven

The Economic & Political Thought of Southern Revivalism

It is difficult to believe that the common man of the South, who possessed few slaves, little education, and a provincial outlook, could have held even the rudiments of a conscious economic and political theory. His was largely a world of planting, reaping, and hunting; of the ax and plow; of monotony and loneliness. For the great majority the only acquaintance they had with abstractions and theories was through the sermons of the local minister or itinerant preacher. In an age of almost negligible newspaper circulation, only lawyers, merchants, large commercial planters, and politicians clustered in state capitals were interested in any but purely local affairs. Their concern with politics and economics was more a matter of status and location (within the zone of commercial farming or not), than of governmental philosophy; of provincial rather than national interests. Intricately spun webs of political theory were the preoccupations of planter-philosophers like Jefferson and John Taylor of Caroline. The thoughts of such men did transcend local needs. But these were not common men, and theirs was not a religious outlook. Pietistic revivalism was not the seedbed of politico-economic reform.

Certainly, however, even the most isolated farmer had some kind of vague awareness that political and economic issues existed. But for him these were not theoretical statements of governmental policy toward which he maintained a solid understanding and an obstinate position. If he voted at all—and the chances are he did not—he voted strictly according to his local, pragmatic interests. Usually he followed the lead of the several influential and respected men in his county. The South was overwhelmingly rural, and despite class and sectional differences, it was remarkably homogeneous politically. Most people were Jeffersonians: planters, small farmers, Episcopalians, deists, and evangelicals, they all generally voted Republican. Religion does not seem to have been an important, much less decisive factor in party affiliation. There definitely was no monolithic religious position as such on either political or economic matters.

To whatever extent common people apprehended their workaday world intellectually, they probably did so in the pietistic formulations of their evangelical ministers. Preachers on occasion spoke out against waste and prodigality. They warned against endangering one's soul by putting a disproportionate interest in wealth. Only rarely did clergymen articulate the barest essentials of an economic philosophy. Their preeminent concern was saving souls. In a tangential manner economics came under their focus, and whenever it did so, it was wholly subsidiary to their primary purpose. They emphasized that economic considerations among the populace should be subordinated to the individual's real concern, which was living in proper relationship to God. Economics was a reality that had to be met, not a matter of state or national policy. The pietist concerned himself with the Blackstoneian concept of "domestic economy"—the business affairs of a household. He was too individualistic and anti-institutional to theorize about how the government should stand on matters of "political economy."

In their comparatively few references to economics, the revivalists reveal that they were not committed to poverty in and for itself. Ultimately economic considerations were secondary. "Happy the man," wrote an early Baptist historian, "though poor in this world, who is rich in faith and an heir of the kingdom of heaven."[1] Because poverty seemed to offer fewer temptations and distractions, it was thought better for the soul. Affluence was attacked only for its propensity to draw one's attentions away from religion. Nevertheless, this was a severe criticism of wealth for the majority of southern pietists.

The ideal economic situation was to be between the two extremes of destitution and opulence. Poverty itself was not a virtue. Henry Holcombe expressed this belief in a funeral oration for one of his deceased members: "He enjoyed the enviable medium betwixt penury and affluence."[2] The churches reminded those who had made some progress toward "honorable affluent and happy situations in life" that God was the author of their success. He should be given thanks for allowing temporal happiness.[3] Moreover, the clergy pointed out that Christian habits gave believers an advantage over others in acquiring a comfortable position in this life: "where there is no inequality in other things, the habits of diligence, sobriety, punc-

---

[1] William Fristoe, *A Concise History of the Ketocton Baptist Association* (Staunton, [Va.], 1808), p. 154.

[2] Henry Holcombe, *A Sermon, Occasioned by the Death of Mr. Charles Bealer* (Charleston, S. C., 1793), p. 9.

[3] Furman, ed., *History of the Charleston Association of Baptist Churches*, "On Religious and Civil Duties—1800," p. 147.

tuality, and economy, in a religious man, commonly give him an ascendency over dissimilar characters, in point of wealth." [4]

Since the moderation characteristic of a pious life contributed to financial betterment, the Charleston Baptist Association urged that there was no excuse for any Christian not gaining the minimum property necessary for voting. [5] It is significant here both that the association had to promote political participation and that it even made a public statement relating to politics. Only in the coastal regions of South Carolina and Georgia was the Baptist Church influential among the propertied classes. From this region, then, one would expect clerical statements on politics and economics—and, to some extent, this expectation is justified. Henry Holcombe, who preached first in the sea island district of South Carolina and later at Savannah, was perhaps the leading lowland Baptist minister and also the most outspoken on economics and politics. [6] Even so, issues of this kind represent a very minute portion of his published writings.

The foremost concern of the ministers was the conversion of unbelievers and the prosperity of the kingdom of God. Economics was considered only to the extent that it affected this larger and more important consequence—salvation. Certainly God through his mercy and love did not restrict Christians from worldly success. Neither did he make redemption available as a reward for those who found no material prosperity. In a very real sense, economics was irrelevant to the Christian plan of salvation. William Fristoe thus explained the attitude of a Virginia Baptist Association toward "worldly circumstance": "Not that we suppose that poverty in itself is any qualification for embracing the gospel, or the reception of grace, neither does their being poor, lay the Almighty under obligation to bestow his grace upon them—neither do we suppose, a person being rich in this world, though surrounded with the most valuable property, can be a preventative to their conversion, if God should see fit in his good pleasure to operate on them by his unfrustrable [*sic*] grace." [7]

It seems that prosperity was accepted when it was the silent by-product of hard work, moderation, and sobriety. In other words, if living an exemplary Christian life gained for a person not only eternal life but also a comfortable life, then so much the better. It was not wise, however, to

[4] Holcombe, *Primitive Theology*, p. 169.

[5] Furman, ed., *History of the Charleston Association of Baptist Churches*, "On the regard, due from Christians, to Civil and Political Interests—1796," pp. 110–11.

[6] John B. Boles, "Henry Holcombe, A Southern Baptist Reformer in the Age of Jefferson," *Georgia Historical Quarterly* 54 (Fall 1970): 381–407.

[7] Fristoe, *History of Ketocton Baptist Association*, p. 149.

make worldly success a predominant goal in life. Here was the danger that evangelicals saw in wealth. So often, they argued, prosperity turns the soul from piety. For example, although a Presbyterian divine argued that a man rightly worked to provide his family some degree of "temporal comfort," he warned: "It is doubtful whether any christian parent ought to form and attempt to execute plans having for their chief object an independent fortune either for himself or for his children. All agree that such a spirit cherished in a christian minister is utterly incompatible with his character."[8]

The pursuit of prosperity conflicted with the avid desire of evangelical pietists "to go on to perfection." It seemed irrefutable that although there was nothing evil about wealth in itself, the urge for it was corrupting. It led one away from religious devotion. James McGready spoke of the effect of materialism on men: "The world is in all their thoughts by day and night. All their conversation is of corn and tobacco, of land and stock. The price of merchandise and negroes are inexhaustible themes of conversation. But for them the name of Jesus has no charms; and it is rarely mentioned unless to be profaned."[9]

As early as 1783 David Rice despaired of Kentucky, for he foresaw that the rampant land office business would submerge much of the potential religious life. "I saw," he wrote, "that the spirit of speculation was flowing in such a torrent that it would bear down every weak obstacle that stood in its way."[10] Robert B. Semple observed that "Nothing is more common, than for the increase of riches, to produce a decrease of piety. Speculators seldom make warm christians."[11] David Barrow, finding it impossible on his exhausted Virginia farm to meet his debts, provide for his family, and offer the hospitality which a minister should, decided to move to Kentucky. But he was careful to make clear that he was not chasing materialistic aspirations. I am not leaving, he wrote, "to accumulate great stores of wealth for my children. For we are informed by the lip of inspiration, *That they who will be rich fall into temptation, and a snare, and into many foolish and hurtful lusts, which drown men in destruction and perdition.*"[12]

Francis Asbury, riding through South Carolina in the fall of 1801, just before the Great Revival revitalized the region, noted that he could

---

[8] Bishop, *Outline of the History of the Church*, p. 65.

[9] McGready, *Posthumous Works*, 1:165.

[10] Quoted in Bishop, *Outline of the History of the Church*, p. 66.

[11] Semple, *A History of Baptists in Virginia*, pp. 35–36.

[12] Barrow, *Circular Letter*, p. 4. See also Fristoe, *History of Ketocton Baptist Association*, pp. 150–51.

not "record great things upon religion in this quarter; *but cotton sells high. I fear there is more gold than grace.*"[13] In numerous such statements, the southern pietists gave evidence of their concern with one's personal relationship to God. Too much interest in money and prosperity squeezed religious considerations out of daily life. For devotees of pietistic religion, conversion was a continuing, everyday event. The urge for perfection, for an imitation of Christ, was strong. Such a pietistic mind could hardly coexist with a business mind.

Perhaps if one were already religious, he could somehow adjust to prosperity.[14] But still one had to be careful of the temptations of wealth. As with everything God provided, the revivalists thought, prosperity—good in itself—could be misused by fallible man and serve as an enemy of true religion.

Ministers early recognized that the level of affluence affected receptivity to and choice of religion. The "*poor . . . will,* the rich *may possibly,* hear the truth," wrote Asbury.[15] Henry Holcombe observed that "the important concerns of religion have been conducted, with a few honorable exceptions, through the instrumentality of the lower and middle classes of society."[16]

Social standing had some effect on religious affiliation. The economic differentiation between the three dominant denominations was nowhere near as pronounced in 1800 as it was to be several decades later. But even by this period, ministers were aware of subtle class differences. In ascending order of affluence were the Methodists, Baptists, and Presbyterians, although at this date local circumstances often shifted the ranking.

The Methodists appear to have been particularly aware of the status of those to whom they were most attractive. On several occasions Asbury remarked that "it is our duty to condescend to men of low estate"; at another date he wrote that "the poor . . . are the people we are more immediately called to preach to." Once in coastal South Carolina, where the old Regular Baptists were powerful among the wealthy, he remarked that the Baptists "take the rich; and the commonalty and the slaves fall to us."[17]

In most localities, the Baptists too were drawn from "the common people" who were "low in circumstances [of] the world," according to the Reverend William Fristoe. "In a general way those among us who

---

[13] Asbury, *Journal and Letters*, October 24, 1801, 2:311.

[14] Ibid., October 10, 1785, 1:497.

[15] Ibid., June 19, 1789, 1:601.

[16] Holcombe, *First Fruits*, p. 213.

[17] Asbury, *Journal and Letters*, January 5, 1805; March 5, 1797; and June 29, 1804; all in 2:456, 122, and 423–24.

have been wrought upon under the preaching of the gospel, and professed conversion to Christ, have been of the mediocrity, or poorer sort among the people—instances have been very few, of persons being called who were rich in this world." [18]

The Presbyterians represented the class above the Methodists and Baptists. Although a Methodist could say of them, "They were the aristocracy and we the poor people," the Presbyterians in general were not the wealthiest planters and merchants. [19] In most instances these remained in the feeble Episcopal Church. In later years, however, the Presbyterians gained increasing strength from this quarter.

Because social stratification was already present, the Methodists, Baptists, and even Presbyterians were quick to mention when those of wealth, education, or position attended divine services or a camp meeting. Such unusual attendance always made news, and the Methodists and Baptists in particular seized the chance to enhance their own reputations by publicizing the worthies who worshiped with them.

But the most common economic observation made by the revivalists was that poverty was congenial to religious commitment. This of course in part represented a valid sociological fact; it emphasized the otherworldly aspirations of southern pietists; and it probably bespoke some degree of self-rationalization. The huge majority of churchgoers were of the common sort, habituated to work and poverty. Very likely the clergy ministered to their acceptance of a less-than-comfortable life by minimizing the importance of affluence in the long run. This may have been an unconscious method of defusing any possible class antagonisms, for doubtless such sermons as that preached by George Reed lessened the urge for economic betterment.

> Since all we have is ye [the] gift of God, let this teach us, "in what ever state we are, therewith to be content." "Our heavenly Father knoweth what we have need of before we ask him." . . . It were as easy for him to give you large estates, as to supply you with ye bread you eat, or to continue ye breath in your nostrils; but he sees poverty best for you; he sees prosperity might prove your ruin; therefore he has appointed you ye

[18] Fristoe, *History of Ketocton Baptist Association*, pp. 57 and 148.

[19] Jacob Young, *Autobiography of a Pioneer, Or the Nativity, Experience, Travels, and Ministerial Labors of Jacob Young* (Cincinnati, Ohio, [1857]), p. 138. John M. Wilson, a Presbyterian missionary to a district of North Carolina in 1794, reported that "the higher rank of people" looked down upon the Baptists, and although "these generally call themselves Episcopalians, . . . they would not be backward to favor the presbyterian interest." Synod of the Carolinas, "Minutes," "Missionary Report of John M. Wilson," March 6, 1794.

honour of being in this respect comformable to our Lord, who, when on earth, "had not where to lay his head." [20]

Hence for the revivalists of the South, economic considerations were not a major issue in their lives. They were too individualistic, too anti-institutional, too provincial in their thinking for economics to mean more than the very personal finances of actual and potential believers. For them economics did not transcend the individual level to assume a role in governmental decision making. There was at this time no evangelical position on banking, economic growth, tariffs, or manufacturing. These were matters simply beyond the purview of their primary concern—effecting individual conversions and nurturing Christians in the life of Jesus Christ. Economics was of consequence only to the extent that it affected one's religious development.

There is no solid evidence that revivalistic religion was a spur either to political philosophizing or political participation. There is no indication that religious beliefs were a predominant force in political decisions. If anything, pietistic revivalism on the individual level decreased concern with politics. Indeed, an examination of voting results reveals a surprising lack of public participation. The state of Virginia, the most populous and perhaps the most influential state in 1800, is a case in point. With a long history of some degree of representative government, a remarkable kaleidoscope of gifted political leaders, and a provincial stake in the Jefferson-Adams election, voter response was small. This had been a bitterly contested, highly publicized campaign. The Republican majority in Virginia operated a statewide machine, with a "corresponding committee" in practically every county. The General Assembly's "Committee on Elections" provided publicity, advice, and printed ballots.[21] Nevertheless, only 27,000 votes were cast out of a total white population of over a half million.

Several factors explain these figures. For one thing, women, who played an active part in the religious life of every locality, were not eligible to vote. Less than a third of the white males were old enough to vote, and

[20] Reed, "Sermon," unpaged Ms in Reed Papers.

[21] See the Circular Letter sent to Charles Wingfield, an Episcopalian of Albemarle County, by the Committee on Election, Charles Wingfield Ms, Alderman Library, University of Virginia, Charlottesville, Va. See also Noble Cunningham, *The Jeffersonian Republicans: The Formation of Party Organization, 1789–1801* (Chapel Hill, N. C., 1967), pp. 149–54, 194–95; and Harry Ammon, "The Jeffersonian Republicans in Virginia: An Interpretation," *Virginia Magazine of History and Biography* 71 (April 1963): 153–67.

of these, property requirements prevented some from political participation. Computing from census figures and voting results, it appears that approximately 28 percent of the adult white males voted in the Jefferson-Adams election. If one makes the assumption that the church age population consists of all those of both sexes over ten years of age, then only 8 percent of the Virginia population old enough to have some kind of religious affiliation voted.[22] So religious life necessarily had a modest impact on politics.

There is much impressionistic evidence to suggest that southern evangelicals took little interest in or had little knowledge of political activities. The biographer of David Caldwell, a prominent North Carolina Presbyterian who educated many ministers in his academy (McGready had been a close associate of his), wrote that although Caldwell was chosen by his county to attend the constitutional ratification convention of 1788, he took a very small part in the debates. He possessed little knowledge of the complexities of government because of his rural background and almost total preoccupation with church work. He was such a localist that it was only with hesitation that he voted for the federal constitution.[23] Another Presbyterian minister, writing from Virginia in the midst of the 1787–1789 revival and in the very year of the Virginia contest over ratification, remarked that he had heard "Not a word scarcely about politics; but all religion in public and private. They run far and near to sermons, sacraments, and societies."[24]

On several occasions Francis Asbury indicated that neither he nor the denomination he represented took much interest in the political world. Visiting the nation's capital in 1806, he wrote in his *Journal*: "congress does not interest me: I am a man of another world, in mind and calling."[25] A year before this statement, Asbury had again denied James O'Kelly's accusation that the Methodists were dictatorial and power-hungry: "The Methodists have but two of their very numerous society members of Congress; and until these democratic times [1805] we never had one. I ques-

---

[22] See the excellent discussion of early political practices in Virginia in Charles G. Sydnor, *American Revolutionaries in the Making* [original title, *Gentlemen Freeholders*] (New York, 1962), chapt. 3 and Appendixes 1 and 2. I have computed the voting percentage from the figures given by W. Edwin Hemphill, " 'In a Constant Struggle': How and Why Virginians Voted for Thomas Jefferson in 1800," *Virginia Cavalcade* 2 (Spring 1953): 14–15; and the U. S. Census for 1800, *Return of the Whole Number of Persons Within . . . the United States*, pp. 2H–4H.

[23] Caruthers, *Life of David Caldwell*, pp. 246–48.

[24] Robert Smith to "a Lady in Philadelphia," October 26, 1788, reprinted in Foote, *Sketches of Virginia*, 1: 422.

[25] Asbury, *Journal and Letters*, March 5, 1806, 2: 497.

tion if, in all the public legislative bodies in the seventeen United States, there are more than twenty members Methodists. No; our people are a very independent people, who think for themselves; and are as apt to differ in politics (so do the preachers), and divide at the hustings, as those of any other denomination; and surely, they are not seekers of the offices of this world's profit or honour." [26]

Another Methodist itinerant, Henry Boehm, wrote a telling comment on the Methodist political position. He relates in his autobiography that in 1801, when the General Conference met in Philadelphia, there was "great political excitement" in the air. He was pressured to make a stand on the issues, but refused because he saw that political disputes could disrupt the church. He consulted with Asbury's equal, Bishop Richard Whatcoat, who warned Boehm against any kind of political statements. He said, according to Boehm, "that our different political sentiments should never affect our Christian fellowship and affections; that each had a right to his own peculiar views, and we should make no man an offender because his views of politics were different from ours." [27] In a city where politics was a major topic of discussion, Methodist ministers steered away from taking a position.

Back in the predominantly rural South, it is significant that Henry Holcombe found it necessary to urge Christians to take even a minimum of interest in politics. Because some Christians in past times confused the church-state issue by erecting a religious establishment, Holcombe argued, their error was no reason to bar present Christians from performing their civil duty. It "by no means follows" that because they "paid a disproportionate attention to politics . . . we should not regard [political affairs and responsibilities] with the attention they deserve." [28] If his congregations had been already voting and paying close attention to political matters, Holcombe would not have felt the need to promote involvement. This was not the case. In 1802 he urged Baptist friends to "attend to the political affairs of our country, as far as will consist with our other, and more important duties." [29]

Religious duties were the reason southern evangelicals did not actively contribute to regional politics. The political arena was simply outside their

[26] Ibid., February 13, 1805, 2:459–60.

[27] Henry Boehm, *Reminiscences, Historical and Biographical, of Sixty-four Years in the Ministry*, ed. Joseph B. Wakeley (New York, 1865), p. 65.

[28] Holcombe, *First Fruits*, p. 127.

[29] Holcombe, "Address, to the Friends of Religion, in the State of Georgia, on their Duties, in reference to Civil Government, by the Editor," *Georgia Analytical Repository* 1 (September-October 1802): 97.

primary concern. Jeremiah Moore, a Baptist leader in Virginia, presents a noteworthy example of the revivalists' indifference to politics. On July 12, 1800, in the thick of the presidential election campaign, with accusations and pledges filling the air, with pamphlets and broadsides cluttering the desks of the influential in each county, Moore wrote a letter to the candidate he should have known best, Thomas Jefferson. Declaring himself to have been an advocate "of republican principles" since the American Revolution, he wanted to know Jefferson's stand on the issues of the day. He knew and appreciated Jefferson's efforts two decades ago to establish religious freedom. Nevertheless, he told Jefferson, he had "heard it hinted a few days ago that you must be more aristocratical in your disposition than Mr. Adams." [30] If a prominent Virginia Baptist leader, often moderator of the Ketocton Baptist Association, had to inquire of Jefferson's political position in 1800, this does not suggest a high level of political awareness on the part of Baptists. As a matter of fact, Jefferson himself seems to have been somewhat surprised, for although he courteously replied to Moore, he wrote, "I have been so long on the public theater that I supposed mine [political principles] to be generally known." [31]

This exchange of correspondence indicates that ministers, and by inference the people they represented, were not politicized. In fact, there is no evidence to suggest that the Great Revival had any appreciable effect on politics, except perhaps even to lessen political participation. For example, Samuel Keene, Jr., an Episcopalian, returned to Kentucky in late 1801 and found things there very much as they had been before "except that they have substituted the Rage of Religion for the Rage of Politicks." [32] He then proceeded to describe how "the Religionists (principally Presbyterian)" were spending days in monstrously large meetings of "eight and ten thousand People." The Methodists he reported were completely "put out of countenance by them." This was a far different Kentucky from that of several years before—a Kentucky agitated by debates over a new constitution and the repressive Alien and Sedition Acts.

In terms of voter response, Charles S. Sydnor found a decline in the number of voters participating in Virginia elections. Citing figures from the 1740s to the 1840s, he could discover no significant increase in voting. After 1785, when the church was disestablished, and hence religion "could

---

[30] Jeremiah Moore to Thomas Jefferson, July 12, 1800, typescript in the Virginia Baptist Historical Society, University of Richmond.

[31] Thomas Jefferson to Jeremiah Moore, August 14, 1800, photostat of the original in the Virginia Baptist Historical Society, University of Richmond.

[32] Keene to Rev. James Kemp, December 6, 1801, in the Maryland Diocesan Archives, Maryland Historical Society, Baltimore, Md.

no longer be a ground for disfranchisement," one might have expected an increase of votes. Instead, reported Sydnor, "in 19 elections held in nine counties from 1786 to 1800," "there was a slight decrease" in actual votes cast.[33] Religion precipitated no revolution in politics.

One of the few religious spokesmen who made any sort of an attempt to express a political philosophy was Henry Holcombe of Savannah. Situated in the commercial and political capital of Georgia, Holcombe undoubtedly had to confront politics more often than did the huge majority of southern religious leaders. As editor of the *Georgia Analytical Repository*, he felt the need of defining the Christian response to the governmental issues of the day.[34] How representative his statement was is difficult to say. The scattering of other references to politics is convincing evidence that Holcombe did include in his printed address the essential beliefs accepted by other proponents of popular religion in the South. Although very few had thought as deeply about politics as Holcombe, most appear to have shared his reluctant acceptance of government as a necessity.

Because mankind had fallen from grace, government was essential, he stated. Government was possible because man, through Jesus Christ, had the potentiality for virtue and progress toward perfection. Thus pietistic religion led to a Jeffersonian concept of government: it was needed, but the less the better. Since it was founded on man's failure, Holcombe warned Christians that their expectations of civil government "should not be too sanguine." After all, "It is not capable, in its most perfect form, of rectifying many of the most formidable existing evils; and, is at once, a consequence, and demonstration, as well as a punishment of sin. Had man continued, as he was created, in the image, and subject to the laws of GOD, there could have been no necessity for punitive justice; and were all men genuine, and consistent Christians, there would now be no use for coercive power: But in the present state of our morals, coercion is essentially necessary to the good, perhaps, to the very existence of society."[35]

Typical of the southern religious propensity to see Providence working in everything, Holcombe assumed that the political offices and their holders were positioned by God. Christians owed them respect and dutiful response. Although there might be individual cases where laws seemed unfair, all

[33] Sydnor, *American Revolutionaries in the Making*, pp. 121–24.

[34] Holcombe's "Address, to the Friends of Religion, in the State of Georgia, on their Duties, in reference to Civil Government, by the Editor," was printed in several successive issues of the *Georgia Analytical Repository* 1, numbers 3, 4, and 5 (September–October, 1802, through January–February, 1803). The *Repository* folded after one year, hence there is only one volume.

[35] Ibid. (September–October 1802): 98–99.

citizens should remain subject to the ordained laws as long as they were not contrary to the will of God. (Holcombe did not spell out how one was to be certain of God's will.) Some form of stable government, founded on law, based on representation, and devoted to liberty, was absolutely essential to human happiness. Because men were corruptible, a degree of injustice was inevitable. But, he warned, "even the worst form of government, and that badly administered, is preferable to entire anarchy."[36]

Holcombe had fought in the American struggle for independence and had long subscribed to the tenets of the Declaration. Now, in 1802, he argued that government existed to preserve and protect those certain basic rights phrased by Jefferson in 1776. "The principal of our natural rights," Holcombe wrote, "as well defined in this immortal instrument ["our memorable declaration of Independence"], are 'LIFE, LIBERTY, AND THE PURSUIT OF HAPPINESS.' "[37] From this tradition he recognized that in some instances government might finally become repressive and opposed to God's will. Christians should be patient and hesitant to draw the sword. Yet revolution was always a last resort to uphold the rights of Christians. "As the laws of a country can never accord, in all respects, with strict justice, in their application to every individual, the generous spirit of Christianity will enable us to bear many inconveniences, rather than disturb the public peace. ... [But] if governments become grievously oppressive, to effect a reform, or even a *revolution* may be a desirable and important object; but it should always be done, *if possible*, by constitutional, and moderate means."[38]

There was absolutely nothing original or creative about Holcombe's political statements. He accepted the body of beliefs common to the generation that promoted the revolution and established a new nation. Like Franklin, Washington, Jefferson, and others, he firmly believed "that virtue is as essential to the *genuinely Republican*, as it is to the *Christian* character."[39] In addition, he also believed with the founding fathers that virtue and morality were necessary for the continuation of representative government. As he stated in his address: "I need not prove, for it is evident, that without Religion there can be no virtue; and it is equally incontestible, that without virtue, there can be no liberty. At least, it is allowed, on all hands, that a *large Republic*, especially, cannot long subsist without virtue."[40]

Hence Christianity had an indispensable role to play in the future of

[36] Ibid.; and (November–December 1802): 169–70.
[37] Ibid. (September–October 1802): 101.
[38] Ibid. (November–December 1802): 170.
[39] Ibid. (January–February 1803): 230.
[40] Ibid.

this nation. However, Holcombe spoke of the virtue of individual Christians—he abhorred the idea of a state church. Moreover, he openly opposed party spirit, believing it led to needless dispute and dissipation of energy. Christians should remain open minded and support virtue wherever it was found. Perhaps because of his innate conservatism and the political climate of his congregation in Savannah, Holcombe supported property requirements for voting. He thought wealth and population should be represented, otherwise "the poor are liable to oppression, or property is insecure."[41] Quite obviously, the Calvinistic notion of man's nature was central to Holcombe's statements on politics.

Near the middle of his address Holcombe wrote that the United States were "the enlightened favorites of divine Providence."[42] Here was a point upon which all evangelicals would agree. They also accepted Holcombe's idea that government was a necessary evil, that virtue was indispensable for republicanism, and that man possessed certain inalienable rights. Probably most pietists, removed from the centers of commerce and government, would not have agreed with Holcombe's defense of property requirements for voting. But certainly it was clear to evangelicals in every region that in their government they possessed a blessing. On infrequent occasions church associations expressed their thanks, and whenever they did, they were contented because in practice, the government defended political and religious liberty.

In its pastoral letter for 1802, the Synod of the Carolinas challenged the world to find a government "now existing, in which there is a more sure foundation laid for the security of the civil and religious rights of its subjects."[43] Five years later, the Holston Baptist Association of Tennessee (an organization descended from the North Carolina Separate Baptists who fled as a result of the Regulator troubles in 1771 and 1772) in its minutes for 1807 praised the existing system: "We are blest with a free Republican government, and are privileged to act as a free people in making laws for the benefit of civil Society as Rational beings."[44] But in every instance of

---

[41] Ibid., 228–29; and (November–December 1802):168–69. Richard Hofstadter discusses the centrality of Calvinist interpretations of man to the political theorizing of the founding fathers in Chapter 1 of his *American Political Tradition and the Men Who Made It* (New York, 1947).

[42] Holcombe, "Address, to the Friends of Religion," *Georgia Analytical Repository* 1 (November–December 1802):171.

[43] Synod of the Carolinas, *A Pastoral Letter from the Synod of the Carolinas* (Salisbury, [N. C.], 1802), p. [3].

[44] Holston [Baptist] Association, *Minutes* ([n.p., n.d.]), p. 99, on microfilm at the library of the Historical Commission, Southern Baptist Convention, Nashville, Tenn.

this kind, the religious groups were not taking a position on any party issue. They were supporting the form of government under which they lived. They had seen that it was good, and expressed their thanks. In no way were they really engaging in political theorizing or participating as an organization in politics. They simply realized that government was necessary, that theirs was functioning satisfactorily, and that they should be appreciative.

Because southern evangelicals were individualistic and basically otherworldly, they preferred to leave active politics alone. For the majority of common folk in the South, political considerations hardly ever entered into their everyday lives. The government was something far away that essentially served them better than any other people's government. The only experience they often had with politics was on election days. The unchristian disorder observed then often solicited the only comments a minister would make on politics, and in such a situation few found much good in political participation.

Jeremiah Norman, a Methodist itinerant, happened to be in Ebenezer, North Carolina, in November 1800, when the people were voting for an elector for the presidential race. The pious Norman was "greatly distressed to see & hear so much quaraling & fighting, cursing, & Swearing. They seemed as if they had recently come out of the bottomless Pit. . . . Satan seems to have raised all his forms." [45] In 1790 Presbyterian missionary William Hill witnessed the revelry of election day in Franklin County, Virginia. He recorded in his journal: "I saw much wickedness this day, & felt much concerned to see my poor fellow mortals drinking—& degrading themselves below the brutes that perish, & to hear them cursing & swearing & using the language of Hell. Some were stripping & fighting, & tearing each other to pieces like the Devil incarnate." [46]

This was the politics the plain folk knew best in their homely world of work and worship. Politics no doubt at times appeared even more evil than necessary. For those bent on seeking some small degree of perfection in a world defined as sinful, political participation presented a dilemma: whether to isolate oneself completely from matters of state or to inject virtue into the body politic. Perhaps the great majority never really considered the alternatives. It would probably be easy to overintellectualize the common response. Most, no doubt, were practically untouched by politics. Geographic isolation, bad weather, planting or harvest times, difficult traveling conditions, all took their toll, along with essential indifference, from voter

[45] Norman, "Diary," November 3, 1800, p. 985, in the Stephen B. Weeks Collection.

[46] Hill, *Journal*, September 6, 1790, p. 31.

participation. For example, Hill voted for the first time in 1790 only in response to what he felt was the barbarity of electioneering.

> I saw one of the Candidates walk thro' the court yard with a large wooden can of stiff grog & inviting the voters to come & drink with him, & what made the matter worse, this candidate had been an Episcopal clergyman before the revolution. I was so disgusted at this sight, that I determined to go in & vote against him, & did so, tho' it was the first vote I ever gave, & I had no intention whatever of voting when I came to the place, altho' the property I had in the country entitled me to vote.[47]

It is significant that he voted not for political reasons but purely for moral ones.

To whatever extent the proponents of revivalistic religion participated in politics—and it seems to have been very little—there is incontrovertible though largely impressionistic evidence that they were Jeffersonian in party outlook. Of course, the South as a region was preponderantly pro-Jeffersonian, so the pietists were not distinguishable in political affiliation. But it is important that they were not pro-Jefferson for essentially religious reasons. Instead, most Baptists, Methodists, and Presbyterians lived in rural areas, depended upon agriculture for their livelihood, were individualistic and provincial in outlook, and emphasized the importance of personal decision making (particularly in what was for them the key life event—conversion). Each of these evangelical characteristics were shared by Jefferson himself and his political-philosophical coterie. In many of the most important ways, the pietistic world outlook was similar to the Jeffersonian.

Before quickly concluding that all those most susceptible to revivalism were at heart Jeffersonian Republicans, we must consider the oft-repeated campaign slander that Jefferson was a gross infidel. How telling were these mainly New England and Congregationalist-inspired charges against Jefferson in the South? There is little evidence that the insidious pamphlet warfare against him was waged very intensely in the region below the Potomac. One can infer that a very small percentage of the common folk would have read such attacks even if they had been available. In the South where there was no established church whose position would be jeopardized by a devotee of religious liberty, the Baptists and to a lesser extent the Presbyterians remembered Jefferson as the founder of their own religious freedom.

A letter from an "Old Soldier" printed in the *Raleigh Register and North-Carolina Gazette* in 1804 indicates that at least some in the South

[47] Ibid.

felt that the revivals following Jefferson's election by a year or so proved that he was no enemy of religion. However, the "Aristocratical Prophets" and "Dissenters" referred to could very well have been those to the northward. Nevertheless, in the aftermath of a tremendous upsurge of revivalism in North Carolina, the "Old Soldier" wrote triumphantly:

> I think I would not be amiss to observe that our Aristocratical Prophets made a mistake, when they predicted that Thomas Jefferson would burn all our Churches and Bibles, if he became our President. As it is now well known to all Americans that there never was so great a stir of religion since the day of Pentecost, as there has been in America during Jefferson's administration, and it still goes on with rapidity throughout the union. . . . I hope our Christians in general, and our Dissenters in particular, are now well convinced that they have treated their best friend Jefferson with ingratitude, when they joined those Aristocrats to curse his political interests.[48]

In Philadelphia, where politics were more discussed, the circulation of newspapers, pamphlets, and rumors more advanced, and party feeling more provoked, there are indications that many Methodists opposed Jefferson for fear he would inaugurate a reign of godlessness.[49] This Methodist position was not duplicated anywhere in the South. Some wealthy planters—commercial farmers—who were Episcopalian were opposed to Jefferson. For example, Charles Pettigrew of eastern North Carolina, a warm defender of the Episcopal faith, bitterly attacked Jefferson and his supposed infidel accomplice, Thomas Paine, in a letter to an Episcopal minister. Pettigrew, however, was against Jefferson for more than religious reasons. Moreover, on second thought he decided not to send his partisan letter "on account of the political part."[50]

Party affiliation in the South seems to have depended more on whether one lived within the sphere of commercial farming than on one's religion. But since most of those who participated in the excitement and fervor of camp meetings lived beyond the commercial zone, they very probably were Jeffersonian in political sentiment. This is not to say that the Jeffersonian

[48] Letter from "Old Soldier," Carwell County, North Carolina, September 12, 1804, in the *Raleigh Register and North-Carolina Gazette*, October 1, 1804. In pietistic terms, Jefferson was privately an "infidel."

[49] See "Extract of a Letter from the Rev. George Roberts, of Philadelphia, to Mr. William Myles, Minister of the Gospel, in London, November 17, 1802," *Methodist Magazine* [London] 26 (1803): 417; and the *Philadelphia Aurora General Advertiser*, August 5 and 18, 1803.

[50] Charles Pettigrew to Rev. N[athaniel] Blount, August 23, 1803, in the Pettigrew Papers.

ascendancy was rooted in the flood of revivalism that rolled over the South after Gasper River. After all, the election was practically decided by May 1800, when New York went for Jefferson—and the Gasper River revival took place in June 1800. Not until August 1801 did the revival really gain momentum at Cane Ridge. By then, Jefferson was already safely ensconced in the White House. In 1802 and 1803 the revival roared through the South, drawing thousands to tumultuous camp meetings. All this, though, was long after the presidential campaign and the charges of deism and infidelity. There is no available evidence to suggest that the Great Revival in any way affected the outcome of the election of 1800.

Yet because the evangelicals were basically republican in outlook (as opposed to aristocratical), provincial-minded (rather than centralist), individualistic (not collectivist), and pietistic (as compared to mercantile or commercial), they no doubt tended toward Jeffersonianism. David Barrow, traveling through Kentucky in 1795, found the Baptist elder he was visiting as well as "many others in this country . . . very clear in theory concerning the rights of man, [they] are what are commonly called good republicans."[51] Francis Asbury in 1805 indirectly praised Jefferson and Madison when he said of a fellow minister that had he possessed the "advantages of education, he would have displayed abilities not inferior to a Jefferson or Madison."[52] In Maryland, where the situation was not unlike Virginia, a Federalist Episcopalian accused the Methodists of being radicals and supporters of Republican Samuel Smith. "I have been fully convinced for some time," the Reverend Joseph Bend wrote, "of the Jacobinic principles of the Methodists: nor is this fact wonderful. They are, for the most part, persons of the lower classes in life, & distinguished by that ignorance, upon which the Jacobin chiefs work so successfully."[53]

The situation was different to the north and northwest. Especially in New England, where there was an established church, the Baptists, Methodists, and to a lesser extent Presbyterians, were "dissenters" and suffered disadvantages in their secondary position. Here there *were* religious reasons for getting involved in politics—they had grievances to redress. Under completely different circumstances in New England, evangelical Baptists like Elder John Leland and Isaac Backus fought long and hard for Jefferson.[54] Leland even delivered to the White House a cheese four feet in

[51] David Barrow, "Diary," July 19, 1795, p. 19, typescript, in the Filson Club.

[52] Asbury, *Journal and Letters*, February 17, 1805, 2:462.

[53] Rev. Joseph G. J. Bend to Rev. William Duke, November 3, 1798, in the Maryland Diocesan Archives, Maryland Historical Society, Baltimore, Md.

[54] See Lyman H. Butterfield, "Elder John Leland, Jeffersonian Itinerant," *American Antiquarian Society* 62 (October 1952): 155–242; and McLoughlin, *Isaac*

diameter, seventeen inches thick, and weighing 1,235 pounds, in appreciation for Jefferson's republican principles and celebration of his victory.[55] These were the "bawling, itinerant, field and barn preachers" primarily referred to in such bitter Federalist pamphlets as "Christopher Caustic's" *Democracy Unveiled, or Tyranny Stripped of the Garb of Patriotism.*[56]

There were no figures in the South of 1800 comparable to Leland or Backus. Henry Holcombe wrote a purposely nonpartisan address urging Christians to uphold their form of government. David Barrow of Virginia included a "Summary of my Political Beliefs" in his farewell *Circular Letter* before leaving for Kentucky. He abstracted in twenty-six tenets his political philosophy, and the result was strikingly Jeffersonian.[57] But never in any way did Barrow actively participate in politics in order that his beliefs might be put into practice. Indeed, after disestablishment was effected in the South, no religious leader played a significant role in politics. Their only experience or memory of politics intertwined with religion was in the form of a state church. So disagreeable was this memory that evangelicals seemed studiously to avoid overt political participation. There was not the slightest tendency of a theocracy in the Jeffersonian South—there was not even a practice of "election sermons." This was a distinctive New England custom.

Popular religion in the South was conversion-centered; economic and political formulation was not its forte. To the extent that it was a religion catering to the common people, its supporters formed the bulk of republican-democratic strength in the South. But this was independent of religious considerations. Ministers strove with all their energy to change the lives and habits of their congregation; the issues, however, were virtue, conversion, and conforming to Jesus Christ. They aspired to a more complete other-worldliness. Even had the pietists been more secular, their firm insistence on separation of church and state would have carried overtones that decreased political participation. In the South especially, political economy was the province of large planters and lawyers. Religion was a thing not of this world; it was concerned with souls, not society; with personal salvation, not the body politic.

Backus, esp. p. 229. Richard D. Birdsall, "The Reverend Thomas Allen: Jeffersonian Calvinist," *New England Quarterly* 30 (June 1957): 147–65, relates the career of a Congregational minister devoted to republicanism.

[55] C. A. Browne gives a detailed account of the making of the cheese, and its delivery, in "Elder John Leland and the Mammoth Cheshire Cheese," *Agriculture History* 28 (October 1944): 145–53.

[56] [Thomas Green Fessenden], *Democracy Unveiled, or Tyranny Stripped of the Garb of Patriotism. By Christopher Caustic*, 3d ed. (New York, 1806), p. 174n.

[57] Barrow, *Circular Letter*, pp. 8–10.

Chapter Twelve

Revivalism & the Southern Evangelical Mind

The revival movement declined rapidly after 1805. By that time practically everyone who could be reached and moved by the evangelical message had enjoyed the opportunity. Unlike upstate New York two decades later, the South had not reached the stage of agrarian maturity that could sustain almost continuous revivalism.[1] Nevertheless, at hundreds of camp meetings and innumerable rural churches scattered across the South, thousands of common people had felt their consciences pricked and had experienced a feeling of conversion. Churches were crowded afterwards, and most observers seemed satisfied that there had been a great moral reformation wherever the revival fires had burned. But increased church membership and improved manners were the most transitory legacy of the movement.

More importantly, the Great Revival was a watershed in the religious history of the South. It predetermined the eventual failure of Unitarianism which Thomas Jefferson at one time hoped would become the dominant southern religion. The deistic liberalism of the revolutionary era soon faded into the past. This awakening at the turn of the century helped set into motion the diverse forces that by the decade of the 1830s had created an orthodox South, a South resistant to change and criticism in every form. An evangelical pietism came to characterize southern religion and as such contributed significantly to that perhaps amorphous outlook labeled "the southern mind."

In an important review essay several years ago, Henry F. May noted that "the recovery of American religious history has restored a knowledge of the mode, even the language, in which most Americans, during most of American history, did their thinking about human nature and destiny."[2] If this is true for the nation as a whole—and it seems to be—it is particularly valid for the South, that region known even today as the Bible Belt. Writing of the period just before World War II, Francis B. Simkins stated, "Conservatism in religion did not rank far behind traditional racial attitudes as significant causes for the South's retention of its regional distinctiveness."[3]

Simkins continued: "The great masses of both races remained virtually untouched by the winds of modernism that swept in from the outside world."[4] This religious viewpoint, like a clinging fog, descended over the South in the decades following the Great Revival and, with its peculiar pietistic vagaries, has only now begun to lift. "Nowhere else, almost surely," wrote Kenneth K. Bailey, "is there a Protestant population of equal size so renowned for its piety or for its commitment to old-fashioned Scriptural literalism."[5] Much of the southern response to history is partially explained by this strong revivalistic heritage.

The numerical impact of the revival is difficult to measure with exactness. All accounts of camp meetings agree that the attendance was absolutely stupendous for a rural region. Revivalists, rigid opponents, unconcerned travelers, laymen, all reported crowds that seemed to average between four and ten thousand. Many estimates of the Cane Ridge meeting, which was unique, place the number there at near 25,000. Undoubtedly these figures were inflated; perhaps if the quoted figures were halved, they would indicate the attendance more accurately.

There was great duplication in the crowds, for the same people attended different meetings in their vicinity. The total number of individuals who experienced a camp meeting is far less than the sum of the attendance figures given for the meetings. The percentage of worshipers who professed conversion was probably relatively small. Conversions were more numerous at the beginning of the revival in each locality, then gradually declined as the number readily susceptible to pietistic faith was exhausted. Even though some were repulsed by the emotionalism or reputation of the Baptists and Methodists, the majority of people appear to have accepted the major beliefs of the revivalists. Very likely a rather large proportion of the "believers" never quite felt the convincing "conversion experience"

[1] Whitney R. Cross has written a classic account of this development in *The Burned-Over District*.

[2] Henry F. May, "The Recovery of American Religious History," *American Historical Review* 70 (October 1964): 79.

[3] Francis Butler Simkins, *A History of the South*, 3d ed. (New York, 1963), p. 425.

[4] Ibid.

[5] Kenneth K. Bailey, *Southern White Protestantism in the Twentieth Century* (New York, 1964), p. ix. My conclusion that revivalistic religion has been unusually influential in shaping the southern response to history, though arrived at independently, is comparable to the general theme of Samuel S. Hill, Jr., in his thought-provoking study *Southern Churches in Crisis* (New York, 1967).

thought necessary to merit official church membership. In addition, it is probably safe to assume that many of those who felt conversion were either too individualistic or isolated to join a church. Much of the South was too sparsely settled to make membership feasible.

The quantification of membership constitutes a definite problem in itself. The various churches defined their members in different ways. For some only those adult, baptized converts were considered bona fide members; others counted infants and children.[6] To make matters more difficult, many of the records are either incomplete or nonexistent. For example, it is impossible to estimate the strength of the Presbyterian Church. Up until about 1750, churches were few enough to keep account of; after that, it was not until 1850 that census figures included denominational affiliation. Edwin S. Gaustad's helpful religious atlas has maps which indicate the location of each church in 1750. The records did not permit similar completeness until 1850, and for this date Gaustad delineated religious membership county-by-county throughout the nation. So any kind of statement about the numerical result of the Great Revival is by necessity imperfect and approximate.

As fragmentary as the evidence is, there is enough to indicate a significant spurt in church growth. Between 1800 and 1802 the six Baptist associations in Kentucky grew in membership from 4,766 to 13,569.[7] In the five years following the beginning of the revival, the Western Conference of the Methodist Church, which consisted of the districts in Kentucky and Tennessee, expanded from 3,030 members to 10,158. During the same time the number of Methodist ministers tripled, from eleven to thirty-three.[8] The camp meetings did not appear in South Carolina until 1802, but between that date and 1805 the Methodist membership doubled, from 7,443 to 16,089.[9] Bethel Baptist Association in South Carolina increased from 2,690 to 4,029 converts in the three years following the inception of the revival.[10] Georgia's Sarepta Baptist Association more than

[6] See Edwin S. Gaustad, *Historical Atlas of Religion in America* (New York, 1962), pp. x–xi.

[7] S. H. Ford, "History of the Kentucky Baptists: Chapter IX, The Great Revival. —Camp-Meetings.—The Jerks.—Barton W. Stone.—New Lights," *The Christian Repository* 5 (December 1856): 346.

[8] Computed from the *Minutes of the Methodist Conferences, Annually Held in America; from 1773 to 1813, Inclusive* (New York, 1813), passim.

[9] Shipp, *Methodism in South Carolina*, p. 603.

[10] Bethel [Baptist] Association, *Minutes*, on microfilm, library of the Historical Commission, Southern Baptist Convention, Nashville, Tenn.

tripled in the first four years of the cenutry, leaping from 797 in 1800 to 2,903 in 1804.[11]

Throughout the South, Methodist membership almost doubled in six years, growing from approximately 30,000 in 1800 to 59,000 in 1806.[12] The Presbyterians prospered slightly, but many of their early converts in Kentucky were lost by the several schisms in the church. In all states of the South, the Baptists and Methodists beat the Presbyterians in the race for church membership. These three groups, along with the Cumberland Presbyterians and the Christians (Disciples of Christ) have completely dominated southern religion for the past century and a half. For example, in 1850 there were in the twelve southern states 5,298 Baptist churches, 6,061 Methodist churches, 1,647 Presbyterian churches, and only 408 Episcopalian (315 of them were in the four seaboard states: Virginia, both Carolinas, and Georgia), 179 Catholic, 166 Lutheran, 52 Quaker, 26 German Reformed, and two Congregational churches. The new Christian denomination already claimed 267 churches in the region.[13] As late as the 1920s, when Edmund Brunner made a detailed study of church life in the rural South, he discovered that "the number of adherents of all non-evangelical faiths is negligible. They total only about 2 per cent of the entire church membership, and, except in Louisiana, are to be found exclusively in the cities."[14]

For many contemporaries, unable to see that the South's future was to be evangelically orthodox, the most significant result of the Great Revival was the pietistic reformation of morals which it seemed to effect. George Baxter, a prominent Virginia Presbyterian, visited the West in late 1801 and wrote back to a colleague: "On my way to Kentucky I was told by settlers on the road, that the character of Kentucky travellers was entirely changed, and that they were now as distinguished for sobriety as they had formerly been for dissoluteness: and indeed, I found Kentucky the most moral place I had ever been in; a profane expression was hardly heard, a religious awe seemed to pervade the country, and some deistical characters

[11] Sarepta [Baptist] Association, *Minutes*, on microfilm, Historical Commission, Southern Baptist Convention, Nashville, Tenn.

[12] Computed from the *Minutes of the Methodist Conferences*. The figures given are approximate because the conference boundaries did not always coincide with state lines.

[13] Adopted from Gaustad, *Atlas of Religion*, Appendix C, p. 168. The figures for the Christian Church are from J. B. DeBow, *A Compendium of the Seventh Census* (Washington, D. C., 1854).

[14] Edmund deS. Brunner, *Church Life in the Rural South* (New York, 1923), p. 41.

had confessed that, from whatever cause the revival might originate, it certainly made the people better."[15]

David Thomas lived through the various stages of the revival in Kentucky and wrote a ringing rebuttal of Adam Rankin's charges that it was a work of delusion. The bulwark of Thomas's defense was his contention that "A great change of manners . . . has taken place in this part of the world. This is too evident for any one to deny, who takes notice of the most common events that happen in the place where he lives."[16] Eastward across the mountains, in Bath County, Virginia, the revival was hailed for drastically changing society for the better. There, where the revival was never even relatively strong, a Presbyterian wrote in 1805 that whereas "formerly, when [people] collected together, drinking, swearing, horseracing, fighting, and such like practices, were common among them—But now. . . you will seldom see one pursuing any of these practices. Those who make no pretensions to religion, still appear under great restraint."[17]

There is of course a tendency for divines to overestimate the good that results from a revival, but it is probable that the religious awakening served as a strong civilizing factor in the rural South, and more especially in the westernmost regions. For one thing, each of the major churches put great emphasis on Christian living after conversion. This perfectionist-pietistic urge shaped much of the religious activity, for the congregations were constantly upbraiding those among their members who had fallen into profanity, drunkenness, adultery, or wife-beating. The Baptists made each member responsible for the behavior of every other Baptist; the Methodists met weekly in classes organized to keep each member under close spiritual and temporal surveillance; and the Presbyterians maintained a watch over their collective morality through the Elders sitting in quarterly sessions to examine members' behavior.[18]

Undoubtedly this close surveillance sometimes led to puritanical excess. For example, Wheeley's Baptist Church, Person County, North Carolina,

---

[15] "Letter from the Rev. George Baxter to the Rev. A. Alexander, dated Washington Academy, Virginia, January 1, 1802," *New York Missionary Magazine* 3 (1802) : 87. Baxter later turned against the revival when it seemed to become extreme. See Davidson, *Presbyterian Church in Kentucky*, p. 185n.

[16] Thomas, *The Observer Trying the Great Reformation*, p. [7].

[17] "Extract of a letter from a Missionary to his friend in Rockbridge County," *Virginia Religious Magazine* 1 (July 1805) : 232.

[18] Sweet, "Churches as Moral Courts of the Frontier," pp. 3–21; Cortland V. Smith, "Church Discipline in North Carolina," passim; and W. D. Blands, "Corrective Church Discipline in the Presbyterian Churches of the Nineteenth Century South," *Journal of Presbyterian History* 44 (June 1966) : 89–105.

in May 1804, heard bad reports of "Br. Bailor Burch." He was called to testify before the church business session, where he "informed the church that there was some reports circulating in respect of his kissing of Sister Susannah Clayton which he deneyed but confessed that he rubbed his beard in her face in the night at her bedside." For this heinous crime a committee of seven, after much consideration, expelled both Burch and Sister Clayton as "heathen . . . & publicans." [19]

Nevertheless, the churches acting as moral courts helped make society less barbaric and uncouth. A certain modicum of order, concern for education, respect for others, self-discipline, and even virtue was necessary if the backcountry South were to move from semi-frontier to stable society. In 1808 David Ramsay, the early secular historian of South Carolina, appraised the consequence of the spread of revivalistic religion:

> To presume that nothing improper has ever occurred in their frequent, numerous and unseasonable meetings, would be contrary to the ordinary course of things; but that great good has resulted from the labors of the Methodists is evident to all who are acquainted with the state of the country before and since they commenced their evangelisms in Carolina. Drunkards have become sober and orderly—bruisers, bullies, and blackguards, meek, inoffensive and peaceable—profane swearers, decent in their conversation. In the cause of religion the Methodists are excellent pioneers and prepare the way for permanent moral improvement. . . . They are particularly suited to the state of society in South Carolina, in which large tracts of poor land afford such a scanty return to its dispersed cultivators as to be incompetent to their own support, and also that of learned stationary clergymen. To multitudes of such persons the methodists have given religious instructions which they never enjoyed before and among such they have produced a great diminution of gross immoralities. Similar zeal and activity have been displayed by the Baptists, and their labors have been followed with correspondent success in civilizing and evangelizing remote and destitute settlements.[20]

Evangelical religion captured the popular mind during the era of the Great Revival. It offered the hope, the feeling, the finality desired by the common people. Philosophical deism, which drew support from the upper classes of the revolutionary generation, was unable to slow the proliferation of pietism. Even if there had been no great emotional outburst of revivalism, Clement Eaton has written, deism would not have survived long into the nineteenth century. "It was not suited," he stated, "to the romantic

[19] Wheeley's Baptist Church, "Minute Book," p. 30, typescript, North Carolina State Archives, Raleigh, N. C.

[20] David Ramsay, *Ramsay's History of South Carolina, from its first Settlement in 1760 to the year 1808* (Newberry, S. C., 1858), pp. 20–22.

spirit that conquered the South. Deism was too cold, too philosophic and reasonable to satisfy the emotional needs of the people. When the colonial-bred aristocracy died out, deism faded imperceptibly from Southern society."[21]

The three decades after the beginning of the revival saw a gradual tightening of orthodoxy. Two liberal college presidents, Horace Holley of Transylvania University and Thomas Cooper of the University of South Carolina, received unrelenting criticism, and Holley finally resigned.[22] The University of Virginia was harassed for its secular structure. As liberal theology in the North came increasingly to be associated with Unitarianism and various reform interests, the southern clergy determined to maintain an unbending conservatism. This tendency was greatly intensified after 1830 by the growing unity of northern religion and abolitionism. The "cotton curtain," as it has been called, was dropping around the South, shutting it off from the winds of change and criticism.

Francis B. Simkins has written, "After 1830 the Southern mind was captured . . . by a group of orthodox Presbyterian theologians."[23] And he should have included Baptist and Methodist ministers as well. The enlightenment ideas which had gained some degree of currency among the revolutionary generation had died out with them. "By 1830," wrote Clement Eaton, "there were few deists and freethinkers left in the Southern states. . . . Indeed, a profound religious orthodoxy had settled upon the South."[24] A good indication of this changed affection is given by Thomas R. Dew's address at the opening of classes at William and Mary College in 1836. Forty years before these halls had resounded with huzzas for the French Revolution; students greeted each other as "citizen" and discussed the most liberal ideas about Christianity. Now Dew spoke in a totally different age:

[21] *The Freedom-of-Thought Struggle in the Old South,* rev. ed. (New York, 1964), pp. 303–4. See also Eaton's article, "The Ebb of the Great Revival," *North Carolina Historical Review* 23 (January 1946): 1–12, which draws similar conclusions.

[22] For the complete account, see Sonne, *Liberal Kentucky,* and Dumas Malone, *The Public Life of Thomas Cooper, 1783–1839* (New Haven, Conn., 1926).

[23] Simkins, "The Rising Tide of Faith," in *The Lasting South, Fourteen Southerners Look at Their Home,* ed. Louis D. Rubin, Jr., and James Jackson Kilpatrick (Chicago, 1957), p. 88.

[24] Eaton, *The Growth of Southern Civilization: 1790–1860* (New York, 1963), p. 14. Others have noted this change which occurred around 1830. Cf. Rollin G. Osterweis, *Romanticism and Nationalism in the Old South* (New Haven, Conn., 1949), p. 21; and Samuel S. Hill, Jr., "An Agenda for Research in Religion," in *Perspectives on the South: Agenda for Research,* ed. Edgar T. Thompson (Durham, N. C., 1967), p. 205.

I would advise you particularly to be punctual in your attendance on divine service every Sabbath. . . . Be always respectful in your conversation towards religion, not only from regard to the feeling of others, but for the sake of your own reputation. Avowed infidelity is now considered by the enlightened portion of the world as a reflection both on the head and the heart. The Atheist has long since been overthrown by the light of nature, and the Deist by that of revelation. The Infidel and the Christian have fought the battle, and the latter has won the victory. The Humes and Voltaires have been vanquished from the field. . . . The argument is closed forever, and he who now obtrudes on the social circle his infidel notions, manifests the arrogance of a literary coxcomb, or that want of refinement which distinguishes the polished gentleman.[25]

The rise of an evangelical orthodoxy mirrors the corresponding decline of Unitarianism in the South. During the 1820s and early 1830s, Unitarian churches were established in several southern cities. The parent organization was in Baltimore, where Jared Sparks was the first minister. Although the other churches were not nearly so well staffed, the few scattered liberals left hoped for a while that their struggling groups in Richmond, Charleston, Savannah, Louisville, and seven other cities would effect a long overdue revolution in southern religion. But their dreams were premature.

Unitarianism never took deep root among Southerners. Few wanted a coldly intellectual religion. It was too closely associated with New England, and later with abolitionism, to have much indigenous popularity in the slave states. Recognizing this, by the 1830s the Unitarian strongholds in the North sent most of their missionaries to the Midwest. Moreover, in the southern mind Unitarianism became equated with those other "isms," socialism, Fourierism, and Transcendentalism. Even at its height in the South, the bulk of Unitarian support probably came from Northerners living in the commercial centers. There never was a firm basis for growth and prosperity, and by the end of the 1830s Unitarianism was sinking. "Had Thomas Jefferson lived in the 1840's," wrote Clarence Gohdes, "he would have bowed his head in futile rage as the power of religious conservatism cast a blacker and blacker cloud over the scattered lights of liberalism in the South."[26]

[25] Thomas R. Dew, "An Address, Delivered before the Students of William and Mary, at the Opening of the College, on Monday, October 10th, 1836," *Southern Literary Messenger* 2 (November 1836): 768.

[26] Clarence Gohdes, "Some Notes on the Unitarian Church in the Ante-Bellum South: A Contribution to the History of Southern Liberalism," in *American Studies in Honor of William Kenneth Boyd, by Members of the Americana Club of Duke University*, ed. David K. Jackson (Durham, N. C., 1940), p. 366. My discussion of

As the South became more self-consciously a distinct section, with a different way of life and different aspirations, evangelical orthodoxy clamped itself more firmly on the southern conscience. To protect her sons from the seditious influence of northern social and religious ideas, the pious churchmen erected a string of denominational colleges like fortresses to keep out the enemy—new ideas. The Presbyterians, long advocates of an educated clergy, had founded five colleges by 1794. Not until 1819 was another denominational college established in the South, and then it (Centre College) was the orthodox Presbyterian response to Horace Holley's liberalizing effect on Transylvania University. Ten years passed before the Baptists decided that education could facilitate their evangelism. Until this time, most devout Southerners had sent their sons to Princeton, Brown, Yale, or Harvard. By the 1830s, it was considered dangerous to the southern way to expose students to northern "isms." In addition, the Baptists and Methodists had reached a level of social acceptance and power where education was seen to be advantageous.

The result was a great expansion in southern denominational colleges. Ten colleges were founded by the evangelical groups in the decade of the 1830s—more than the total for all preceding years. Eleven more were established in the following decade, and nine were begun in the decade before the Civil War. In all, only six permanent denominational institutions of higher education were founded in the South before 1828; thirty-one were established in the next three decades.[27] Religious orthodoxy was entrenched in the southern colleges, and few indeed were outside the influence of evangelical pietism.

Many factors were at work adjusting the southern mind to an orthodoxy which barricaded itself against change. To a certain extent denominational competition led the various churches to pour their funds into education, but the result was the same—church colleges guaranteed that the rising youth would have the classics and moral philosophy arrayed on the side of "Christian truths."[28] Similarly, technological advancements in

Unitarianism is drawn primarily from Gohdes, pp. 327–66, and also George H. Gibson, "The Unitarian-Universalist Church of Richmond," *Virginia Magazine of History and Biography* 74 (July 1966): 321–35.

[27] These figures are based on computations from data in Donald G. Tewksbury, *The Founding of American Colleges and Universities before the Civil War, With Particular Reference to the Religious Influence Bearing upon the College Movement* (New York, 1965), pp. 93–95, 104–5, 115–16, 129–32. Only those private colleges established by the Baptists, Disciples of Christ, Methodists, and Presbyterians are here counted. But the Episcopalians also erected "safe" colleges for their sons.

[28] Starting from a different position and different assumptions, William R. Tay-

printing and the production of paper, the increase in literacy, the growth of population, all contributed to a multiplication of newspapers and periodicals. But these circumstances did not dictate the subject matter. A glance at religious publications in the South again shows how evangelical orthodoxy was enlarging its sway.

Henry Holcombe's short-lived *Georgia Analytical Repository* (1802–1803) was the first religious periodical in the South, and that decade saw the introduction of but two more magazines, both of which soon folded. Nine more were introduced during the next decade, yet only three were being published in 1820. The following decade seventeen were established; by 1830 only seven were still in existence. Then in the decade of the 1830s, thirty were founded, thirty-six in the decade of 1840, and forty-two in the ten years before the war. Between 1830 and 1840, the number in current publication tripled, from seven to twenty. From none current in 1810, the periodicals in print expanded to thirty-six in 1860.[29] Despite the collapse of dozens of journals, the orthodox reading public after the 1830s had an ample and continuing supply of home-grown religious literature.

Of course, not all the denominational literature published in the South represented the efforts of the evangelicals, but the vast majority did. As the entire "freedom-of-thought struggle" in the Old South ended in intellectual thralldom, new ideas became a rarity. The separate denominations maintained a strict watch over theology, and the Presbyterian Church in particular countenanced no deviation. Religion was fast becoming a dogma accepted faithfully—it was not a matter to be investigated or reasoned over. Subjection to the status quo marked the southern response to religion as well as society. There was neither an indigenous movement of critical thinking nor an importation of northern and European ideas. Foreign immigration was practically nonexistent; urbanization and industrialization were so

---

lor has arrived at similar conclusions regarding the conservative role of education in the Old South. He has written that southern education became a "means of social control." After examining much of the educational literature of the ante bellum South, he concluded: "Instead of conceiving of the educational process as the introduction of the young to a process of inquiry and questioning, these writings speak in increasingly strident tone about the urgent necessity of preparing the young to do battle for the very orthodoxies that it had become heretic to question or examine." "Toward a Definition of Orthodoxy: The Patrician South and the Common Schools," *Harvard Educational Review* 36 (Fall 1966): 413.

[29] Based on the data in H. S. Stroupe, *The Religious Press in the South Atlantic States 1802–1865: An Annotated Bibliography with Historical Introduction and Notes* (Durham, N. C., 1956), pp. 139–40.

slight as to solicit no new response from the de facto religious establishment.

The basic characteristics of evangelical Protestantism which were to dominate the South for more than a century were thoroughly entrenched by the final decades before the Civil War. As a matter of fact, one commentator has remarked that "the Southern people reached the eve of the Civil War one of the few religious peoples left in the Western World."[30] Certainly this is an exaggeration, for religion had played a major role in the developing antislavery sentiment of the North, but the southern states did possess a more homogeneous, more conservative religion. Theirs was a pietism based on the individual, nurtured in revivalism, stirred by emotional fervor, and energized by almost universal acceptance. Clement Eaton, in his *Mind of the Old South*, rightfully noted that by the end of the era, "there was little disagreement between the fundamental beliefs of the lower and upper classes of the South, in contrast with the dichotomy that had existed in the early American republic and in many creative periods of history; all classes in the South adhered to a conservative faith, a common orthodoxy. . . . In the beliefs that mattered . . . there was virtually no disagreement."[31]

The emphasis of popular religion in the Old South was totally personal. Sermons were aimed at single unconverted "sinners"; ministers called persons, not the society, to account for their transgressions. There was no communal or abstract approach. The revivalist always had in mind the individual whom God would judge. The all-encompassing purpose of the ministers was to bring such persons to conversion. A felt conversion, one that was fixed in time and place and memory, was the primary object of evangelical preaching. After conversion it was thought essential that the new believer push himself ever nearer to that perfection which he would attain in full splendor only with death. This southern perfectionist impulse in practice was largely ethical. One tried to live in imitation of the New Testament Christ. One hoped to abstain from alcohol, from profanity, from fornication. In other words, it was a personally oriented ethical code, divorced from society. Although occasionally a denomination would support an orphanage or care for a widow, there was never anything closely resembling a social gospel. The only way to cure society, it was believed, was to cure souls.

The ultimate worldly allegiance of southern ministers was seeking out

[30] R. M. Weaver, "The Older Religiousness in the South," *Sewanee Review* 51 (Spring 1943): 248.

[31] Rev. ed. (Baton Rouge, La., 1967), pp. 222–23.

and converting "those that were lost." Basically noninstitutional, they continued to hold that the church was composed of all those experientially converted who voluntarily joined together for fellowship. Therefore interdenominational warfare had little meaning. Such feuding did exist, but on nearly every major issue the southern evangelicals lined up on the same side. Their shared orthodoxy was so supreme that peripheral skirmishes were essentially unimportant.

Individualistic, conversion-oriented, provincial, and anti-institutional, the evangelical groups in the South took comparatively little notice of political and social matters. Providence had decreed the various political offices into existence, and to some extent the officeholders owed their position to God and were ultimately responsible to him. The role of the church was almost completely religious, except after 1830 when it seemed that outside forces were trying to dismantle the southern political and social structure. Then the ruling denominations sprang to the defense of slavery and the southern way of life. For decades the evangelicals had often spoken against the South's peculiar institution, but as their churches had grown both in influence and affluence, and slavery had expanded in proportion to cotton production, the clergymen had gradually come to accept slavery as part of this world's affairs. As such, this institution—like political offices—was under the providence of God. He would eventually judge men's errors.

The cardinal tenet of orthodox biblicism had always been absolute scriptural literalism. Every sermon, every point, every action, was supposedly based on biblical injunction—and more likely than not the verse was cited if not quoted. Especially after the New Light schism in Kentucky, creative theological thought was throttled. Theology became only the exposition of received truths, the elaboration of dogma. Within this nonabstract, strictly literal framework, the Bible quite obviously condoned slavery. For the ministers of the popular southern churches, the Bible was the guide to every act—personal and public. They called erroneous if not atheistic that liberal reading of the Scriptures given by northern abolitionist ministers. The southern clergy emphasized the letter of the gospel law, not its spirit. An abstract, conceptual interpretation of religious truths was alien to southern pietism. Given such an outlook, it was not difficult for evangelicals to turn the Scriptures into a sharp-edged defense of slavery.

In another sense, the southern evangelical had so developed his individual emphasis that he often failed to see slavery as an abstract evil. Instead he was apt to reply that individual slaves were usually better off than northern "wage slaves." The inability to conceptualize in part hid the ugly reality of a labor system which deprived slaves of their own individuality. But Southerners of good conscience could never completely hide this ugliest of realities. No one who reads deeply in the history of the region can miss the pervasive, though often disguised, feelings of guilt for perpetuating an institution which denied both the ideals of the Declaration of Independence and the Golden Rule. George B. Tindall has written, "A consciousness of God's justice and a sense of sin have always been sources of uneasiness among Southerners about their peculiar institutions." Charles G. Sellers spoke of this tension when he wrote of "the travail of slavery": "No analysis that misses the inner turmoil of the antebellum Southerner can do justice to the central tragedy of the southern experience." [32]

The set of religious beliefs which undergirded the Great Revival soon characterized the southern religious outlook. Religion was a matter of faith and emulation. A critical spirit was totally absent. One accepted his faith along with his position in life. The southern Christian was taught to accept the world and try to perfect his soul. It is significant that although the South was perhaps the most "religious" section of the nation, it could boast no great theologians. The North, where critical ideas were accepted, produced the Emersons, Channings, and Theodore Parkers. Who could imagine a southern Orestes Brownson? Southern religious life had become so static and orthodox that it became almost totally a heart religion, not a head religion. This attitude carried over into all realms of the southern comprehension of and response to historical events, public and private. Henry Adams observed that "strictly, the Southerner had no mind; he had temperament." W. J. Cash similarly remarked that the Southerner "did not (typically speaking) think; he felt." [33] Arrogant perhaps, but more than a little true, for the ante bellum South was not a region in which ideas had free play. They were not even allowed in the marketplace.

A South rich in revival heritage and buttressed by denominational colleges exhibited a pitifully weak heritage of social concern and reform. Except for a pietistic acceptance of the temperance movement, the reform ferment of the 1830s and 1840s was practically nonexistent in the South. In this region, religious commitment did not lead to an awareness of the need for intellectual and social reformation. As R. M. Weaver concluded in his essay on southern orthodoxy: "It seems an inescapable inference that in the

[32] George B. Tindall, "The Central Theme Revisited," in *The Southerner as American*, ed. Charles G. Sellers (New York, 1966), p. 119; and Charles G. Sellers, "The Travail of Slavery," in ibid., p. 40.

[33] Henry Adams, *The Education of Henry Adams* (New York, 1931), p. 57; and W. J. Cash, *The Mind of the South* (New York, 1941), p. 99.

sphere of religion the Southerner has always been hostile to the spirit of inquiry. He felt that a religion which is intellectual only is no religion. His was a natural piety, expressing itself in uncritical belief and in the experience of conversion, not in an ambition to perfect a system, or to tidy up a world doomed to remain forever deceptive, changeful, and evil." [34]

It has been one of the tragedies of southern religion that it never progressed intellectually or in social awareness past that orthodoxy which solidified several decades before the Civil War. The major denominations had perfected their institutional identities soon after the American Revolution. Within two decades they had managed to accept a reasonably sophisticated theological system which explained for their time the role of God, man, and history. They were so successful in preaching these doctrines and charging both their ministers and listeners with zeal that a vigorous revival swept over the South in the five years after 1800. But the southern evangelical movement grew little qualitatively after this. Colleges were established and periodicals published, thousands of sermons were preached. Yet the same content, scope, and approach persisted. Individual conversion remained the paramount issue. The dominant religious denominations in the South became so wedded to orthodoxy that they were unable to adjust creatively to the changes wrought by passing time. [35]

Along with the continual nearness and influence of the frontier and a modified agrarianism, the church has greatly helped to shape that "exaggerated individualism" which W. J. Cash considered the identifying characteristic of the southern mind. None of these factors contributed a posture receptive to change. At least until the Second World War, southern religious, racial, and political attitudes remained comparatively stationary. From his depression outlook Cash wrote: "It was the total effect of Southern conditions, primary and secondary, to preserve the Southerner's original simplicity of character as it were in perpetual suspension." [36]

This resistance to change—except occasionally that which was self-imposed, like the New South movement of the post-reconstruction years—has been a central theme of southern history. In a very real sense the dedication to maintaining white supremacy and the desire to preserve the regional

[34] Weaver, "The Older Religiousness in the South," p. 248.

[35] The Presbyterian James Henley Thornwell was perhaps the preeminent ante bellum theologian of the South, yet his writings betray a profound doctrinal rigidity and extreme political conservatism. Larry Philip Leonard has written a good introduction to Thornwell's thought, "'The Contributions of Presbyterian Orthodoxy to the Pro-Slavery Argument as Exemplified by the Writings of James Henley Thornwell, 1838–1860" (M.A. thesis, University of Virginia, 1967).

[36] Cash, *The Mind of the South*, p. 99.

agrarian identity can be subsumed under this theme.[37] The outcome of the freedom-of-thought struggle in the ante bellum South meant that new ideas and outlooks were largely forbidden. The unchanging presence of a large Negro population kept racial fears alive. Religious orthodoxy was vigorously self-correcting, and its practitioners ferreted out every inference of aberration. "Scratch any sectarian skin," wrote a Baptist university president, "and the same orthodox blood flows."[38] The South had no avalanche of immigrants to build up competing forms of religion and labor. Industrialization and urbanization were so late coming to the South that they had little influence on most of the region's history. In contrast with the rest of the nation, there has been little to force the South to change and adapt its mental attitudes. Defeat and its aftermath only served to reinforce the traditional southern way, for in defeat the Old South gained a glory and a piety much greater than in reality.

In 1902 Walter Hines Page, the gifted journalist, returned to the South to see firsthand what twenty years had done to his homeland. It was as if not a week had passed. Away from the immediate presence of railroads and isolated cities, people lived and thought "as men and women did fifty years ago, or eighty years ago, or even a hundred."[39] Page sensed that three factors locked the South to its past: slavery, politics, and the church. Slavery had "pickled" southern life and kept it unchanged, politicians stumped the South telling everyone that their way of life was the ideal situation, and the ever-present minister did his best to convince the faithful that this life and its hardships were of little importance. The life after death should be the real concern. "Thus gagged and bound," wrote Page, "Southern rural society has remained stationary longer than English-speaking people have remained stationary anywhere else in the world."[40]

This attachment to traditional attitudes has, in the opinion of economist William H. Nicholls, been a notable stumbling block to southern industrialization and economic growth. He says unequivocally that "the South

[37] The search for a theme to southern history has solicited some of the best essays in the field. See U. B. Phillips, "The Central Theme of Southern History," *American Historical Review* 34 (October 1928): 30–43; Twelve Southerners, *I'll Take My Stand* (New York, 1930); C. Vann Woodward, "The Search for Southern Identity," in his *Burden of Southern History* (Baton Rouge, La., 1960), pp. 3–26; and George B. Tindall, "Mythology: A New Frontier in Southern History," in *The Idea of the South*, ed. Frank E. Vandiver (Chicago, 1964), pp. 1–15.

[38] Edwin McNeill Poteat, Jr., "Religion in the South," in *Culture in the South*, ed. W. T. Couch (Chapel Hill, N. C., 1935), p. 261.

[39] "The Rebuilding of Old Commonwealths," *Atlantic Monthly* 89 (1902): 653.

[40] Ibid., p. 654.

must choose between tradition and progress."[41] C. Vann Woodward has also shown the inhibiting force of southern customs on capital formation, a necessity for indigenous economic growth. His own impressionistic evidence and the statistical studies of others suggest that Southerners have long had near extravagant spending habits, or rather, a higher propensity to consume than comparable income groups elsewhere in the nation. Woodward discusses the effect of the planter syndrome and slave labor on this relative southern unwillingness to save.[42] In addition to these factors, the otherworldliness of southern pietism and the resultant lessened concern with the economic future have probably contributed to a lowered desire to save for the future.[43] With smaller per capita savings, southern prosperity had to await the intrusion of large-scale investments from northern entrepreneurs. So in a compounded sense, the economic growth that has come to the region since the Second World War has often not been southern in character.[44]

One might argue today that at least parts of the South have accepted, indeed grasped for, a substantial degree of industrialization, urbanization, and economic growth, but this has usually not resulted in a wholesale overthrow of old values. Southerners to a peculiar degree have maintained an ambivalent coexistence with both modernity and tradition because, as David M. Potter has written, "they could not bear either to abandon the patterns of the Old South or to forego the material gains of modern America."[45] They have welcomed the affluence, not the influence, of change. Perhaps they have somehow recognized the inherent antipathy between the old and the new.

In many ways the South fits perfectly the definition of a "sacred" (not to be confused with holy) society given by the eminent sociologist Howard Becker. "A sacred society," he described, "is one that elicits from or imparts to its members . . . an unwillingness and/or inability to respond to the culturally new." He proceeded to elaborate his definition. "Formulated differently: a society that incorporates and sustains an impermeable value-

---

[41] *Southern Tradition and Regional Progress* (Chapel Hill, N. C., 1960), p. x.

[42] "The Southern Ethic in a Puritan World," *William and Mary Quarterly* 25 (July 1968): 357–58. Woodward discounts the laziness thesis of David Bertelson, *The Lazy South* (New York, 1967).

[43] See Nicholls, *Southern Tradition*, p. 163n., and the review of Nicholls by Robert H. Woody, *Mississippi Valley Historical Review* 47 (December 1960): 535.

[44] In very recent years, Atlanta, Dallas, and Houston banks have begun financing regional growth.

[45] "On Understanding the South," *Journal of Southern History* 30 (November 1964): 460.

system is sacred." [46] Both forms of his idea seem to include the southern response to historical forces. Two absolutes—a large black population and a firm evangelical orthodoxy—have not permitted adaptability.

"The impermeability of a value-system depends on the absence of effective intersocietal communication," [47] and this has been the region's experience. Until recently the South has been predominantly rural and isolated. For decades there was little critical communication between the North and South. Even Southerners of long standing who attempted to work for changed attitudes often met bitter opposition in what was labeled a "closed society." [48] This southern awareness of being out of step with the mainstream, this awareness of a subtle unity of religious and racial beliefs, has helped the South to respond almost as one to change dictated by extraregional forces. Most southern Protestants felt their individual faiths challenged by the Scopes trial; every southern state felt challenged by the Little Rock school episode of 1957.

The form of religion popular in the South has contributed as much as any other factor to the creation of the distinct southern mind and its characteristic unity of response to the threat of change.[49] C. Vann Woodward spoke of the "bonds of mind and spirit" which distinguished and unified the region on the eve of the First World War.

> Neither learning nor literature of the secular sort could compare with religion in power and influence over the mind and spirit of the South. The exuberant religiosity of the Southern people, the conservative orthodoxy of the dominant sects, and the overwhelming Protestantism of all but a few parts of the region were forces that persisted powerfully in the twentieth century. They were a large element in the homogeneity of the people and the readiness with which they responded to common impulses. They explained much of the survival of a distinctive regional culture, and they went far toward justifying the remark that the South was solid religiously as well as politically.[50]

[46] "Sacred and Secular Societies," *Social Forces* 28 (May 1950): 363–64.

[47] Ibid., p. 364.

[48] See James W. Silver's book, an enlargement of his presidential address to the Southern Historical Association, *Mississippi: The Closed Society* (New York, 1966).

[49] For an interesting comment on the southern propensity to overreact to change, see Frank E. Vandiver, "The Southerner as Extremist," in *The Idea of the South*, ed. Vandiver, pp. 43–56. An able study of the Protestant opposition to change, especially that represented by the "monkey trial" and Alfred E. Smith's presidential campaign, is Bailey, *Southern White Protestantism in the Twentieth Century*.

[50] Woodward, *Origins of the New South, 1877–1913* (Baton Rouge, La., 1951), p. 448.

Woodward here suggests another paradoxical feature of the enigmatic South. A society that persistently emphasized individual and provincial attachments nevertheless reached beyond these seemingly limiting ingredients to produce a regional loyalty, a "folk culture," unique in the nation. This concept is usually associated with David M. Potter, who stated in an essay in 1961: "On the face of it, it seems a matter of observation and not of theory to say that the culture of the folk survived in the South long after it succumbed to the onslaught of urban-industrial culture elsewhere. It was an aspect of this culture that the relation between the land and the people remained more direct and more primal in the South than in other parts of the country. . . . this culture retained a personalism in the relations of man to man which the industrial culture lacks."[51]

Whatever it is that in reality characterizes those who are native to the region, most would agree that it includes an intangible feeling of union with the land and people, a certain felt "southernness." The intense particularism of the separate states somehow is subsumed in a larger loyalty strikingly pervasive. In another essay Potter showed that group loyalty arises not by smothering all lesser attachments but instead by absorbing them "in a mutually supportive relation to one another." Many aspects of the southern past are poured into the form, each to harden into a portion of "southernness." "The strength of the whole," he wrote, "is not enhanced by destroying the parts, but is made up of the sum of the parts. The only citizens who are capable of strong national loyalty are those who are capable of strong group loyalty, and such persons are likely to express this capacity in their devotion to their religion, their community, and their families, as well as in their love of country."[52]

The uniformity of religious emphases and traditions throughout the South have contributed notably to this perceived sameness which has united Southerners. Contrary to logic, a people whose religion stresses individuals, whose outlook is provincial, and whose aversion to abstractions is legendary, have nevertheless produced a regional folk culture that, for all its failures, exhibits a "relatedness and meaning" which the national culture often lacks.[53]

[51] "The Enigma of the South," *Yale Review* 51 (Autumn 1961): 150.

[52] "The Historian's Use of Nationalism and Vice Versa," in Potter, *The South and the Sectional Conflict* (Baton Rouge, La., 1968), pp. 48–49. C. Vann Woodward has discussed these matters in "The Southern Ethic in a Puritan World," esp. pp. 347–48. Over twenty years ago Frank L. Owsley described the southern people as a "genuine folk" bound by common "ties of race, language, tradition and history." *Plain Folk of the Old South* (Baton Rouge, La., 1949), p. 90.

[53] Potter, "Enigma of the South," p. 151.

The rapid growth of cities and industry after the Second World War has brought surprisingly little accommodation on the part of religion. Skyscrapers have sprung up in Atlanta, Memphis, Houston, and Dallas, and a sophisticated space-age industrial complex has developed along the Texas and Florida coasts, but still emotional, personal revivalism resounds from most pulpits. In "Space City, U.S.A.," as Houston calls itself, one can still hear ministers fighting the century-old battle against science and evolution. Population and technological change, John Ezell and Francis B. Simkins have noted, only aid old-time religion. The people composing the booming urban populations are still basically rural people, and they prefer a rural religion. The concentration of people only makes larger crowds possible, and radio and television mean that the evangelical message can span the region every Sunday and any weeknight.[54]

During the last two decades, the major denominations in the South have begun to reevaluate their social ethic. While the Presbyterians and Methodists have taken the lead, the Southern Baptist Convention has hesitatingly started to move beyond the purely individual social matters such as drinking, dancing, and cursing. Relative to the rest of the nation the southern churches still seem far too singleminded in their solicitude for spiritual issues, but compared to their past, the 1960s in particular saw the beginning of perhaps a kind of southern social gospel. To date one of the foremost quandaries has been how to diffuse this newfound concern of denominational leaders and theologians among the millions of complacent churchgoers.[55]

Many have remarked on the failure of the white evangelical churches of the South to work together in the communities to break down the patterns of segregation. Recently the major denominations have indicated that their Christian conscience does include Negroes. Yet too often on the local level their paramount concern with salvation has led them to see the dilemmas of racism as only transitory, only minor as compared to the "real" issue of eternal life. And again the southern propensity to individualize has helped produce the stereotyped Southerner of today who professes to see

[54] John S. Ezell, *The South since 1865* (New York, 1963), p. 355; and Simkins, "The Rising Tide of Faith," passim. Cf. Alfred O. Hero, Jr., *The Southerner and World Affairs* (Baton Rouge, La., 1965), pp. 435–49; Harry Lefever, "The Church and Poor Whites," *New South: A Quarterly of Southern Affairs* 25 (Spring 1970): 20–32; and William C. Martin, "The God-Hucksters of Radio," *Atlantic Monthly* 225 (June 1970): 51–56.
[55] See the excellent articles by Donald W. Shriver, Jr., "Southern Churches in Transition," *New South: A Quarterly Review of Southern Affairs* 25 (Winter 1970): 40–47; and James H. Smylie, "On Being Presbyterian in the South," *Christian Century* 87 (August 5, 1970): 936–40.

no evil in the institution of segregation and insists instead that "some of my best friends are Negroes." The numerous independent, missionary, and Bible churches—all emphatically fundamentalist and unaffiliated with the major denominations—insure that the old-time religion will not fade away. Unfortunately, there does seem to be a definite correlation between evangelical religion in the South and at least tacit racism. As Alfred O. Hero, Jr., has written, "Apparently even when Southerners of similar education have been compared, those of more fundamental denominations have been more segregationist." He cites the results of a study made in the 1950s that showed Baptist undergraduates at the University of Texas to be "significantly more opposed to desegregation and generally racist on a variety of questions" than those of any other religious group.[56] Often the southern brand of Christian ethics has just not included the social immorality of segregation.

The Southern Baptist Convention is today the nation's largest Protestant denomination and also the one most indigenous to the South. Today this church, like its sister evangelical denominations, is facing a crisis.[57] Its ministers for the most part persist in preaching a literalism so strict it suffocates biblical relevancy. Their emphasis is almost wholly individualistic, patently ignoring social ills and injustices. Modern scientific and intellectual currents are often shunned, and the faithful are held to a pietism which obeys the letter of the Scriptures and misses the broader implications. The proudly autonomous local congregations calmly ignore the modernist social pronouncements which they know denominational leaders cannot enforce. Recently a small group of liberal dissenters tried to goad the Southern Baptist Convention into recognizing that changed times require changed programs. *The National Observer* quoted one of the modernists as saying: "We have lost our legitimacy with young people. . . . The stuff they are fed at the Sunday-school level hasn't got it. Most ministers are not being Scripturally honest with the kids. The (college students) who hold on to the old stuff usually crack before they get out."[58]

Perhaps the advocate of creative adaptation exaggerates the issues, but certainly the dominant southern denominations have lagged behind other

[56] Hero, *Southerner and World Affairs*, p. 443.

[57] See the eloquent work by Samuel S. Hill, Jr., *Southern Churches in Crisis*; see also Harold Lindsell, "Whither Southern Baptists?" *Christianity Today* 14 (April 24, 1970): 667–69.

[58] Terrence Shea, "Dissent Bubbles among the Southern Baptists," *National Observer* 8 (June 9, 1969): 6, quoting Robert Alley of the University of Richmond. The current (1971–1972) Jesus Movement may be stimulating anew the evangelical spirit among the young.

groups in reconciling their message with modernity. Southern churches have never been in the vanguard of social service, yet in the opening decades of the new nation they rapidly adapted themselves to the exigencies they faced. Institutional identities were shaped and belief systems spread. They perceived a situation of apparent crisis and energetically took both intellectual and practical steps to counter it. In their own terms they met the emergency. A vigorous revival effort swept across the southern states, dispelling clerical fears that religion was collapsing in the face of change and secular ideas. It is indeed ironic that out of such a heritage the current evangelical denominations have been so hesitant to move beyond religious concepts developed more than a century and a half ago.

Selected Bibliography

WRITINGS BY CONTEMPORARIES

Manuscripts

Anderson, Henry. Mss. Kentucky Historical Society, Frankfort, Ky.

Barrow, David. "Diary, May 5, 1795–September 1, 1795." The Filson Club, Louisville, Ky.

Botsford, Edmund. Letters. South Carolina Baptist Historical Society, Furman University, Greenville, S. C.

Carter, Robert. Mss. Virginia Baptist Historical Society, University of Richmond, Richmond, Va.

Caruthers, Eli W. "Richard Hugg King and His Times. Reminiscenses of Rev. Eli Caruthers of Orange Presbytery, N. C." North Carolina State Archives, Raleigh, N. C.

Draper Collection. Kings Mountain Papers. Wisconsin Historical Society. Microfilm, Tennessee State Archives, Nashville, Tenn.

Dromgoole, Edward. Papers. Southern Historical Collection, University of North Carolina, Chapel Hill, N. C.

Fishback, James. Collection. Lexington Theological Seminary, Lexington, Ky.

Furman Family Papers. Mss. South Carolina Baptist Historical Society, Furman University, Greenville, S. C.

Furman, Richard. Papers. South Carolina Baptist Historical Society, Furman University, Greenville, S. C.

———. "A Sermon on the Constitution and Order of the Christian Church. Preached before the Charleston Association of Baptists by Richard Furman, Pastor of the Baptist Church of Charleston, 1789." Mss. South Caroliniana Collection, University of South Carolina, Columbia, S. C.

Gaffney, Michael. "Journal, 1797–1854." South Caroliniana Collection, University of South Carolina, Columbia, S. C.

Glenn, L. C. Collection. Southern Historical Collection, University of North Carolina, Chapel Hill, N. C.

Gratz, Simon. Collection. Historical Society of Pennsylvania, Philadelphia, Pa.

Hammett, Revd. William. "Journal, 1787–1803." South Caroliniana Collection, University of South Carolina, Columbia, S. C.

Hemphill, W. R., J. C., and D. R. Papers. Duke University, Durham, N. C.

Hickman, William. "A Short Account of My Life and Travels." Typescript, Southern Baptist Theological Seminary, Louisville, Ky.

Kershaw, James. "Diary with Meteorological Observations." South Caroliniana Collection, University of South Carolina, Columbia, S. C.

Lyle, John. "Diary, June, 1801–July, 1803." Mss. Kentucky Historical Society, Frankfort, Ky. Typescript owned by Dr. Robert Stuart Sanders, Lexington, Ky.

McGready, James. "Letter." Pittsburgh Theological Seminary, Pittsburgh, Pa.

McHenry, James. Mss. University of Virginia, Charlottesville, Va.
Maryland Diocesan Archives. Maryland Historical Society, Baltimore, Md.
Mead, Stith. Letterbook. Virginia Historical Society, Richmond, Va.
Michaux-Randolph Papers. North Carolina State Archives, Raleigh, N. C.
Moore, Jeremiah. Mss. Virginia Baptist Historical Society, University of Richmond, Richmond, Va.
Norman, Jeremiah. "Diary." Stephen B. Weeks Collection, Southern Historical Collection, University of North Carolina, Chapel Hill, N. C.
Ormond, William. "Journals, 1791–1803." Duke University Library, Durham, N. C.
Patterson Mss. Shane Collection, Presbyterian Historical Society, Philadelphia, Pa.
Pettigrew Papers. North Carolina State Archives, Raleigh, N. C.
Pocket Plantation Mss. University of Virginia Library, Charlottesville, Va.
Reed, George A. Papers. Duke University Library, Durham, N. C.
Rice, David. Letters. Shane Collection, Presbyterian Historical Society, Philadelphia, Pa.
Watts, James. "Diary." University of Virginia Library, Charlottesville, Va.
Williamson Papers. Shane Collection, Presbyterian Historical Society, Philadelphia, Pa.
Wingfield, Rev. Charles. Mss. University of Virginia Library, Charlottesville, Va.

Church Records

Bethel [Baptist] Association, South Carolina. "Minutes." Microfilm, Historical Commission, Southern Baptist Convention, Nashville, Tenn.
Charleston [Baptist] Association, South Carolina. "Minutes." Microfilm, Historical Commission, Southern Baptist Convention, Nashville, Tenn.
Chestnut Grove Baptist Church, Albemarle County, Virginia. "Minute Book, 1773–1811." Ms in Virginia Baptist Historical Society, University of Richmond, Richmond, Va.
Goshen [Baptist] Association, Virginia. "Minutes." Virginia Baptist Historical Society, University of Richmond, Richmond, Va.
Hanover Presbytery. "Minutes." Photocopy, Union Theological Seminary in Virginia, Richmond, Va.
Holston [Baptist] Association, Tennessee. "Minutes." Microfilm, Historical Commission, Southern Baptist Convention, Nashville, Tenn.
[Methodist Episcopal Church]. *Minutes of the Methodist Conferences, Annually Held in America; from 1773 to 1813, inclusive.* New York, 1813.
Orange Presbytery. "Minutes." Mss in the Historical Foundation of the Presbyterian and Reformed Churches, Montreat, N. C.
Presbyterian Church in the United States. *Minutes of the General Assembly, A.D. 1789 to A.D. 1820 inclusive.* Philadelphia, 1847.
Sarepta [Baptist] Association, Georgia. *Minutes.* [n.p., n.d.], Microfilm, Historical Commission, Southern Baptist Convention, Nashville, Tenn.
Synod of the Carolinas. "Minutes." Mss in Union Theological Seminary in Virginia, Richmond, Va.
Synod of Kentucky. "Minutes." Mss in Louisville Presbyterian Seminary, Louisville, Ky.

Synod of Virginia. "Minutes." Photocopy, Union Theological Seminary in Virginia, Richmond, Va.

Transylvania Presbytery. "Minutes." Mss in Louisville Presbyterian Seminary, Louisville, Ky.

Wheeley's Baptist Church. "Minute Book." Typescript, North Carolina State Archives, Raleigh, N. C.

Pamphlets & Printed Sermons

A Brief History of the Rise, Progress, and Termination of the Proceedings of the Synod of Kentucky, Relative to the Late Cumberland Presbytery . . . as Taken from Official Documents and Facts in Possession of Synod. Lexington, Ky., 1823.

A Circular Letter Addressed to the Societies and Brethren of the Late Cumberland Presbytery; in Which There is a Correct Statement of the Origin, Progress, and Termination of the Differences between the Synod of Kentucky, and the Former Presbytery of Cumberland, 1810. Russellville, Ky., 1810.

[Anonymous]. *Gospel News, or A Brief Account of the Revival of Religion in Kentucky, and Several Other Parts of the United States. . . .* Baltimore, Md., 1801.

[Anonymous]. *Increase of Piety, or the Revival of Religion in the United States of America; Containing Several Interesting Letters Not Before Published. Together With Three Remarkable Dreams. . . . Collected by the Publisher.* Philadelphia, 1802.

[Anonymous]. *Two Letters Written by a Gentlemen [sic] to his Friend in Kentucky.* Lexington, Ky., [1804].

Barrow, David. *Circular Letter, February 14, 1798.* Norfolk, Va., 1798.

[Birch, Thomas L.]. *Letters addressed to the Revs. Messrs. John Cree, John Anderson, William Wilson, and Thomas Alison, members of the Associate Presbytery of Pennsylvania in Answer to Their Pamphlet, entitled Evils of the Work Now Prevailing in the United States Under the Name of a Revival of Religion. . . .* Washington, Pa., 1805.

[Cree, John; Anderson, John; Wilson, William; Alison, Thomas; Henderson, E.] *Evils of the Work Now Prevailing in the United States of America, under the Name of a Revival of Religion; Shewn by a Comparison of that Work, as it is Represented by its Friends and Promoters, with the Word of God.* Washington, Pa., 1804.

Furman, Richard. *America's Deliverance and Duty. A Sermon Preached at the Baptist Church, in Charleston, South-Carolina, on the Fourth Day of July, 1802, Before the State Society of the Cincinnati, the American Revolution Society; and the Congregation Which Usually Attends Divine Service in the Said Church.* Charleston, S. C., 1802.

Gildersleeve, Cyrus. *A New-Year Sermon, Delivered at MIDWAY* [Georgia], *January 1st, 1798. . . .* Savannah, Ga., [1798].

Haggard, Rice. *An Address To the Different Religious Societies On the Sacred Import of the Christian Name.* Lexington, Ky., 1804. Reprinted in *Footnotes to Disciple History,* Number 4, Nashville, Tenn., The Disciples of Christ Historical Society, 1954.

Hall, James. *A Narrative of a most extraordinary work of religion in North Carolina; also, a collection of interesting letters from the Rev. James M'Corkle, to which is added the agreeable intelligence of a revival in South Carolina.* Philadelphia, 1802.

Holcombe, Henry. *Primitive Theology, in a Series of Lectures.* Philadelphia, 1822.

————. *A Sermon, Occasioned by the Death of Mr. Charles Bealer, Who Cheerfully Resigned his Soul to God, in the Fifty-fifth year of His Age. Delivered at Euhaw.* Charleston, S. C., 1793.

Jarratt, Devereux. *Sermons on Various and Important Subjects in Practical Divinity, Adapted to the Plainest Capacities, and Suited to the Family and Closet.* 3 vols., Philadelphia, 1793–1794.

McGready, James. *The Posthumous Works of the Reverend and Pious James M'Gready, Late Minister of the Gospel, in Henderson, Kentucky.* Edited by James Smith. 2 vols. Vol. 1, Louisville, Ky., 1831; vol. 2, Nashville, Tenn., 1833.

Marshall, R., and Thompson, J. *A Brief Historical Account of Sundry Things in the Doctrines and State of the Christians, or as it is Commonly Called, The Newlight Church.* Cincinnati, Ohio, 1811. Reprinted in Levi Purviance, *Biography of Elder David Purviance. . . .* Dayton, Ohio, 1848, pp. [253]–274.

Pattillo, Henry. *Sermons, &c.* Wilmington, [N. C.], 1788.

Rankin, Adam. *A Review of the Noted Revival in Kentucky, Commenced in the Year of our Lord, 1801.* Lexington, Ky., 1802.

Rice, David. *An Epistle to the Citizens of Kentucky, Professing Christianity; Especially Those That Are, or Have Been, Denominated Presbyterians* [1805]. In Robert H. Bishop, *An Outline of the History of the Church in the State of Kentucky.* Lexington, Ky., 1824.

————. *A Second Epistle to the Citizens of Kentucky, Professing the Christian Religion, Especially Those Who Are, or Have Been, Denominated Presbyterians* [1808]. In Bishop, *History of the Church in Kentucky.*

————. *A Sermon on the Present Revival of Religion, &. in this Country; Preached at the Opening of the Kentucky Synod.* Lexington, Ky., 1803.

Stone, Barton W. *An Address to the Christian Churches in Kentucky, Tennessee, & Ohio on Several Important Doctrines of Religion.* 2d ed. Lexington, Ky., 1821.

————, et al. *An Apology for Renouncing the Jurisdiction of the Synod of Kentucky, To which is Added, a Compendious View of the Gospel, and a Few Remarks on the Confession of Faith. By the Presbytery of Springfield.* Lexington, Ky., 1804.

————. *Atonement. The Substance of Two Letters Written to a Friend.* Lexington, Ky., 1805.

Synod of the Carolinas. *A Pastoral Letter from the Synod of the Carolinas, Through the Medium of their Commission to the Churches Under their Care.* Salisbury, [N. C.], 1802.

Thomas, David. *The Observer trying the Great Reformation in This State and Proving it to have been originally a work of Divine Power with a survey of Several Objections to the contrary as being chiefly comprised in Mr. Rankin's Review of the Noted Revival lately published.* Lexington, Ky., 1802.

Periodicals & Newspapers

The Arminian Magazine: consisting of extracts and original treatises on general redemption. Philadelphia, 1789–1790.
The Connecticut Evangelical Magazine and Religious Intelligencer. 1808–1815.
The Georgia Analytical Repository. 1802–1803.
The Kentucky Gazette. 1795–1805.
The Massachusetts Baptist Missionary Magazine. 1803–1805.
The Methodist Magazine. London, 1802–1804.
The New York Missionary Magazine, and Repository of Religious Intelligence. 1800–1803.
Philadelphia Aurora General Advertiser. 1803.
Raleigh Register and North-Carolina State Gazette. 1799–1813.
The Virginia Religious Magazine. 1804–1807.
The Western Missionary Magazine; and Repository of Religious Intelligence. Washington, Pa., 1803–1805.

Memoirs, Biographies, & Journals

Asbury, Francis. *The Journal and Letters of Francis Asbury.* Edited by Elmer T. Clark, et al. 3 vols. Nashville, Tenn., 1958.
Boehm, Henry. *Reminiscences, Historical and Biographical, of Sixty-four Years in the Ministry.* Edited by Joseph B. Wakeley. New York, 1865.
Cartwright, Peter. *Autobiography of Peter Cartwright, The Backwoods Preacher.* Edited by William P. Strickland. Cincinnati, Ohio, 1856.
Caruthers, Eli W. *A Sketch of the Life and Character of the Rev. David Caldwell, D. D.* Greensborough, N. C., 1842.
Channing, William Ellery. *Memoir of William Ellery Channing, with Extracts from His Correspondence and Manuscripts.* Compiled by William Henry Channing. 3 vols. Boston, 1848.
Coke, Thomas. *Extracts of the Journals of the Rev. Dr. Coke's Five Visits to America.* London, 1793.
Cossitt, F. R. *The Life and Times of Rev. Finis Ewing.* Louisville, Ky., 1853.
Dow, Lorenzo. *History of Cosmopolite: or, The four volumes of Lorenzo's journal. Concentrated in one: containing his experience & travels, from childhood to 1814, being upwards of thirty-six years.* New York, 1814.
Finley, James B. *Autobiography of Rev. James B. Finley; or, Pioneer Life in the West.* Edited by William P. Strickland. Cincinnati, Ohio, 1856.
Hill, William. *Autobiographical Sketches and Other Papers of William Hill of Winchester.* Historical Transcripts No. 4. Richmond, Va., 1968.
Holcombe, Henry. *The First Fruits, in a Series of Letters.* Philadelphia, 1812.
Hovey, Alvah. *A Memoir of the Life and Times of the Rev. Isaac Backus.* Boston, 1859.
Humphrey, Edward P., and Cleland, Thomas A. *Memoirs of the Rev. Thomas Cleland: Compiled from his Private Papers.* Cincinnati, Ohio, 1859.
Jarratt, Devereux. *The Life of the Reverend Devereux Jarratt, rector of Bath parish, Dinwiddie county, Virginia. Written by himself, in a series of letters addressed to the Rev. John Coleman, one of the ministers of the Protestant Episcopal Church, in Maryland.* Baltimore, Md., 1806.

Jeter, J. B. *The Sermons and Other Writings of the Rev. Andrew Broaddus, with a Memoir of His Life.* New York, 1852.

Keever, Homer M., ed. "A Lutheran Preacher's [Paul Henkel] Account of the 1801–02 Revival in North Carolina." *Methodist History* 7 (October 1968): 38–55.

Lee, Jesse. *A Short Account of the Life and Death of the Rev. John Lee, A Methodist Minister in the United States of America.* Baltimore, Md., 1805.

Lee, LeRoy M. *The Life and Times of the Rev. Jesse Lee.* Louisville, Ky., 1848.

Leland, John. *The Life and Writings of Elder John Leland.* Edited by L. F. Greene. New York, 1845.

Mallary, C. D. *Memoirs of Elder Jesse Mercer.* [n. p.], 1844.

Purviance, Levi. *The Biography of Elder David Purviance, with his memoirs: containing his views on baptism, the divinity of Christ, and the atonement. Written by himself: with an appendix: giving biographical sketches of elders John Hardy, Reuben Dooley, . . . Together, with a historical sketch of the great Kentucky revival.* Dayton, Ohio, 1848.

Rankin, John. "Autobiographical Sketch, written in 1845, prefacing the church records of the Shaker Community at South Union, Logan County, Kentucky." In J. P. McLean, "The Kentucky Revival and its Influence on the Miami Valley." *Ohio Archaeological and Historical Publications* 12 (April 1903): 279–81.

Sandford, P. P. *Memoirs of Mr. Wesley's Missionaries to America.* New York, 1843.

Smith, Henry. *Recollections and Reflections of an Old Itinerant.* New York, 1848.

Stuart, Robert. "Reminiscences, Respecting the Establishment and Progress of the Presbyterian Church in Kenutcky." In Robert Stuart Sanders, *The Reverend Robert Stuart, D. D. 1772–1856: A Pioneer in Kentucky Presbyterianism and His Descendants.* Louisville, Ky., 1962.

Stone, Barton Warren. *A Short History of the Life of Barton W. Stone.* In James R. Rogers, *The Cane Ridge Meeting-House.* Cincinnati, Ohio, 1910.

Thomas, Joseph. *The Life of the Pilgrim Joseph Thomas, containing an accurate account of his trials, travels, and gospel labors, up to the present date.* Winchester, Va., 1817.

Young, Jacob. *Autobiography of a Pioneer, Or the Nativity, Experience, Travels, and Ministerial Labors of the Rev. Jacob Young, with Incidents, Observations, and Reflections.* Cincinnati, Ohio, [1857].

Travel Accounts

Bayard, Ferdinand Marie. *Travels of a Frenchman in Maryland and Virginia . . . in 1791; or Travels in the Interior of the United States, to Bath, Winchester, in the Valley of the Shenandoah . . . during the summer of 1791.* Translated and edited by Ben C. McCary. Ann Arbor, Mich., 1950.

Melish, John. *Travels in the United States of America, in the Years 1806 & 1807, and 1809, 1810, & 1811; Including an Account of Passages Betwixt America and Britain, and Travels Through Various Parts of Great Britain, Ireland, and Upper Canada.* 2 vols. Philadelphia, 1812 and 1815.

Michaux, Francois André. *Travels to the Westward of the Allegany Mountains, in the States of the Ohio, Kentucky, and Tennessee.* . . . Translated by B. Lambert. London, 1805.

Rouchefoucault, Duc De La. *Travels through the United States of North America, The Country of the Iroquois, and Upper Canada, in the Year 1795, 1796, and 1797.* . . . 2 vols. London, 1799.

[Smith, Daniel]. *A Short description of the state of Tennassee [sic], lately called the Territory of the United States, south of the river Ohio.* . . . Philadelphia, 1796, reprint ed., Boston, 1938.

Smith, James. "Tours into Kentucky and the Northwest Territory: Three Journals by the Rev. James Smith of Powhatan County, Virginia, 1783–1795–1797." *Ohio Archaeological and Historical Publications* 16 (1907): 348–401.

[Steiner, Abraham, and De Schweinitz, Frederick C.]. "Report of the Journey of the Brethren . . . Steiner and Schweinitz . . . to the Cherokees and the Cumberland Settlements, 1799." Reprinted in Samuel Cole Williams, *Early Travels in the Tennessee Country, 1540–1800.* Johnson City, Tenn., 1928, pp. 445–525.

Weld, Isaac. *Travels through the States of North America, and the Provinces of Upper and Lower Canada, during the years 1795, 1796, and 1797.* London, 1799.

Miscellaneous

Armenius, Theophilus [pseud.]. "Account of the Rise and Progress of the Work of God in the Western Country." *Methodist Magazine* 2 (1819): 184–87, 221–24, 272–74, 304–8, 349–53, 393–96, 434–38.

Asbury, Francis. "A Letter to [Nelson Reed], February 11, 1796." *World Parish* 8 (October 1960): 24.

Asplund, John. *The Annual Register of the Baptist Denomination, in North-America; to the First of November, 1790. Containing an Account of the Churches and their Constitutions, Ministers, Members, Associations, their Plan and Sentiments, Rule and Order, Proceedings and Correspondence. Also Remarks Upon Practical Religion.* [n. p.], 1792.

Backus, Isaac. *An abridgement of the church history of New-England, from 1602 to 1804.* . . . *With a concise account of the Baptists in the Southern parts of America.* . . .Boston, 1804.

Baird, Robert. *Religion in America; or, an Account of the Origin, Progress, Relation to the State, and Present Condition of the Evangelical Churches in the United States.* New York, 1844.

Benedict, David. *A General History of the Baptist Denomination in America and other parts of the world.* 2 vols. Boston, 1813.

Bishop, Robert Hamilton. *An Outline of the History of the Church in the State of Kentucky, during a period of 40 years; containing the memoirs of Rev. David Rice, and sketches of the origin and present state of particular churches.* . . . Lexington, Ky., 1824.

Burkitt, Lemuel, and Read, Jesse. *A Concise History of the Kehukee Baptist Association.* . . . Halifax, [N. C.], 1803.

Carr, John. *Early Times in Middle Tennessee*. Nashville, Tenn., 1857. Reprint ed., Nashville, Tenn., 1958.

Coke, Thomas, and Asbury, Francis, intro. *A Pocket Hymn-Book, Designed As a Constant Companion for the Pious. Collected From Various Authors*. 9th ed. Philadelphia, 1790.

Davidson, Robert. *History of the Presbyterian Church in the State of Kentucky*. New York, 1847.

Dew, Thomas R. "An Address, Delivered before the Students of William and Mary, at the opening of the College, on Monday, October 10th, 1836." *Southern Literary Messenger* 2 (November 1836): 760–69.

Dow, Lorenzo, comp. *A Collection of Spiritual Songs Used at the Camp Meetings in the Great Revival in the United States of America*. London, 1806.

Dow, Lorenzo, ed. *Extracts from Original Letters, to the Methodist Bishops, Mostly from their Preachers and Members, in North America: giving an Account of the Work of God, Since the Year 1800. Prefaced with a Short History of the Spread and Increase of the Methodists; with a sketch of the Camp Meetings*. Liverpool, 1806.

[Fessenden, Thomas Green]. *Democracy Unveiled, or Tyranny Stripped of the Garb of Patriotism. By Christopher Caustic*. . . . 3d ed. 2 vols. in 1. New York, 1806.

Foote, William Henry. *Sketches of North Carolina, Historical and Biographical*. New York, 1846.

————. *Sketches of Virginia, Historical and Biographical*. 2 vols. Philadelphia, 1850–1855.

Ford, S. H. "History of the Kentucky Baptists: Chapter IX, The Great Revival.—Camp Meetings.—The Jerks.—Barton W. Stone.—New Lights." *The Christian Repository* 5 (December 1856): 331–46.

Fristoe, William. *A Concise History of the Ketocton Baptist association: wherein a description is given of her constitution, progress, and increase*. . . . Staunton, [Va.], 1808.

Furman, Wood, comp. *A History of the Charleston Association of Baptist Churches in the State of South-Carolina; With An Appendix Containing the Principal Circular Letters to the Churches*. Charleston, S. C., 1811.

Gallaher, James. *The Western Sketch-Book*. Boston, 1850.

[Green, Calvin, and Wells, Seth Y.]. *A Summary View of the Millennial Church, or United Society of Believers, Commonly Called Shakers, Comprising the Rise, Progress, and Practical Order of the Society, Together With the General Principles of Their Faith and Testimony*. Albany, N. Y., 1823.

Hawks, Francis L. *Contributions to the Ecclesiastical History of the United States of America*. 2 vols. New York, 1836.

Hymn Book. [n.p., n.d.]. Michaux-Randolph Papers. North Carolina State Archives, Raleigh, N. C.

Lee, Jesse. *A Short History of the Methodists, in the United States of America; beginning in 1766, and Continued till 1809*. Baltimore, Md., 1810.

McAfee, Robert B. "The Life and Times of Robert B. McAfee and his Family Connections." *Kentucky State Historical Society Register* 25 (May 1927): 5–37, 111–43, 215–37.

McGready, James. "Extract of a Letter from the Rev. James M. Gready [*sic*], a Presbyterian Minister, in Logan County, Kentucky, to the Rev. Dr. Coke." *Methodist Magazine* [London] 26 (1803): 181–84.

―――. "Narrative of the Commencement and Progress of the Revival of 1800. . . . In a Letter to a Friend, Dated Logan County, Kentucky, October 23, 1801." In McGready, *Posthumous Works*, 1: ix–xvi.

―――. "A Short Narrative of the Revival of Religion in Logan County, in the State of Kentucky, and the adjacent Settlements in the State of Tennessee, from May 1797, until September 1800." *New York Missionary Magazine* 3 (1802): 74–75, 151–55, 192–97, 234–36.

M'Nemar, Richard. *The Kentucky Revival, or, A Short History of the Late Extraordinary Out-Pouring of the Spirit of God, in the Western States of America, Agreeably to the Scripture-Promises, and Prophecies Concerning the Latter Day: With a Brief Account of the Entrance and Progress of What the World Call [sic] Shakerism, Among the Subjects of the Late Revival in Ohio and Kentucky, Presented to the True Zion-Traveller, As a Memorial to the Wilderness Journey.* Cincinnati, Ohio, 1807; later ed., 1846.

Marshall, Humphrey. *The History of Kentucky.* 2 vols. 1, Frankfort, Ky., 1812; 1 and 2, Frankfort, Ky., 1824.

Mercer, Jesse. *A History of the Georgia Baptist Association.* Washington, Ga., 1838.

Methodist Episcopal Church. *A Form of Discipline, For the Ministers, Preachers, and Members of the Methodist Episcopal Church in America, Considered and Approved at a Conference Held at Baltimore, in the State of Maryland, On Monday the 27th of December, 1784. . . .* 5th ed. New York, 1789.

Peck, John M. "Baptists of the Mississippi Valley." *The Christian Review* 17 (October 1852): 482–514.

Presbyterian Church in the United States of America. *The Constitution of the Presbyterian Church in the United States of America. Containing the confession of faith, the catechisms . . .* [as approved in] *1805.* Philadelphia, 1815.

Ramsay, David. *Ramsay's History of South Carolina, from its first Settlement in 1760 to the year 1808.* Newberry, S. C., 1858.

Rippon, John. *The Baptist Annual Register.* 4 vols. [n.p.], 1793–[1803].

―――. *A Selection of Hymns From the Best Authors, Intended to be an Appendix to Dr. Watt's Psalms and Hymns.* Philadelphia, 1802.

Rumple, Jethro. *The History of Presbyterianism in North Carolina.* Historical Transcripts Number 3. Richmond, Va., 1966.

Semple, Robert Baylor. *A History of the Rise and Progress of the Baptists in Virginia.* Richmond, Va., 1810.

Smith, James. *History of the Christian Church (including a history of the Cumberland Presbyterian Church).* Nashville, Tenn., 1835.

Smith, Joseph. *Old Redstone; or, Historical Sketches of Western Presbyterianism, its early ministers, its perilous times, and its first records.* Philadelphia, 1854.

Sprague, William B. *Annals of the American Pulpit; or, Commemorative Notices of Distinguished American Clergymen of Various Denominations.* 7 vols. New York, 1859.

Stone, Barton Warren. *A History of the Christian Church in the West.* Reprinted from the *Christian Messenger*, 1827. Foreword by Roscoe M. Pierson. Lexington, Ky., 1956.

Taylor, John. *A History of Ten Baptist Churches*. Frankfort, Ky., 1823.

Watts, Isaac. *Hymns and Spiritual Songs, in Three Books. . . . Corrected, And Accommodated to The Use of The Church of Christ in America*. Bound in Watts, *The Psalms of David. . . .* Norwich [Eng.], [1793].

Welch, James E. "Early Preachers of Kentucky." *Christian Repository* 5 (May 1856): 289–94.

Woodmason, Charles. *The Carolina Backcountry on the Eve of the Revolution: The Journal and Other Writings of Charles Woodmason, Anglican Itinerant*. Edited by Richard J. Hooker. Chapel Hill, N. C., 1953.

Woodward, William W. *Surprising Accounts of the Revival of Religion in the United States*. Philadelphia, 1802.

SECONDARY SOURCES

Books

Adams, Henry. *The Education of Henry Adams*. New York, 1931.

Addison, James Thayer. *The Episcopal Church in the United States, 1789–1931*. New York, 1951.

Albright, Raymond W. *A History of the Protestant Episcopal Church*. New York, 1964.

Andrews, Edward Deming. *The People Called Shakers: A Search for the Perfect Society*. New York, 1953.

Arnold, W. E. *A History of Methodism in Kentucky*. 2 vols. Louisville, Ky., 1935–1936.

Bailey, Kenneth K. *Southern White Protestantism in the Twentieth Century*. New York, 1964.

Beard, Richard. *Brief Biographical Sketches of Some of the Early Ministers of the Cumberland Presbyterian Church*. Nashville, Tenn., 1867.

Bertelson, David. *The Lazy South*. New York, 1967.

Bridenbaugh, Carl. *Myths & Realities: Societies of the Colonial South*. Baton Rouge, La., 1952.

Brunner, Edmund deS. *Church Life in the Rural South*. New York, 1923.

Brydon, G. MacLaren. *Virginia's Mother Church and the Political Conditions Under Which It Grew*. 2 vols. Richmond, Va., 1947–1952.

Bucke, Emory Stevens, ed. *The History of American Methodism*. 3 vols. New York, 1964.

Buckley, James Monroe. *A History of Methodists in the United States*. *The American Church History Series*, vol. 5. 2d ed. New York, 1907.

Case, Shirley J. *The Millennial Hope: A Phase of War-Time Thinking*. Chicago, 1918.

Cash, W. J. *The Mind of the South*. New York, 1941.

Cleveland, Catharine Cleveland. *The Great Revival in the West, 1797–1805*. Chicago, 1916.

Cohn, Norman. *The Pursuit of the Millennium*. New York, 1957.

Cunningham, Noble. *The Jeffersonian Republicans: The Formation of Party Organization, 1789–1801*. Chapel Hill, N. C., 1967.

Davenport, Frederick M. *Primitive Traits in Religious Revivals*. New York, 1905.

DeBow, J. B. *A Compendium of the Seventh Census*. Washington, D. C., 1854.

Dick, Everett. *The Dixie Frontier*. New York, 1948.

Dorchester, Daniel. *The Problem of Religious Progress*. New York, 1881.

Eaton, Clement. *The Freedom-of-Thought Struggle in the Old South*. Rev. ed. New York, 1964.

———. *The Growth of Southern Civilization, 1790–1860*. New York, 1963.

———. *The Mind of the Old South*. Rev. ed. Baton Rouge, La., 1967.

Eckenrode, H. J. *The Separation of Church and State in Virginia*. Richmond, Va., 1909.

Ezell, John S. *The South since 1865*. New York, 1963.

Foster, Charles I. *An Errand of Mercy: The Evangelical United Front, 1790–1837*. Chapel Hill, N. C., 1960.

Foster, R. V. *A History of . . . the Cumberland Presbyterian Church. . . . The American Church History Series*, vol. 11. 2d ed. New York, 1904.

Garrison, Winfred Ernest, and DeGroot, Alfred T. *The Disciples of Christ, A History*. St. Louis, Mo., 1948.

Gaston, Paul M. *The New South Creed: A Study in Southern Mythmaking*. New York, 1970.

Gaustad, Edwin Scott. *Historical Atlas of Religion in America*. New York, 1962.

Gewehr, Wesley M. *The Great Awakening in Virginia*. Durham, N. C., 1930.

Goen, C. C. *Revivalism and Separatism in New England, 1740–1800; Strict Congregationalists and Separate Baptists in the Great Awakening*. New Haven, Conn., 1962.

Griffin, Clifford S. *Their Brothers' Keepers: Moral Stewardship in the United States, 1800–1865*. New Brunswick, N. J., 1960.

Guthrie, Dwight Raymond. *John McMillan, The Apostle of Presbyterianism in the West, 1752–1833*. Pittsburgh, Pa., 1952.

Harrell, David Edwin, Jr. *Quest for a Christian America: The Disciples of Christ and American Society to 1866*. Nashville, Tenn., 1966.

Heimert, Alan. *Religion and the American Mind from the Great Awakening to the Revolution*. Cambridge, Mass., 1966.

Hero, Alfred O., Jr. *The Southerner and World Affairs*. Baton Rouge, La., 1965.

Hill, Samuel S., Jr. *Southern Churches in Crisis*. New York, 1967.

Hofstadter, Richard. *The American Political Tradition and the Men Who Made It*. New York, 1948.

———. *Anti-Intellectualism in American Life*. New York, 1966.

Hudson, Winthrop S. *American Protestantism*. Chicago, 1961.

———. *Religion in America*. New York, 1965.

Jackson, George Pullen. *White and Negro Spirituals: Their Life Span and Kindship*. New York, 1943.

Koch, G. Adolf. *Republican Religion: The American Revolution and the Cult of Reason*. New York, [1933].

Kilgore, Charles F. *The James O'Kelley Schism in the Methodist Episcopal Church*. Mexico, D. F., [1963].

Lumpkin, William L. *The Baptist Foundations in the South, Tracing through the Separates the Influence of the Great Awakening, 1754–1787*. Nashville, Tenn., 1961.

MacClenny, William E. *The Life of Reverend James O'Kelley, and the Early History of the Christian Church in the South.* Raleigh, N. C., 1910.

MacLean, John Patterson. *The Life and Labors of Richard McNemar.* Franklin, Ohio, 1905.

Malinowski, Bronislaw. *Magic, Science, and Religion and Other Essays.* Glencoe, Ill., 1948.

Malone, Dumas. *The Public Life of Thomas Cooper, 1783–1839.* New Haven, Conn., 1926.

Manross, William Wilson. *The Episcopal Church in the United States, 1800–1840.* New York, 1938.

———. *A History of the American Episcopal Church.* 3d ed. New York, 1959.

Marty, Martin E. *The Infidel: Freethought and American Religion.* Cleveland, Ohio, 1961.

McDonnold, W. B. *History of the Cumberland Presbyterian Church.* Nashville, Tenn., 1888.

McFerrin, John Berry. *History of Methodism in Tennessee. From the Year 1783 to the Year 1840.* 3 vols. Nashville, Tenn., 1874–1875.

McLoughlin, William G. *Isaac Backus and the American Pietistic Tradition.* Boston, 1967.

McNeil, John T. *Modern Christian Movements.* Rev. ed. New York, 1968.

Melcher, Marguerite Fellows. *The Shaker Adventure.* Princeton, N. J., 1941.

Miller, Perry. *The Life of the Mind in America, From the Revolution to the Civil War.* New York, 1965.

———. *The New England Mind: From Colony to Province.* Cambridge, Mass., 1953.

Miyakaya, T. Scott. *Protestants and Pioneers: Individualism and Conformity on the American Frontier.* Chicago, 1964.

Moore, Matthew H. *Sketches of the Pioneers of Methodism in North Carolina and Virginia.* Nashville, Tenn., 1884.

Morais, Herbert M. *Deism in Eighteenth Century America.* New York, 1934.

Neal, Julia. *By Their Fruits; The Story of Shakerism in South Union, Kentucky.* Chapel Hill, N. C., 1947.

Nicholls, William H. *Southern Tradition and Regional Progress.* Chapel Hill, N. C., 1960.

Norbeck, Edward. *Religion in Primitive Society.* New York, 1961.

Osterweis, Rollin G. *Romanticism and Nationalism in the Old South.* New Haven, Conn., 1949.

Owsley, Frank Lawrence. *Plain Folk of the Old South.* Baton Rouge, La., 1949.

Porter, Herschel S. "History of the Cumberland Presbyterian Church." In *An Original History of All the Religious Denominations in the United States,* edited by I. Daniel Rupp. Harrisburg, Pa., 1849.

Posey, Walter Brownlow. *The Baptist Church in the Lower Mississippi Valley, 1776–1845.* Lexington, Ky., 1957.

———. *The Development of Methodism in the Old Southwest, 1783–1824.* Tuscaloosa, Ala., 1933.

———. *Frontier Mission. A History of Religion West of the Southern Appalachians to 1861.* Lexington, Ky., 1966.

————. *The Presbyterian Church in the Old Southwest, 1778–1838.* Richmond, Va., 1952.

Price, R. N. *Holston Methodism. From its Origin to the Present Time.* 5 vols. Nashville, Tenn., 1912.

Rankin, S. M. *History of Buffalo Presbyterian Church and Her People.* Greensboro, N. C., 1934.

Redford, A. H. *The History of Methodism in Kentucky.* 4 vols. Nashville, Tenn., 1868–1870.

Shipp, Albert M. *The History of Methodism in South Carolina.* Nashville, Tenn., 1883.

Silver, James W. *Mississippi: The Closed Society.* New York, 1966.

Simkins, Francis Butler. *A History of the South.* 3d ed. New York, 1963.

Smith, George Gilman. *History of Methodism in Georgia and Florida, from 1785 to 1865.* Macon, Ga., 1877.

Smith, Timothy L. *Revivalism and Social Reform in Mid-Nineteenth-Century America.* New York, 1957.

Sonne, Niels Henry. *Liberal Kentucky 1780–1828.* New York, 1939.

Speer, William. *The Great Revival of 1800.* Philadelphia, 1872.

Spencer, J. H. *A History of Kentucky Baptists from 1769 to 1885, including more than 800 Biographical Sketches.* 2 vols. Cincinnati, Ohio, 1886.

Stroupe, H. S. *The Religious Press in the South Atlantic States 1802–1865: An Annotated Bibliography with Historical Introduction and Notes.* Durham, N. C., 1956.

Sweet, William Warren. *Men of Zeal: The Romance of American Methodist Beginnings.* New York, 1935.

————. *Religion in the Development of American Culture, 1765–1840.* New York, 1952.

————. *Religion on the American Frontier,* vol. 1, *The Baptists.* New York, 1931; vol. 2, *The Presbyterians.* New York, 1936; vol. 3, *The Congregationalists.* Chicago, 1939; vol. 4, *The Methodists.* Chicago, 1946.

————. *The Story of Religion in America.* New York, 1950.

————. *Virginia Methodism: A History.* Richmond, Va., 1955.

Sydnor, Charles S. *American Revolutionaries in the Making* [original title, *Gentleman Freeholders.* Chapel Hill, N. C., 1952]. New York, 1962.

Tewksbury, Donald G. *The Founding of American Colleges and Universities before the Civil War, with Particular Reference to the Religious Influence Bearing upon the College Movement.* New York, 1965.

Thompson, Ernest Trice. *Presbyterians in the South.* Richmond, Va., 1963.

Thompson, Robert Ellis. . . . *A History of the Presbyterian Churches in the United States.* The American Church History Series. Vol. 6. 2d ed. New York, 1902.

Torbet, Robert George. *A History of the Baptists.* Philadelphia, 1950.

Townsend, Leah. *South Carolina Baptists, 1760–1805.* Florence, S. C., 1935.

Turner, Herbert Snipes. *Church in the Old Fields: Hawfields Presbyterian Church and Community in North Carolina.* Chapel Hill, N. C., 1962.

Tuveson, Ernest Lee. *Redeemer Nation: The Idea of America's Millennial Role.* Chicago, 1968.

Twelve Southerners. *I'll Take My Stand.* New York, 1930.

[United States Census]. *A Century of Population Growth, From the First Census to the Twelfth, 1790–1900.* Washington, D. C., 1909.

————. *Return of the Whole Number of Persons Within the Several Districts of the United States, according to "An act providing for the second Census or Enumeration of the Inhabitants of the United States."* [Washington, D. C., 1800].

Weisberger, Bernard A. *They Gathered at the River: The Story of the Great Revivalists and Their Impact upon Religion in America.* Boston, 1958.

West, William Garrett. *Barton Warren Stone: Early American Advocate of Christian Unity.* Nashville, Tenn., 1954.

Woodward, C. Vann. *Origins of the New South, 1877–1913.* In *A History of the South* series, vol. 9. Baton Rouge, La., 1951.

Wright, Conrad. *The Beginnings of Unitarianism in America.* Boston, 1966.

Articles

Ammon, Harry. "The Jeffersonian Republicans in Virginia: An Interpretation." *Virginia Magazine of History and Biography* 71 (April 1963): 153–67.

Barber, Theodore Xenophon. "Who Believes in Hypnosis?" *Psychology Today* 4 (July 1970): 20–27, 84.

Becker, Howard. "Sacred and Secular Societies." *Social Forces* 28 (May 1950): 361–76.

Birdsall, Richard D. "The Reverend Thomas Allen: Jeffersonian Calvinist." *New England Quarterly* 30 (1957): 147–65.

Blanks, W. D. "Corrective Church Discipline in the Presbyterian Churches of the Nineteenth Century South." *Journal of Presbyterian History* 44 (June 1966): 89–105.

Boles, John B. "Henry Holcombe, A Southern Baptist Reformer in the Age of Jefferson." *Georgia Historical Quarterly* 54 (Fall 1970): 381–407.

Brown, Ira V. "Watchers for the Second Coming: The Millenarian Tradition in America." *Mississippi Valley Historical Review* 29 (Dec. 1952): 441–58.

Browne, C. A. "Elder John Leland and the Mammoth Cheshire Cheese." *Agricultural History* 28 (October 1944): 145–53.

Butterfield, Lyman H. "Elder John Leland, Jeffersonian Itinerant." *American Antiquarian Society, Proceedings* 62 (October 1952): 155–242.

Eaton, Clement. "The Ebb of the Great Revival." *North Carolina Historical Review* 23 (January 1946): 1–12.

Foster, Robert V. "A Sketch of the History of the Cumberland Presbyterian Church." In *American Church History*, 11: 257–309. New York, 1904.

Gabriel, Ralph H. "Evangelical Religion and Popular Romanticism in the Early Nineteenth Century." *Church History* 19 (March 1950): 34–47.

Gewehr, Wesley M. "Some Factors in the Expansion of Frontier Methodism." *Journal of Religion* 8 (January 1928): 98–120.

Gibson, George H. "The Unitarian-Universalist Church of Richmond." *Virginia Magazine of History and Biography* 74 (July 1966): 321–35.

Goen, C. C. "Jonathan Edwards: A New Departure in Eschatology." *Church History* 28 (March 1959): 25–40.

————. "The 'Methodist Age' in American Church History." *Religion in Life* 34 (Autumn 1965): 562–72.

Gohdes, Clarence. "Some Notes on the Unitarian Church in the Ante-Bellum South: A Contribution to the History of Southern Liberalism." In *American Studies in Honor of William Kenneth Boyd, by Members of the Americana Club of Duke University*, edited by David K. Jackson, pp. 327–66. Durham, N.C., 1940.

Hemphill, W. E. " 'In a Constant Struggle': How and Why Virginians Voted for Thomas Jefferson in 1800." *Virginia Cavalcade* 2 (Spring 1953): 8–15.

Hill, Samuel S., Jr. "An Agenda for Research in Religion." In *Perspectives on the South: Agenda for Research*, edited by Edgar T. Thompson, pp. 195–213. Durham, N. C., 1967.

Howe, John R., Jr. "Republican Thought and the Political Violence of the 1790s." *American Quarterly* 19 (Summer 1967): 147–65.

Hughes, N. C. J. "The Methodist Christmas Conference: Baltimore—December 24, 1784–January 2, 1785." *Maryland Historical Magazine* 54 (September 1959): 272–92.

Johnson, Guion Griffis. "The Camp Meeting in Ante-Bellum North Carolina." *North Carolina Historical Review* 10 (April 1933): 95–110.

———. "Revival Movements in Ante-Bellum North Carolina." *North Carolina Historical Review* 10 (January 1933): 21–43.

Lefever, Harry. "The Church and Poor Whites." *New South: A Quarterly of Southern Affairs* 25 (Spring 1970): 20–32.

Lindsell, Harold. "Whither Southern Baptists?" *Christianity Today* 14 (April 24, 1970): 667–69.

Loetscher, Lefferts A. "The Problem of Christian Unity in Early Nineteenth Century America." *Church History* 32 (March 1963): 3–16.

Martin, William C. "The God-Hucksters of Radio." *Atlantic Monthly* 225 (June 1970): 51–56.

Mathews, Donald G. "The Second Great Awakening as an Organizing Process, 1780–1830: An Hypothesis." *American Quarterly* 21 (Spring 1969): 23–43.

May, Henry F. "The Recovery of American Religious History." *American Historical Review* 70 (October 1964): 79–92.

Mead, Sidney E. "Denominationalism: The Shape of Protestantism in America." *Church History* 23 (December 1954): 291–320.

———. "The Rise of the Evangelical Conception of the Ministry in America (1607–1850)." In *The Ministry in Historical Perspectives*, edited by H. Richard Niebuhr and Daniel D. Williams, pp. 207–49. New York, 1956.

Miller, Perry. "Declension in a Bible Commonwealth." *Proceedings of the American Antiquarian Society* 51 (1941): 37–94.

———. "Errand into the Wilderness." In Miller, *Errand into the Wilderness*, pp. 1–15. New York, 1964.

Morrow, Ralph E. "The Great Revival, the West, and the Crisis of the Church." In *The Frontier Re-examined*, edited by John Francis McDermott, pp. 65–78. Urbana, Ill., 1967.

Nash, Gary B. "The American Clergy and the French Revolution." *William and Mary Quarterly* 22 (July 1965): 392–412.

Nichols, Robert Hastings. "The Influence of the American Environment on the Conception of the Church in American Protestantism." *Church History* 11 (September 1942): 181–92.

Opie, James, Jr. "James McGready: Theologian of Frontier Revivalism." *Church History* 34 (December 1965): 445–56.

Page, Walter Hines. "The Rebuilding of Old Commonwealths." *Atlantic Monthly* 89 (1902): 651–61.

Persons, Stow. "The Cyclical Theory of History in Eighteenth Century America." *American Quarterly* 6 (Summer 1954): 147–63.

Phillips, U. B. "The Central Theme of Southern History." *American Historical Review* 34 (October 1928): 30–43.

Posey, Walter B. "The Shakers Move West." *Emory University Quarterly* 18 (Spring 1962): 38–45.

Poteat, Edwin McNeill, Jr. "Religion in the South." In *Culture in the South,* edited by W. T. Couch, pp. 248–69. Chapel Hill, N.C., 1935.

Potter, David M. "The Enigma of the South." *Yale Review* 51 (Autumn 1961): 142–51.

———. "The Historian's Use of Nationalism and Vice Versa." In Potter, *The South and the Sectional Conflict,* pp. 34–83. Baton Rouge, La., 1968.

———. "On Understanding the South." *Journal of Southern History* 30 (November 1964): 451–62.

Sellers, Charles G. "The Travail of Slavery." In *The Southerner as American,* edited by Charles G. Sellers, pp. 40–71. New York, 1966.

Shea, Terence. "Dissent Bubbles among the Southern Baptists." *National Observer* 8, no. 23 (June 9, 1969): 6.

Shriver, Donald W., Jr. "Southern Churches in Transition." *New South: A Quarterly Review of Southern Affairs* 25 (Winter 1970): 40–47.

Simkins, Francis Butler. "The Rising Tide of Faith." In *The Lasting South, Fourteen Southerners Look at Their Home,* edited by Louis D. Rubin, Jr., and James Jackson Kilpatrick, pp. 84–103. Chicago, 1957.

Singer, David. "God and Man in Baptist Hymnals 1784–1844." *Midcontinent American Studies Journal* 9 (Fall 1968): 14–26.

Smith, David E. "Millenarian Scholarship in America." *American Quarterly* 17 (Fall 1965): 535–49.

Smylie, James H. "On Being Presbyterian in the South." *Christian Century* 87 (August 5, 1970): 936–40.

Sweet, William Warren. "The Churches as Moral Courts of the Frontier." *Church History* 2 (March 1933): 3–21.

———. "The Rise of Theological Schools in America." *Church History* 6 (September 1937): 260–74.

Tarver, Jerry L. "Exhortation among Early Virginia Baptists." *Virginia Baptist Register* 5 (1966): 228–36.

Taylor, William R. "Toward a Definition of Orthodoxy: The Patrician South and the Common Schools." *Harvard Educational Review* 36 (Fall 1966): 412–26.

Tindall, George B. "The Central Theme Revisited." In *The Southerner as American,* edited by Charles G. Sellers, pp. 104–29. New York, 1966.

———. "Mythology: A New Frontier in Southern History." In *The Idea of the South,* edited by Frank E. Vandiver, pp. 1–15. Chicago, 1964.

Vandiver, Frank E. "The Southerner as Extremist." In *The Idea of the South,* edited by Frank E. Vandiver, pp. 43–56. Chicago, 1964.

Wallace, Anthony F. C. "Handsome Lake and the Great Revival in the West." *American Quarterly* 4 (Summer 1952): 149–65.

———. "Revitalization Movements." *American Anthropologist* 58 (1956): 264–81.

Weaver, R. M. "The Older Religiousness in the South." *Sewanee Review* 51 (Spring 1943): 237–49.

Woodward, C. Vann. "The Search for Southern Identity." In Woodward, *The Burden of Southern History*, pp. 3–26. Baton Rouge, La., 1960.

———. "The Southern Ethic in a Puritan World." *William and Mary Quarterly* 25 (July 1968): 343–70.

Woody, Robert H. Review of William H. Nicholls, *Southern Tradition and Regional Progress*. In *Mississippi Valley Historical Review* 47 (December 1960): 535–36.

Theses & Dissertations

Allen, Carlos Richard. "The Great Revival in Virginia, 1783–1812." M.A. thesis, University of Virginia, 1948.

Barrus, Ben Melton. "A Study of the Factors Involved in the Origin of the Cumberland Presbyterian Church: 1800–1813." Ph.D. diss., Vanderbilt University, 1964.

DesChamps, Margaret Burr. "The Presbyterian Church in the South Atlantic States, 1801–1861." Ph.D. diss., Emory University, 1952.

Gaebler, Nancy. "Devereux Jarratt: Anglican Evangelist of the Virginia Great Awakening." M.A. thesis, University of Virginia, 1967.

Ham, F. Gerald. "Shakerism in the Old West." Ph.D. diss., University of Kentucky, 1962.

Kirkpatrick, Jerald Lee. "The Effect of the Shaker Conversions on the Christian Church in Kentucky and Ohio, 1805–1810." B.A. honors thesis, Texas Christian University, 1967.

Leonard, Larry Philip. "The Contributions of Presbyterian Orthodoxy to the Pro-Slavery Argument as Exemplified by the Writings of James Henley Thornwell, 1838–1860." M.A. thesis, University of Virginia, 1967.

Long, Ronald W. "Religious Revivalism in the Carolinas and Georgia, 1740–1805." Ph.D. diss., University of Georgia, 1968.

Lykins, Noel Ray. "North Carolina Separate Baptists: A Study in Frontier Baptist Expansion in the Eighteenth Century." Th.M. thesis, Southeastern Baptist Theological Seminary, 1961.

Mikkelson, Dwight Lawrence. "*Kentucky Gazette*, 1787–1848: 'The Herald of a Noisy World.'" Ph.D. diss., University of Kentucky, 1963.

Morgan, David T., Jr. "The Great Awakening in the Carolinas and Georgia, 1740–1775." Ph.D. diss., University of North Carolina, 1968.

Sims, John Norman. "The Hymnody of the Camp Meeting Tradition." D.S.M. diss., Union Theological Seminary, 1960.

Smith, Cortland Victor. "Church Organization as an Agency of Social Control: Church Discipline in North Carolina, 1800–1860." Ph.D. diss., University of North Carolina, 1967.

Stokes, Durward T. "Religious Denominations in North Carolina and the Great Revival." M.A. thesis, University of North Carolina, 1965.

Index

abolitionism, 190
Adams, Henry, 195
Adams, John, 171
*An Address to the Different Religious
Societies on the Sacred Import of
the Christian Name,* 155
Alamance Presbyterian Church, North
Carolina, 41
Albemarle County, Virginia, 32, 85
Allen, Cary, 8
Allen, Ethan, 12, 18, 21
American Revolution, 19–20, 23
Anderson, Alexander, 160
Anglican Church, 1, 5. *See also*
Episcopal Church
anxious bench, 76
*Apology for Renouncing the Jurisdic-
tion of the Synod of Kentucky,* 152,
153, 154
Armenius, Theophilus, 62
Arminianism, 137, 138
Asbury, Francis: and beginning of
American Methodism, 5, 6; on
decline of religion, 16–17, 29; and
O'Kelly controversy, 23, 146; on
answering of prayers, 32; participates
in and praises Great Revival, 68–69,
72–73, 79–82 passim; on Judgment
Day, 101; suggests revival is beginning of millennium, 104; supports
voluntary concept of denominations,
127, 128; proclaims a pietistic view
of religion, 140; attacks materialism,
168–69; recognizes favorably lower
class appeal of Methodism, 169;
political views of, 172–73, 181;
mentioned, 86, 88, 93
Asplund, John, 132–33
Associate Reformed Presbyterian
Church, 98
Atlanta, Georgia, 198n, 201
atonement, 132–33, 138, 149–50,
153–54
Augusta, Georgia, 81

backcountry, 9–10

backsliders, 11
Backus, Isaac, 15, 84, 181
Bailey, Kenneth K., 184
Balch, James, 48, 160
Baltimore, Maryland, 5, 190
Baptist Church: origin in South, 3, 4;
Separate, Particular, and Regular
divisions of, 3, 4; character of, 4;
supports disestablishment, 4, 127; in
early Virginia revivals, 7, 10; and
church discipline, 11, 187–88; on
eve of Great Revival, 15, 43, 51,
73; involved in intradenominational
controversy, 22; participates in and
supports Great Revival, 62, 65, 72,
75–76, 79, 82, 85; gradually
withdraws from revival extremes,
87–89, 90, 94, 99; and ministerial
education, 119; use of hymns by,
121–24; theological position of,
129, 132–33, 135, 136, 137, 138;
and class appeal, 169–70; relationship to politics, 173, 174, 179;
growth in Great Revival, 185–86;
number in South in 1850, 186;
establishes colleges, 191; racism of,
202; in modern dilemma, 202; mentioned, 1, 101, 111
Barnet, William, 40
Barrow, David: on irreligion and deism
in Kentucky, 10, 18; suggests purpose of decline of religion, 30; discounts materialism, 168; reports
republicanism in Kentucky, 181;
states political views, 182
Bates, Issachar, 156
Bath County, Virginia, 187
Bavarian Illuminati, 12
Baxter, George, 93, 186–87
Bayard, Ferdinand Marie, 11
Bear Creek Baptist Church, North
Carolina, 33
Becker, Howard, 198–99
Bedford County, Virginia, 84, 86, 147
Beecher, Lyman, 12
Bend, Joseph G. J., 181